you
know
everybody!

you

know

everybody!

A CAREER GIRL'S GUIDE TO
BUILDING A NETWORK THAT WORKS

MARCY TWETE

*This book is dedicated to Melanie Griffith,
Diane Keaton, and Dolly Parton. Thank you for showing
a little girl in North Dakota how to dream in big business.*

Table of Contents

Praise for *You Know Everybody!*

"Reading You Know Everybody! *is like hanging out in your sweats to talk shop with a great cup of coffee and a good friend; a friend who will gently tell it like it is but direct you down just the right path and help you pick out the perfect shoes for the journey. Marcy blends tactical tools and advice for networking with tremendous wit, grace, and insight into the realities of today's working woman.* You Know Everybody! *Provides advice that every Career Girl should read and practice at all stages of their career!"*
~Nikki Foster, Chief Corporate Responsibility Officer, Sunrise Community Banks

"Marcy has done a witty job of breaking down the art of networking and providing fresh tools and techniques that even the shyest career climber can put to use. She provides both high level perspective as well as immediate ideas for getting started. The book is perfect for someone looking to up their networking game or for like-minded professionals who will find comic relief in Marcy's trials and tribulations involved in today's crazy, multi dimensional social environment. Marcy's writing and experiences are charming and fun to read. The real surprise is the depth and content she's collected from other women's experiences, which collectively are a treasure."
~Emily Frager, Senior Vice President & Senior Partner, Fleishman-Hillard

"Charming, witty, and fresh, Marcy Twete's voice appeals to women of all career levels. At once educational and entertaining, You Know Everybody! *is a must-read for professional women of any age. Simply a delight!"*
~Stacey Beck, Independent Educational and Career Consultant

"You Know Everybody! *is for any woman who has ever uttered the words "I need to start networking, but..." Knowing what you want, asking for it, and receiving it are completely interconnected. We instinctively understand this, but still don't know where to begin or how to go about meeting the right people and making powerful requests. Twete breaks it down brilliantly and reminds us that it's never too early, or too late, to build a strategic network."*

~Jules Taggart, Kickstart Kitchen

"This is a book whose time has come. Every power networker to aspiring networker should own a copy. There is a connection point for everyone to learn and grow from. Marcy Twete has phenomenally illustrated the path for women and girls to be successful networkers and learn to know everybody!"

~Meredith Douglass-Morales, Senior Diversity Recruiter, Federal Reserve Bank of Chicago

"You Know Everybody! *is a compelling and enlightening book that is downright fun to read. You gain countless tangible tips for networking while gaining inspiration and energy from amazing businesswomen. You'll read, learn, laugh - and then get to work!"*

~Courtney Templin, Author of *Manager 3.0:* *A Millennial's Guide to Rewriting the Rules of Management*

"Marcy Twete has done the impossible: she's written a book on networking that's not only intriguing and insightful, it's incredibly entertaining. Drawing on her own personal experiences, as well as those of her mentors and icons in the business world, Twete manages to teach valuable networking lessons while keeping her reader on the edge of her seat, hungry for the next delightful anecdote. This is not your typical How-To book. Twete offers a fun and unique perspective on the subject of networking. You Know Everybody! *is a highly enjoyable read that I recommend to all business professionals."*

~Kalei Kekuna, Global Marketing Professional

"I wish that I could've read Marcy's book when I started my career. This insightful book offers encouragement and a wealth of advice from her own experience and that of successful business women on how to really excel at networking in today's competitive, online world."
~Barbara K. Mednick, Associate Director Corporate Communications, KPMG LLP

"This book is exactly what I've been looking for to hand off to young women when they ask me about building a professional network. The stories are accessible, the advice is clear, and Marcy's passion for the topic is undeniable. Although technology may change the details of how we connect with one another, this book provides valuable instruction for how to build an authentic and powerful network."
~Lauren Melcher, Digital Strategist

"Oozing with positive energy and valuable tips, this book is a must-read for natural-born networkers and self-professed wallflowers alike. Marcy lays out the process of building a network into clear and manageable steps. She provides plenty of concrete examples, scripts and resources. And she shows how fun and empowering it can all be — both professionally and personally."
~Maureen Glasoe, Owner, Virgo Words

"I met Marcy a few months after she had moved to Chicago and assumed that, like most people in a new city, it would take her years to get her bearings. Instead, I've been so impressed with her ability to figure out how to embed herself in the community–a process that takes most people a lifetime, but took her less than a year. She's a master networker."
~Susanna Negovan, Editor, Chicago Sun Times SPLASH

"Networks–so many people know they need one but aren't sure how or where to begin– OR! a person might have a huge network but has no idea how they might be able to leverage the individuals and the group as a whole to fuel their career dreams and goals. Marcy's approach to understanding the layers of a strong, diverse network plus the practical tips offered to help the reader work within a network are inspiring. I now have an entirely new perspective on how to position my network for personal and professional growth."
~Amy Brenengen, Office of Minority & Women Inclusion, Federal Reserve Bank of Minneapolis

"You Know Everybody! is full of brilliant tips and advice on how to build and grow your network. Marcy teaches women how to improve our 'asking for what we REALLY want' skills in an empowering and effective way. You'll look forward to making powerful requests and no longer 'hem and haw' when asked 'How can I help you?'"
~Althea McIntyre, owner, The Best Career For Me

"What resonated with me in Marcy's book is the notion that it takes practice to hone your asking skills. You have to remind your network what you are doing, you need to find excuses to reach out, and overall, you need to aim for clarity when you are asking for help. This book provides great tools, resources and exercises to keep women moving along a successful career path and ultimately becoming master networkers."
~Jessie Ahlschlager Sandoval, Director of Alumnae Relations, College of Saint Benedict

"Marcy is an amazing lady. She's a rising star who will be very successful because she knows how to make things happen. And of course, She Knows Everybody! I can't wait to order copies of You Know Everybody! for my company's book club to motivate and inspire my staff both personally and professionally."
~Robin Kocina, Owner, Media Relations, Inc.

"A great read for any woman that wants to excel in her career and in her life and to have a real network. Marcy is a spunky woman with a lot of class! You read this book and want to network with her! It's not a book just for those looking to climb the corporate ladder. Networking is up to you and this book will teach you how to get out of the corner of the room and build your network."
~Nicole Middendorf, CDFA, CEO, ProsperWell Financial

"The first few pages of You Know Everybody! *had me hooked as Marcy described the initial struggles and fears she too faced when networking in the Windy City. This book is a powerful testament to Marcy's incredible knowledge of successful networking. Just when you think you've got it all figured out, Marcy reminds you how networking is an art form and breaks down the process into multiple levels in each chapter. Whether you're starting out, looking to expand your current network or trying to think 'outside the box,' as Marcy says, you will learn something invaluable from* You Know Everybody!, *and your new/expanded network will reflect just that."*
~Carrie Williams, Managing/Digital Editor,
Today's Chicago Woman

*"*You Know Everybody! *provides women with actionable and measurable steps to diversify and fortify their networking connections. Marcy reminds me that I need to be bold, show up, and build tighter and more strengths-based relationships with all of my levels of connections. Bearing the boldness to ask and be a strategic networker should be paramount goals for any woman to truly further her career."*
~Gina Truitt, VP Finance, Blue Horizon Management Group

"If you are afraid of networking or think it is just superficial "schmoozing," this book will be a paradigm shift for you! Marcy helps you see networking as an authentic way to create meaningful relationships with cool people, like the friends you met in your freshman college dorm. Who doesn't want to do that?! This accessible redefinition of networking is a relief for the busy professional who can't imagine cramming more into her day."
~Shayna Cook, Partner,
Goldman Ismail Tomaselli Brennan & Baum LLP

"Marcy Twete writes a very smart guide that all professionals, particularly women, can benefit from to build their networks. She provides great personal stories, along with guidance from other accomplished professionals, that are relatable, entertaining, and enlightening to those that are not sure where to start or how to make their network work for them. The book lays out easy to execute, step by step instructions that make the world of networking feel like unlimited opportunity. I cannot wait to share it with my friends and colleagues!"
~Arla Lach, Senior Manager, Audit, Grant Thornton LLP

"You Know Everybody! approaches networking and building relationships in a way other books don't. From her sense of humor to real-life stories and profiles, you feel like you are getting Marcy's advice firsthand over a cup of coffee. I highly recommend this book and its approachable and authentic tips to anyone who is looking to grow her network, make a career change or meet people in a new city. It's fun, it's fresh, it's insightful and makes you realize you really do know everybody!"
~Erika Crowell, Communications Consultant

"It's true that it's not about who you are, it's who you know, and Marcy Twete shares all the secrets that have elevated her to someone worth knowing. You Know Everybody! is a step-by-step guide to figuring out who you need to know and then getting to know them. It's not just about gathering business cards - it's about finding sponsors, mentors, door-openers and loyal clients in a way that doesn't require hours of painful cold-calling and awkward rounds of speed-networking. Marcy proves that the steps she shares really work by interviewing some of the most influential women in business - most of whom she met using these exact steps!"
~**Kelley Long, CPA, CFP, Shepard Schwartz & Harris LLP**

"Whether you are the girl who is looking to move up the corporate ladder, find a new job, start your own business or just meet new people, Marcy does a fantastic job in taking the overwhelming act of networking and chopping it down into sizable bites. You Know Everybody! is not about giving your business card to everyone you meet. This book is about how you not only can meet those people who will be your mentor or have your back, but also how to strengthen the strong networking relationships you already have."
~**Lauren McCabe Herpich, Founder, Why Not Girl!**

Introduction

My *"You Know Everybody!"* A-Ha Moment

It was October of 2009 when the idea for *You Know Everybody!* first came to me. I had been dating a man named Charlie for just a few weeks (he would eventually become my husband). We realized quickly we shared a number of commonalities–a love of music and theater, a dedication to our families, but namely, and most instrumental in the development of our relationship, a deep love of great food. It was that foodie sensibility that brought us on a crisp October evening to Minneapolis' newest hot spot, Bar La Grassa. After opening just days before, a friend of a friend made some calls and got me a 7:00 p.m. seating, which thoroughly impressed my new not-quite boyfriend.

As the host escorted us to our table in the back corner of the bustling dining room, I scanned the faces of those around me. I smiled, nodded, waved here and there, and, upon sitting down, immediately turned to Charlie and said, "This place is like a who's who of Minneapolis/St. Paul." He laughed uncomfortably and asked, "How do you know?" For the next few minutes, I covertly drew my date's attention to the man across the room to the left in the blue suit. That's the CEO of one of the Twin Cities' largest companies. Next, the group of girlfriends dressed to the nines—all members of families with what you'd call "old money" in Minnesota. Next to them, the family of one of the restaurant's partners. And at the bar, hoping for a table, was one of the city's best event planners, sipping a martini with a *Star Tribune* editor and a fashion designer who was rumored to be cast on *Project Runway*. Those people weren't just faces to me. They were my friends, my colleagues, all of whom I could call in a moment's notice if I needed something.

After I gave Charlie the skinny on at least half the room, he turned to me and said the words that would shape the course of my life and, ultimately, inspire this book. He said, "Wow, Marcy. ***You Know Everybody!***" He was right. As much as anyone possibly could, knowing that no one can truly know *everybody*, I had amassed a network in Minneapolis/St. Paul that included everyone from corporate CEOs to chefs, artists, actors, and those you might call socialites.

It surprised me at first to realize how strong my network had become. Like most women in their 20s, I was just trying to get ahead in my field. I wondered, had this *You Know Everybody!* Network been created accidentally or intentionally?

I didn't know that night, or in the months to come, that my networking abilities would soon be tested beyond any measure I could imagine. I had no idea that the appearance of the *You Know Everybody!* idea in my life would actually be an invitation to the universe to throw down the gauntlet: Less than a year later, Charlie and I would pick up our furniture and our cat and move to the Windy City of Chicago.

Fast forward to December 9, 2010. Around noon, I walked into the Union League Club in downtown Chicago, looked around the room, and experienced one of the most terrifying moments of my life. I scanned the faces of the 200 women gathered for the Professional Women's Club of Chicago luncheon, and my feelings were the exact opposite of those at Bar La Grassa the year before. Not a soul in the room was familiar to me. I knew nobody. Despite the fact that I would eventually look back on this PWCC luncheon as a success, that evening I sobbed to Charlie. I asked him how would I ever make friends, how would I ever build the kind of network in Chicago I had in Minneapolis? "How," I asked, "am I ever going to get through this?"

I won't lie to you—there were many more evenings like that one. Evenings when I sobbed and shook and wondered how I would ever get through such a huge transition in my life. There were days filled with unanswered questions about which job to take and which to turn down, which events to go to and which ones seemed more like singles mixers than networking opportunities. But as I'll show you step by step in the rest of this book, I embarked on a process to create the same kind of network in Chicago that I had in Minneapolis. And between the tears and the fear, I had to believe if I did it once, I could do it again.

Fast-forward again to November 16, 2011. That evening, I walked into a room filled with hundreds of Chicago women at the Step Up Women's Network annual Stepping Up in the City event. Everything felt eerily familiar and unfamiliar at the same time. I closed my eyes and thought back to that evening in Bar La Grassa and then to that terrifying first luncheon at PWCC, and compared the two. I realized I felt more like the former than the latter. That night, after introducing some of my guests to Step Up members and networking with Board members, knowing I would be joining the Step Up Board in January, I once again felt invincible when it came to my network. And at one moment in the evening, I was standing next to a new friend who turned to me and exclaimed, "Wow, Marcy. *You Know Everybody!*"

I realized then that my network in Minneapolis wasn't created accidentally and my new network in Chicago hadn't been, either. When I moved to Chicago, I attacked networking intentionally, and with a clear, well-thought-out plan. In less than a year, I went from knowing nobody to knowing (again, as well as anyone can) everybody.

As moments often do, those three moments connected

to one another and produced what Oprah calls an "a-ha moment." I knew when I heard those words a second time—*You Know Everybody!*—that I had to write this book. I knew that other women had no doubt experienced exactly what I had that day at PWCC. It was sheer terror, palpable anxiety, and staring out into the unknown asking myself, "Will anyone like me?" I never wanted to feel that feeling again and I don't want you to feel it, either, which is why this book exists. Just like there's no easy pill to take to lose 100 pounds, there's no surefire, quick and easy way to build a network. It takes hard work and dedication, and it takes actual strategic networking. You can't do it solely by connecting with people on LinkedIn, and you certainly can't do it sitting on your couch or at your desk all the time.

I've created *You Know Everybody!* Networks for myself throughout my career—first in Minneapolis, then in Chicago, and now nationwide as the CEO of Career Girl Network. My mission, and that of my business, is to provide women with clear paths to career success and a large network of women to nurture, mentor, and support their goals. And just like every day on the Career Girl Network website, and through our events and services, this book is about fulfilling that mission. It's about giving you the network you need to succeed.

I know what you're thinking. Networking sucks, right? If I had a dime for every time a woman said to me, "I need a bigger network, but I hate networking," I'd be a millionaire by now. I get it. No one wants to walk into a room full of strangers, drink bad wine, listen to some greasy guy's pitch about his auto detailing business, and pass out countless business cards in the hope that one of the people you meet will ultimately help you get ahead. Even the best networkers in the world get a little nervous before a big event or an important networking meeting, not because they're scared to fail, but because they're scared it's going to suck.

But even if you're one of those people who hates

networking, I beg you to stay with me. Because if there's one thing I know for sure, it's that relationships aren't built in the ways we've always been taught to network. You won't bond with your potential new best friend over mini corn dogs passed out by a cheap catering company, and you won't meet your new boss in an icebreaker in which everyone shares their favorite movie. In this book, I'm going to teach you about *real* networking, not the kind we see on television and in movies. I'm going to teach you about *real* relationship building that will not only create your own *You Know Everybody!* moment, but will provide you with friendships, trusted mentors, and the advice of industry leaders you need to get everything you want in your career.

In the next ten chapters, I'll guide you step by step through the process of building a network that works for you. You'll learn how to clarify what you need and what you want, and how to build a wish list that keeps you on track in finding those resources. I'll also teach you how to perfect your pitch, speak honestly about who you are, and learn to make powerful requests of those in your network. In truth, the only thing that got me through that terrifying day at PWCC was my ability to sell myself and adequately articulate what I needed.

From there, we'll cover how to get the right folks on your side, and how to get your foot in what can seem like very heavy doors. Often the biggest challenge in networking, especially for women, that we assume someone "doesn't have time." They have time. You just have to learn how to get them to give it to you. I'll guide you through the art of nailing a meeting with someone you never thought would speak to you, and show you ways to continue relationships beyond first meetings to create mentorships and sponsorships.

Along the way, I'll weave in both my experience and the advice and experience of other powerful women whose networks and reputations are simply the best in the business. From TV personalities to corporate CEOs, you'll find that you likely have more in common with these women than you think. They face the same struggles in networking, building relationships, and asking for what they want as you do.

I worked for years in nonprofit organizations that support women and girls. And whether I was working with a woman who had just donated $10,000, or a woman who barely made $10,000 last year and is trying to put food on the table for her family, I quickly realized we all have the same need to create success in our businesses, careers, and lives. We need information, we need resources, and above all else, we need a network. Women are social, caring creatures. We want to connect with other women. We want to build relationships that are both meaningful and mutually beneficial. And whether you're the softest, most sensitive person in the world or the hard-nosed tell-it-like-it-is diva, you need a network, too.

I've asked myself countless times during the process of writing this book, "Who is *You Know Everybody!* for?" Is it for the early 20s recent college graduate who has only her college friends and professors on her LinkedIn page and desperately needs to build a network? Is it for the successful 30-something woman whose calendar is overflowing with coffee, lunch, and drink meetings? Is it for the established executive who wants to be more strategic with the connections she already has? The answers: Yes, yes, and yes. I'm not so bold as to say that every woman in the world needs this book or will love it. No matter our profession, the level of our career, or the number of connections we have on LinkedIn, Facebook, and Twitter, we all can get better at networking. We can all improve our strategy and add to our inner circles with individuals and ideas that are new, exciting, and beneficial to our already overly ambitious careers. This book was written so that those who don't know how to network can learn, and those who are experts at networking can sharpen. Consider this both your workbook and your wakeup call. It's time to make the people who surround you just as important as the words on the page of your resume and the reputation you've worked so hard to build. If a tree falls in the forest but no one is there to hear it, does it make a sound? If a woman excels in her career but there's no network there to applaud her success, and no one to follow in her footsteps, is the glass ceiling ever really broken?

There's a reason I called this book *You Know Everybody!* It's not that I want you to add a lot of random connections to your contact list, although you certainly can take that approach. This book is called *You Know Everybody!* because my goal for every woman who reads it is simple: I want you to know everybody you need to in order to be as successful as you want to be. Not all of us will ascend to the C-suite, and not all of us want to. Your own *You Know Everybody!* moment has to come in building the network that works . . . not for everybody, but for you. This is your very own *Career Girl's Guide to Building a Network That Works*, and I know it can guide you and all of the women who read it. I want each of you, after following the steps I'm outlining here and implementing these networking strategies in your life, to have the kind of "a-ha" moment I did when someone turns to you in a crowd and says, "Wow! *You Know Everybody!*" The beauty in that moment isn't in the words being spoken, but in the feeling you'll have inside when you can say, "You bet your ass I do!"

one

Pitching: Inside and Outside the Elevator

Hi, my name is (what?)
My name is (who?)
My name is (wukka wukka) Slim Shady

–MARSHALL BRUCE MATHERS III

You have a glass of wine in one hand, your purse in the other, and a server shoves a tray in your face and says, "Meatball slider?" Simultaneously, the person you've been making small talk with over how much you hate chardonnay says, "Tell me about yourself." Here it is. This is the time. You're ready to shine, right? Probably not. Inevitably, you say something like, "Oh, I work in corporate marketing. What do you do?" You've just given yourself enough time to wolf down that meatball slider, slam that glass of bad champagne, and hopefully run out the door before ever actually having to introduce yourself properly. This is the plight of most people who attend networking events. Sure, you want to make good connections, but wouldn't it be easier if you could do it without ever having to talk about yourself?

Introducing yourself properly requires the use of one of business' favorite buzz words—the elevator pitch. At one time or another, you've probably asked yourself, "What the hell is an elevator pitch? Does anyone really talk in elevators? I mostly look at the screen that displays today's temperatures and the president's approval rating." And you're right. Very few people talk to one another in elevators anymore. But here's where the idea of the elevator pitch came from: The average elevator ride is about 60 seconds (some say it's 90 seconds in New York City, but everything's bigger in New York, right?). The idea of an elevator pitch isn't about being uncomfortable in an elevator, though. It's about asking this question: Can you effectively sell yourself or your business in 60 seconds or less?

If you want to be successful as a networker and build your own *You Know Everybody!* Network, you can't do it without knowing exactly how to pitch yourself, your ideas, your business, and your potential to partners, connections, and yes, the woman standing next to you while you eat your meatball slider.

I started this chapter with a quote from a controversial artist from Detroit. His lyrics are often offensive and his influence widely discussed, but if I stopped most of you on the street and asked you, "Who is Marshall Mathers?" it's likely you wouldn't know the answer. But if I said to you, "Hi, my name is (what?) My name is (who?)" you would likely answer back "Slim Shady!" The vision, name, and persona surrounding Slim Shady are what put Eminem, a.k.a. Marshall Mathers III, on the map. It is as good an elevator pitch as any I've ever heard. Why? First, it's memorable. Anyone who has heard "My Name Is" once could repeat it to you months later. Second, it's unique. No one in the world will ever be mistaken for Eminem. With that song, he quickly and undeniably built his calling card, one that continues to follow him years into the future. This is both an incredible example of success in personal branding and a cautionary tale. Successful because you'll likely remember Eminem decades into the future, but cautionary in the fact that he, as an artist, will never be able to divorce himself from the words "Hi, my name is."

Take another cue from Eminem and ask yourself this: Do you remember the cover of The Slim Shady LP? Can you recall the sequences of the music video for "My Name Is"? Did the song go gold? Or platinum? You likely don't know the answer to any of these questions. Because these questions aren't about Eminem and the elevator pitch that catapulted his personal brand into worldwide recognition: The album art was created by a graphic designer employed by his record company; the music video played on MTV and VH1 and you watched it in the background every now and again; and it's the music business that hands out those gold and platinum records. What you remember is the song's "hook." Because Eminem sold it to you. The record company didn't. The graphic designer didn't. Eminem did–in a way that only he could. And just like Eminem, your boss can't sell you, your spouse can't sell you, your company can't sell you. You are the best and the only sales person for you.

You are the only person who can develop and propagate your brand, and it is your responsibility to distribute your name and your brand in order to build your own *You Know Everybody! Network*. Your personal elevator pitch is the beginning.

Inevitably, there are still a few naysayers at this point in the process. Some of you are ready to put down this book thinking, "I don't need an elevator pitch. Isn't it enough to say 'I'm a lawyer'?" No, it's not. Though you might think an elevator pitch exists only for networking events, that's not its only use.

Imagine you're interviewing for a new job. You shake the hand of the hiring manager, sit down across the table, and the interviewer usually says something like, "Tell me about yourself." Trust me, the interviewer is not asking for your life story. This question is not about where you live, whether or not you're married, or the complete rundown of every job you've ever had. Skilled hiring managers tell me that the most common answer to this question is a two- or three-minute response that essentially guides the hiring manager through the candidate's resume. Somehow in this moment, interviewees forget that the person sitting across from them has already read their resume. What they want to know, and what they're really asking for, is relevant information that isn't in the resume. Saying "Tell me about yourself" is actually asking for your elevator pitch.

Still not convinced? Try this. You're meeting a new client or important stakeholder in your company. This person knows what you do for the company, is connected to you on LinkedIn and likely knows a tiny bit about your background, and has spoken to you via phone regularly. During your first in-person meeting, you might hear something like, "We don't know each other very well. Tell me a little more about you." The same principle applies as above. This is a clear ask for your elevator pitch. All of these individuals want to hear an engaging but succinct description of who you are and why they should be interested.

So, whether you're meeting a potential boss, new client, or just a stranger you're hoping to impress at a networking event, the elevator pitch is crucial to making a great first impression. It shows that you know how to sell yourself and you're comfortable talking about both your background and your future. Hopefully you're still with me at this point and agree: Girl, you need an elevator pitch. Don't worry. I'm going to guide you straight through the process of creating one. So let's get it done!

To craft an elevator pitch, you must first be aware of its intentions. Sixty seconds of mumbo jumbo about your background and your goals does not make an elevator pitch. Clarifying your intentions will help you create a pitch that not only sells you but helps people to remember you, much like you remember Eminem. The tricky thing about intentions, though, is you usually don't have just one. What does that mean? Unfortunately, you can't create a one-size-fits-all elevator pitch to use in every scenario in your life. If your intention is to look for, find, and land a new job, your elevator pitch will be tailored to highlight why you'd be a great investment to a potential employer. If you simply want to network to get ahead in your company or build your skill set, you'll need to be sure your elevator pitch is skill-based and points towards strong leadership development. If you're searching for a mentor, looking for new friends, or searching for that special someone, your elevator pitch will be different for every scenario you're in.

To clarify your intentions around your elevator pitch, you'll need to set some goals. Normally, I hate visioning exercises. However, one of the regular writers on Career Girl Network, Rebecca Niziol, pushes me outside my comfort zone regularly by asking me to close my eyes and envision something about the future. And just like she pushes me, I'm going to push you right now. Take a few minutes to think about where you see yourself in a year. Sit up straight, put your feet on the ground or crossed in a comfortable position, close your eyes, and create a vision. What would your life look like one year from now if everything you dreamed of creating in this year – every person you wanted to connect with, every moment you wanted to savor – happened in the blink of an eye? What would that day or that moment feel like to you? Do you look different? Are you in a different city? Are you in a different job? Really take the time to create your vision, look around within it, and note as many details as you can about your surroundings.

After you open your eyes and come back to reality, think back to your vision. In the left side of the chart below, list all of the specific things in your vision that were different from the way things are today. This might be a change in job, city, your looks, your attitude, or your spouse. If it was different in your vision, list it in the following chart:

First, note what was different.	Then, set the intention.
Example: I'm living in a different city, specifically Washington, DC.	*Example: In the next year, I will accept a position in and move permanently to Washington, DC.*

For the purpose of this exercise, try to keep the number of differences you're noticing to four or five. This will help you to clarify your goals and set the intentions that accompany the elevator pitches you're crafting.

Now that you've noted the differences in your vision, you have to set intentions around those differences. Take the example above. In your vision, if you're standing on the National Mall, wearing a suit and talking on the phone to an aide in a Senator's office about votes and commitments, chances are you need to move to Washington, DC. More importantly, you need to set a deadline and a plan for doing it. Therefore, your intention is clear if you declare, "In the next year, I will accept a position in and move permanently to Washington, DC." That's a clear intention if I ever heard one. While your elevator pitch may not necessarily include that exact intention in every case, it will always have your intentions incorporated into its meaning and goals. Next to your noted differences in the chart in the above, write out your clear intentions to accompany each difference you noted in your vision.

For a moment, now, let's set aside your intentions and focus on the reality of what you hear when you hear an elevator pitch. If you've recently attended a networking event or met someone new, you've heard versions of elevator pitches that are both good and bad, long and short. There's a guy trying to sell you his social media services, a woman looking for a job in technology, and many other individuals you've met and listened to as they describe themselves and their goals. And whether you know it or not, the questions going through your mind during their elevator pitches are the same questions going through the minds of the people to whom you're pitching. They're thinking:

- What's interesting about this person?
- Do I like her?
- Do I want to know more about her?
- Is she someone I could add to my network?
- If so, how? Will we be friends? Would I like to add her on LinkedIn?
- Whom could I introduce her to?
- Whom could she introduce me to?
- Will this person make me money in the future?

The list goes on and on, and the moral of the story is this: No one is really listening to you. They're hearing the words you're saying while simultaneously evaluating which category to put you in – someone I want to know, someone I like, someone I just want to stop talking to, or someone I don't like. Your job in that 60-second pitch is simple: Show that person what's interesting and likable about you, and why you'd be a valuable person to add to her network and to potentially help get ahead.

To combat the questions your listener is silently asking, you first have to be willing to ask yourself the hard questions as you develop your elevator pitch. Let's tackle them one by one.

1. **Who are you?** Sure, this statement will include your name. It might even include your job. But it's much more than just the standard first name and company most people give when they introduce themselves. It's the opportunity to break the ice with the most important key messages of your personal brand, and it gives the listener a reason to keep listening. Who you are isn't just about where you work. It's about what you love, what you're passionate about, and the things that make you whole. Sure, your job is an important part of that equation, but it's not the only part. Examine the following examples:

Example A: *"Hi, I'm Sue. I'm an attorney."*
Example B: *"Great to meet you. I'm Sue. I'm a patent attorney with my own practice. I love my job, but my real passion is fulfilled in my volunteer work mentoring young women who are interested in science and math, just like me."*

It's easy to imagine the follow-up questions you'd ask Sue in Example B. You might wonder which organization she mentors with, what kinds of clients she has in her independent practice, or what made her interested in math and science growing up. She's given you the opportunity for a built-in conversation right off the bat.

In the space below, go ahead and answer that question: Who are you?

_____

_____

_____

_____

2. **What do you want?** –or– **Where are you going?** If you are 100% ecstatic about everything going on in your life right now, from your relationships to your work, from your weight to your bank account, you should congratulate yourself: You are the only person in the world who is. We all have something we want to change about their lives, and everyone is on a path to growth, new opportunities, and, hopefully, success. To reach that success, you have to know your path: What do you want? Or, if it's more suitable and easier for you to answer, where are you going? Consider again our attorney friend, Sue. Here are two examples of how she might answer this question:

    Example A: "I have my own practice, but I hope to join a large firm at some point."
    Example B: "Being a solo practitioner, I'm missing connections with colleagues and the opportunity to be a mentor to young attorneys. So, I'm actively pursuing opportunities to lend my skills to a larger law firm, preferably on the East Coast."

    If you heard Sue say the words in Example A, you'd no doubt be left hanging. She's making no commitment here of when she wants to join a firm, you have no idea why she is interested in firm life, and it may even give you the impression that she's been unsuccessful as a solo practitioner. In Example B, you hear more about what Sue really is passionate about, and how her next move could make her a better lawyer and mentor.

In the space below, go ahead and answer the question that best applies here: What do you want? –or– Where are you going?

_____

_____

_____

_____

3. **What skills are you using to get you there?** Once you've decided where you're going and what you want, the next step is to define your skill set. If you're a financial planner hoping to make the jump into nonprofit management, naturally the person you're speaking to is going to wonder what transferable skills you're going to use to get ahead in a brand new field. When you take Sue's example above, the skill set she wants to highlight may be more about culture than anything else. Consider these examples:

Example A: "I'm good at working with people, so I'm sure I'll fit in fine in a firm."
Example B: "I started my career and spent a decade in a large firm before venturing out on my own. I'm so glad to have had the experience of managing my own company and client docket, and I know it will make me a huge asset to a firm."

If you heard Sue talk through the three questions she's answered in Example B thus far, you'd probably think this woman has a good head on her shoulders, knows where she's going and why, and has a clear path to success. That's what this process can do for you, as well.

In the space below, answer the third question: What skills do you have that will get you to your goals?

_____

_____

_____

_____

4. **What makes you uniquely qualified to achieve your goals?**
    You might think this question is similar to the last question, asking about your skills. It isn't. What makes you uniquely qualified is a very different question than what skills you bring to the table. Your unique qualification is the articulation of the answer to the question "Why you?" Why are you special? Why do you matter? Why would I hire you over someone who brings the exact same experience or qualification? If we were living in a Quentin Tarantino film, the answer to this question would be the "kill shot." Let's keep going with our friend Sue, the patent attorney, and answer this question with two examples below:

    Example A: *"I'm hardworking and business savvy. I learn fast and have passion for what I do."*
    Example B: *"I'm a great patent attorney because I truly love the science of patents. I have a relentless passion for the medical device industry. It's because I love this arena and understand it so well that I can relate to my clients—both those in lab coats and in business suits. I know that kind of mix is exactly what big firms need to guarantee their success."*

News flash, Career Girls: Everyone says "I'm hardworking" when asked why she should get hired. Everyone thinks she's hardworking and savvy. Everyone thinks she's the fastest learner and the best employee. But what puts you head and shoulders above your competition is what you bring to the business or relationship that no one else can. Sue is telling you in Example B that she's the female version of Bill Nye the Science Guy. She loves science and people, and she's going to dig her teeth in. That, combined with her ability to talk to the suits, means she's a perfect candidate for the job she wants.

What is your unique value proposition? What makes you uniquely qualified to achieve your dreams? Answer that question in the space below:

_____

_____

_____

_____

The questions you just answered are tough. They make you really think about who you are and what you want, and they deeply question you about whether or not you have the mettle to get there. And once you've answered the four questions above, you have the first draft of what will be your overarching elevator pitch. The work doesn't end here, but let's go ahead and put it all together for Sue and see what her first draft elevator pitch really looks like.

Sue's Elevator Pitch

I'm Sue. I'm a patent attorney with my own practice. I love my job, but my real passion is fulfilled in my volunteer work mentoring young women who are interested in science and math, just like me. Being a solo practitioner, I'm missing connections with colleagues and the opportunity to be a mentor to young attorneys. So, I'm actively pursuing opportunities to lend my skills to a larger law firm, preferably on the East Coast.

I started my career and spent a decade in a large firm before venturing out on my own. I'm so glad to have had the experience of managing my own company and client docket, and I know it will make me a huge asset to a firm. I'm a great patent attorney because I truly love the science of patents. I have a relentless passion for the medical device industry. It's because I love this arena and understand it so well that I can relate to my clients—both those in lab coats and in business suits. I know that kind of mix is exactly what big firms need to guarantee their success.

Now that you've seen Sue's elevator pitch in full, take some time to put together all of your answers in sequence:

Your Elevator Pitch: The Whole SheBang

Who are you?

_____

_____

_____

_____

What do you want?

_____

_____

_____

_____

Your skills:

_____

_____

_____

_____

Your unique proposition:

_____

_____

_____

_____

If you read Sue's pitch out loud and time it, you'll find it takes about 60 seconds to read. Break out your timer on your phone and read out loud your full elevator pitch as you've written it above. If you're over 60 seconds, comb through it and look for places to cut time. A few places to start:

- Are you repeating yourself anywhere in the pitch?
- Is each thought succinct? Is it taking you more than one sentence to convey one concept?
- Will the information you're sharing help the person you're speaking with get to know you better?

Cut the elevator pitch above as much as you can until you get to 60 seconds. Then, rehearse it a few times. Become familiar with it. Make it as easy to roll off your tongue as it is to state your name and where you work. There's a reason you must become intimately engaged with your elevator pitch. It's not because I want you to memorize it and spout it everywhere you go – it's the opposite, actually. It's because I want you to be able to repeat it in countless ways and countless variations. You see, once you've developed and mastered your main elevator pitch, your work isn't done. Having a single elevator pitch just isn't enough. You're not going to give your "I'm looking for a job" elevator pitch to someone in your company. And you're not going to give your "I'm a great catch. Please marry me." elevator pitch at a professional networking event. Instead, you'll need to tailor your pitch—and ultimately, your intentions—to each audience to get the best chance of success in all facets of your life.

When I told colleagues and friends I was writing a book about networking (a business book, if you will), I heard one universal request from them: no sports analogies. As women, we all know it's commonplace in business to hear about moving the ball down the field and scoring the winning goal, with everything from teamwork to huddles to slaps on the ass as congratulations. And frankly, we're all sick of it. But I hope in illustrating my point here, you'll allow me one small sports analogy and an appropriately girly one at that.

They're referred to as "America's Sweethearts," and every year hundreds of young women flock to Dallas to audition to become one of the lucky few who will call themselves Dallas Cowboys Cheerleaders (DCC). And while, as a professional businesswoman, you might not see where you can relate to a Dallas Cowboys Cheerleader, you might be surprised. On the 2012-2013 DCC squad, you'll find financial analysts, nurses, paralegals, and other women you'll certainly be able to identify with—even if you can't see yourself in white booty shorts and cowboy boots.

But it's not the DCCs' outfits I want you to think about. It's the thinking-on-their-feet skills they develop throughout their training and practice on the field. Just like the players on the field, when game time comes, the Dallas Cowboys Cheerleaders don't rest a moment. They dance during pre-game prep, on the sidelines during the game, at halftime, and more. In any given game, a member of the DCC will combine hundreds of dance elements, 10-15 full routines, game cheers, formations, and much more to appear flawless and prepared in front of an audience of 80,000 in Cowboy Stadium and millions on television. But here comes the most impressive part: They don't know which elements and dance routines are coming. Somewhere far above the field, the music man in the booth decides which songs to play and when to play them. Dallas Cowboys Cheerleaders are trained to recognize one of hundreds of musical elements in a split second and immediately begin the corresponding choreography to accompany that music, which could be any number of the 100 or more dances and combinations they regularly perform.

The same split-second decision-making applies to you and your elevator pitch. When a member of the DCC hears that music, their brains must know the choreography so well that they can simply rely on muscle memory to guide their way. You, too, have to know your elevator pitch so well that when you realize someone is a prospective boss, potential network connection, possible friend, or potential spouse, you'll be able to immediately tailor your pitch to meet the needs of the conversation. It's a thinking-on-your-feet, muscle memory challenge that you can only face if you know the answers to the questions listed above inside out, upside down, backwards, forwards, and sideways.

The changes you'll make to your pitch to accommodate different audiences won't always be drastic, and from day to day, no one but you will notice the nuances you're adding to sell yourself to the right people at the right times. Let's look at a few specific instances when you may want to adjust your elevator pitch to specifically meet the needs of the listener:

1. **Meeting a potential employer before you apply for a job.** It happens all the time. You're at a networking event or hanging out with a friend and meet someone who says, "I'm hiring for (exactly the kind of job you're looking for)." At that moment, maybe you've introduced yourself, talked about the weather, etc., and upon hearing they're looking for someone just like you, you're ready to give them your pitch.

But you certainly can't start the pitch with "Hi, I'm Sue." You have to jump to the meat of your pitch. For a potential employer, you want to focus heavily on your background and what you're looking for in the future. Talk openly about transferable skills and the positions you've held. This is where your unique value proposition comes in handy.

2. Responding to "Tell me about yourself" at a job interview. As I mentioned earlier in this chapter, some version of "Tell me about yourself" is usually the first request made in any interview. And while the interviewer is definitely asking about your elevator pitch, you may want to use a slightly different format here than you would when introducing yourself to someone you've never met. When preparing your interview pitch, recognize that the person you're speaking to has likely reviewed your cover letter and resume, and may have found you on LinkedIn, Twitter, and other social media channels. For this reason, continue to start your pitch with the answer to "Who you are?" then move to your unique value proposition. Think about adding a few sentences to answer two new questions:

- Why are you passionate about the work you'll be doing in this position specifically?
- What drew you to this company or industry?

Again, you'll want to be sure to keep this answer to 60 seconds or less. Rehearse it with your friends or family before the interview, recite it in the shower the morning of, and practice in the car on your way there. It's often the way you'll kick off the interview, and it's your first opportunity to convey both preparedness and excitement effectively.

3.   **Interacting with a person you might want to add to your social circle.** Whether you know it or not, an enormous part of networking is making friends. As adults, many of us carry with us friends from childhood or college and often find it difficult to expand beyond these groups and create new social circles. But if you've ever moved to a new city or away from your core group of friends, you'll know how imperative it is to develop a skill set that addresses this issue. We'll talk more about innovative networking that focuses on building friendships in Chapter 9, but for now, let's tailor your elevator pitch to meet the needs of someone you'd love to add to your Happy Hour list. Here's the order of importance with the friendship pitch:

- Start the conversation with "Who are you?"
- Next, rather than tell where you're going, insert some information that answers the question, "What do you like to do?" You want to find commonality quickly, whether it's your love of yoga or penchant for the White Sox. Drop in some information about your fun passions.
- Finally, mention a specific example of something you've done recently that aligns with what you like to do. Perhaps you went to a fantastic yoga workshop last weekend or a concert last month. Engage in conversation about whether or not the person you're talking to has done something similar.

4.   **Meeting someone you might want to pursue a romantic relationship with.** By no mean is *You Know Everybody!* a book about dating. But in a way, networking and dating are one and the same. You attend events, you connect online, you engage in small talk, and ultimately you decide whether a relationship will work or not, and on what level.

The trick here is to treat this kind of pitch the exact same way you would the pitch above for friendship. Don't ask about past relationships, engage in awkward political discussions, or be "that girl" who asks about marriage and kids in the first five minutes. Instead, look at the encounter as an opportunity to find a potential friend or networking connection, and you may discover a more romantic connection in time.

5.   **Talking to someone who may become a client or a potential business partner.** If you're an entrepreneur or responsible for generating sales or business in your job, you'll naturally run into opportunities where you'll need to pitch your own services or the services of your company quickly after meeting someone. This scenario calls for only a slight tweak in your original elevator pitch in the form of Question 2. Rather than talking about "where you're going," you want to answer this question tactfully, with grace and ease: "What are you selling?" From there, you continue on with your skill set and unique value proposition and voilà, you've pitched your services without breaking a sweat.

Now that we've walked through a few of the most common scenarios in which you might use your elevator pitch, I want you to go back to the beginning of this chapter. Recall the visioning exercise you completed and the intentions you set for yourself in the next year. Does your elevator pitch as it exists now address these intentions? If it does, great. You've done your job and you're ready to get pitching, ladies. If it doesn't, take some time here to go back through those four questions and ask them again, keeping in mind your intentions for the next year. Think of them when you talk to potential employers, connections, and friends. Give them the opportunity to help you fulfill these goals and even become mentors on your journey, because the power of building a network isn't in the elevator speech or the 60 seconds it takes to properly introduce yourself with it. The power of networking is in what happens after the elevator speech is over, which is exactly what we're going to talk about in the rest of *You Know Everybody!*

As we perfect your elevator pitch and move on to other key parts of the networking and relationship building process, I want to give you an image to pair with your elevator pitch—one that you'll take with you as you become accustomed to naturally introducing yourself and selling your unique proposition: Richard Gere in the movie *Pretty Woman*. It sounds strange, but stay with me here and you'll have a great reminder to take with you to every event from here on out.

Near the beginning of Vivian's relationship with Edward in the movie, she asks him, "What do you do, Edward? 'Cause I know you're not a lawyer." He answers, "I buy companies." She responds, "What do you do with the companies after you buy them?" His answer is critical in the elevator pitch process. He says, "I sell them. I don't sell the whole company; I break it up into pieces and then I sell that off. It's worth more than the whole."

Your elevator speech is exactly like the companies Richard Gere buys in *Pretty Woman*. On its own, in its 60-second packaged deal, it's whole, and you can bet it's incredibly valuable because you are incredibly valuable. But sometimes, when broken up into tiny pieces, it can become even more valuable. At times your elevator pitch will not be a 60-second speech. It will become a conversation: In one moment, you talk about your skills and ask about the skills of the person talking with you. In the next, you help each other understand and better convey your unique value propositions.

I told you early in this chapter that your elevator pitch is the beginning. You are the only person who can develop and propagate your brand, and you have the responsibility to distribute your name and your brand in order to build your own

You Know Everybody! Network. So from now on, every time you walk into a networking event, introduce yourself to a stranger at a party, or meet a new client or prospective employer, you should stand at the ready with your elevator pitch at your side. Know, without a doubt, that you're comfortable with it, confident in your ability to sell it, and are ready to use it either in its entirety or broken up into smaller valuable pieces, Richard Gere-style.

She Knows Everybody! Narrative: Chapter 1
Pitching: Inside and Outside the Elevator

Robin Fisher Roffer
CEO, Chief Creative Officer, Big Fish Marketing

Find Robin Online
Website and Blog: www.BigFishMarketing.com
Twitter: @RobinRoffer

Here's the thing about women. We always use the word "know." Someone says, "Do you know Jenny Davis?" You respond, "Oh, sure, I know Jenny Davis. She works at Accenture!" Some of the time, you might really know Jenny Davis. Some of the time, the truth is you "know of" Jenny Davis, but you don't really *know* her. You know what, though? THAT's OK! Because in that moment you say you "know" someone, what you're really saying is you'd like to know that person. THIS is the beginning of the story of how I came to know (for real, though) Robin Fisher Roffer. In 2010, about to embark on a new life in Chicago, my husband and I took a week off between his job in Minneapolis and his new job in Chicago and went to Mexico, where we indulged in a week of beach reading and little else. In that week of beach reading, I read Robin's book *Make a Name for Yourself: Eight Steps Every Woman Needs to Create a Personal Brand Strategy for Success.* THE book changed my life, and in many ways it began this journey of finding out what I really wanted (to start my own business) and my true goals (to write this book) in the journey.

For the next two years, I often told people about this "woman I know" Robin Fisher Roffer. I told everybody about her book. I even found myself saying, "You need to meet Robin Fisher Roffer. You need to read her book. She's fabulous." I followed her on Twitter and Facebook and slowly began to think I "knew" this woman. I didn't. Until writing my own book brought me to interview her and finally be able to say I really do know her.

I tell this story of knowing and not knowing Robin, because it speaks volumes to the hallmark of a great brand. Having an incredible personal brand and phenomenal personal pitch means that it doesn't work only when you're telling it to someone face to face. It works in social media, it works in print, and it works on the phone. That's why I thought I knew Robin so well. Because with everything she did, online and off, she allowed me to get to know her through her brand.

I'm Google! Robin Fisher Roffer's Exercise That Will Change Your Life, Too

With experience building brand strategy for companies, Robin knew how to build a powerful and unforgettable brand. She knew how to craft an incredible marketing and sales strategy. At the time she wrote *Make a Name for Yourself*, it was a revolutionary idea that branding could extend beyond companies to individuals. She asked herself, "Could people flourish in the same way these companies did with real brand strategy behind them?" She started the process by testing the idea in her own life. When Robin began to portray her highest self, staying "on mission" and working every day to achieve her true purpose, she found the evolution of who she really is within her brand.

In her book, Robin takes women through a branding exercise where you first identify a company you are fiercely loyal to (for me, on that beach in Mexico, it was Google) and list a number of that company's branding traits. Who are they, what do they do, and how do they do it? Robin's theory (it worked for me and countless others) is that the company you choose is likely one that also embodies your own brand traits. When you cross out the company's name and input your own, you might find the list rings true. As I sat on a beach in Mexico reading "innovative, fast moving, ever changing, forward thinking," I turned to my husband and said, "I'M GOOGLE!"

Robin says that by articulating your brand purpose by using a company as an example, you're beginning to answer clearly who you are, why you are here, what you do, and how you do it. This exercise forces you to consciously choose the traits you want to include in your brand. To be able to say you made that choice, and thought strategically about the way you're branding, marketing, and pitching yourself? Powerful.

Robin told me about this kind of "I'm Google" exercise, "Women are very logical. They understand, this is how corporate brands do it, and you can, too."

The Answer to "What Do You Do" Isn't "I'm a Lawyer"

I told you in Chapter 1 that the words "What do you do?" don't always mean what you think they do. Sometimes they're a time filler and other times they're truly asking for your pitch. No matter what the question means, the answer should never be "I'm a lawyer" or "I'm a CPA" or "I work for General Mills." Robin Fisher Roffer and I agreed when she said, "Women have a difficult time crisply and clearly articulating who they are and what they do in a way that speaks volumes about their personal values." Did you catch that? What Robin said there is the essence of what a pitch should be – something that speaks volumes about your personal values. It's not about your job or your paycheck or your employer. It's about you and your values, and ultimately, Robin says, it's about your mission.

When someone asks, "What do you do?," don't tell them the name of your company and your title. When we talked about this, Robin said to me, "It's BORING!" I asked Robin what she says when someone asks her that question, and this was her response: "I inspire professionals to achieve their highest potential." Wow, right? If you were standing across from Robin and you heard her say that sentence, how would you react? You'd probably say, "How do you do that?" There, Robin might tell you about her consulting, her business, her clients, and more. She told me, "Put your mission first. When you do, you give the other person the chance to continue the conversation, and it allows you to continue to tell your 'greatest superhero story.'" Robin told me her own superhero story, and I want to tell it to you. She grew up learning business from her father, a single dad who taught her to write headlines and good design in the advertising business. She watched him win business and she learned how to close a deal. Robin told me about the many times she's told that story of her father in networking settings and, suddenly, rather than chomping a slider, the person across from her has heard, seen, and known who she is. The power of your story, and how you've come to be where you are, is much more powerful than the name of your company or your title.

Robin told me, "When you say your company name, you've branded yourself Quaker or Wonder Bread. But who are you after that? Now you're nobody because you never created a value for yourself. A corporation doesn't have arms and legs and a heart to hold you! What a terrible thing to hitch your brand to!"

So go ahead, Career Girls, stop saying "I work for..." or "I'm a...." What is your mission? What makes you tick? In Chapter 1, I gave you the example of our attorney friend, Sue. She led, not with being an attorney, but with her passion for mentoring young women. When she gives her pitch, her audience will hear her passion. She has passion, and so do you. Lead with that and you'll never go wrong.

Robin said, "Your mission has to come first. Tell a great story about you that shows your true character. The 'what' comes last."

Finding Your "Moves Like Jagger"

As I perused Robin's website before our conversation, I noticed that in one section of it, she tells her potential clients she'll help them get "moves like Jagger." Something about it completely stood out to me, and it inspired me to ask Robin about an important part of the pitch process you all might need to hear – confidence! How can you get those moves in your own brand and in your pitch?

- **Get a coach, a mentor, or a guide.** When Robin wanted to up her game in the realm of public speaking, she found a body language coach, a voice coach, and a presentation coach, and enrolled in a 10-week class at UCLA about giving great presentations. When you really want to perfect something, you also need to look for the best coaches to help you. They don't always have to be people you pay—they can be people who are in your network already and will lend their expertise to your cause. Partnerships build confidence.
- **Do an "essence exercise."** This idea from Robin was revolutionary for me. An essence exercise is simple. Robin says, "Call ten people who know you well. Ask them this very simple question: 'When I walk into a

room, what shows up?' Ask them to stay positive. Then, write down all of those adjectives and circle 3-5 of them that will get you into your Jagger (or J-Lo if that works better for you) state of mind." Of course, I asked Robin for her "essence words" and I was inspired by them, as well. What is Robin's essence? Power. Possibilities. Enthusiasm. Grace. Sparkle. Imagine how powerful Robin Fisher Roffer can be when she shows up at every event, every meeting, every encounter, and thinks "sparkle!"

The "Best of the Best" in Networking Advice

I ended each of the interviews completed for You Know Everybody! by asking each woman to provide to this book's readers her best networking tips and advice. Here are Robin's tips and tricks.

- **Dress beautifully!** Robin wants you to know that 65% of all communication is visual. Dressing the part you play is very important. If you don't do this, then the moment you tell people your mission and your "what," there will be an instant disconnect. Robin recommends wearing something that women can visually connect to. Women love to say, "I love those...." So go ahead, wear that great pair of shoes or an interesting pin, belt, or earrings. These can become what Robin calls "descriptor pieces." If you're creative, wear clothes that are creative. If you're a vice president in a major corporation, you're going to wear pieces that are more serious and that's OK. Then, add those signature pieces that can give insights into who you really are.

- **Be intentional about your networking choices.** When attending an event, go in knowing who's in the room already (don't worry, we'll cover this in more detail in Chapter 7) and who you want to connect with. Go ahead and send them LinkedIn messages prior. Take the time to prescreen and find places you can connect strategically with the perfect people – at conferences, research the panelists. Find out where they went to school, the title of their latest books, etc. This kind of prescreening will allow you to have meaningful things to say when you meet them.

- **Follow up. Right away!** Don't be afraid to say something like, "I was the perky blonde in the red jacket." Jog people's memory with your key traits so you'll be memorable in your follow-up. If you loved a speaker at an event and follow up with her, say something to compliment her performance but do it in a very specific way. Never show up generic or you'll be what Robin says is "L.E.E.: Like Everyone Else!"

- **Be unforgettable.** Show up in your highest self every time. You have to be caring and excited, ready to show others respect. How would you want to be approached? Approach people that way. You don't want to be someone beating her chest, but you also don't want to be the shrinking violet. Your networking persona, the person who does your pitch, has to be you. If you're perky or funny or self-deprecating, then be those things all the time!

two

Powerful Requests: Making "The Ask"

If I want transformation, but can't even be bothered
to articulate what, exactly, I'm aiming for, how will it ever occur?
Half the benefit of prayer is in the asking itself,
in the offering of a clearly posed and well-considered intention.
If you don't have this, all your pleas and desires are boneless, floppy,
inert; they swirl at your feet in a cold fog and never lift.

–ELIZABETH GILBERT

What is the purpose of networking? If I were a professor asking this question in a classroom full of eager young students, I might hear answers about building relationships, creating long-term career connections, getting ahead in your industry, becoming a thought leader, and let me go ahead and say it for you, "Blah, blah, blah." Sure, you want to build good relationships. You want to have meaningful connections with individuals in your field. You want to be seen as a connector. But the bottom line is this: networking is largely transactional. You want something from someone–a connection, a recommendation, a job. And they want something from you. The beginning stages of networking, before you build that kind of meaningful relationship, are all about give and take. Unfortunately, though, this is the fact that most people miss in their networking process.

I began this chapter with a quote from Elizabeth Gilbert's *Eat, Pray, Love.* Though she's talking about prayer in this quote, I want you to consider applying it to networking. You've read Chapter 1 and created your elevator pitch. Does this mean you're done? No way. The most important part of any networking connection, especially the first time you meet someone, inevitably comes at the *end* of the elevator pitch. If you've done your job correctly with your elevator pitch, the person you're speaking to likes you, understands who you are and what you do, and wants to help you. You've got them exactly where you want them, at which time they'll usually say something like, "How can I help you?" This is the moment most women fail at networking. Women largely want to be helpful, not helped. We don't want to be a burden or a hassle for anyone. So at this moment, most women say something like, "Oh, gee, I'm not sure. Let me think about that." The connection ends, and often, so does the relationship. Why? Because you didn't make the ask. You weren't able to clearly articulate what you want and why you want it.

This is exactly what Elizabeth Gilbert means when she's talking about prayer. If you really want to make networking connections that help you get a job, get ahead, relocate, or reach other lofty goals in your life, and you can't even be "bothered to articulate" exactly what you want, how can you expect the other person to help you? Just like Ms. Gilbert says about prayer, you have to create a "clearly posed and well-considered intention." Only that will prevent you from standing in front of someone you barely know with your networking hopes and dreams swirling at your feet in a fog while you slink away and hope you do better next time.

Don't get me wrong. Asking for help isn't easy, which is exactly why we don't do it often. We convince ourselves that the person we're asking will say no, will laugh at us, or will think we're utterly ridiculous. But ultimately, what's the worst that can happen? If you ask for something you truly desire, and the person you're asking says no...move on, move up, and find someone else to help you. It's not the end of the world. Easier said than done, right? But let's consider the other side of the coin here. What's the best that can happen? You ask and you receive exactly what you want. And isn't that worth taking the chance?

To illustrate this point, let me tell you a story about an incredibly dynamic Israeli man named Lior Zoref. In May 2010, Lior recorded a video at TEDx Tel Aviv with a single goal in mind. He sat next to his best friend and told him he wanted to speak at the main TED conference some time in the next 10 years. If you're not familiar with the TEDx conferences, they are smaller, locally produced versions of one of the most popular conferences in the world, TED (short for Technology, Entertainment, Design). While speakers all over the world are dazzling audiences at TEDx conferences, the central TED event is held yearly, spanning four to six days in a different location each year, and with a hefty price tag of $7,500 to attend. Attendance carries a big price, and becoming a speaker on the big TED stage is nearly impossible.

Clearly, Lior Zoref's dream was a big one. If he were chosen as a TED speaker, he would join the ranks of great minds like Bill Gates, Stephen Hawking, Tony Robbins, Sheryl Sandberg, and more. But his dream would come true sooner than he ever expected. I was privileged to hear Lior tell the story of his journey to TED in October 2012 and it is truly a remarkable tale. Just a year after making his "I have a TED Talk dream" declaration at TEDx Tel Aviv, a contest emerged at TED, inviting individuals from around the world to submit audition tapes for a chance to speak. With some hesitation, thinking it was too soon, Lior submitted his video and was ultimately chosen to be one of the few who auditioned in person in New York City on May 24, 2011. You can guess what happened next: Lior Zoref was chosen as a TED speaker, only a year after declaring his dream.

But the story of asking for what you want doesn't come in his ability to state a dream and go after it. It comes in his preparation for his TED Talk. Lior's idea for TED was revolutionary. He proposed to have the first ever crowdsourced TED Talk. All along the way, as he prepared for TED, he asked his blog readers, friends, and family for feedback, content, and everything else under the sun, right down to the clothes he would wear to the event. Somewhere in the middle, though, came an incredible suggestion.

In the world of crowd wisdom, there is a famous story about an ox. In it, a group of people is asked to estimate the weight of an ox standing in front of them. Of course, nearly all of them are wrong. But when their answers are averaged, they produced the exact weight of the ox. What's the moral of the story? Crowds are just as powerful as experts. This is exactly the point Lior wanted to make in his TED Talk, and it didn't take long for a 16-year old boy to suggest Lior recreate this experiment in his TED Talk with – you guessed it – a real live ox. Knowing full well he'd be denied, Lior thought it couldn't hurt to ask. So he sent this email to TED:

Lior Zoref's "Ask" Email to TED

Subject: A crazy/fun idea for my on-stage presentation

Hi,

As I'm building my presentation for TED 2012 using crowd sourcing, I asked the crowd for creative ideas that will help me demonstrate crowd wisdom during my talk.

I received more than 100 amazing ideas but one of them stood above all. It came from a fascinating 16 years old teenager.

It all starts with an old story from 1906 that was the foundation for wisdom of crowds theory.

You probably know this story, but here's a summary just in case:

The British scientist Francis Galton stumbled upon an intriguing contest in his village. An Ox was on display, and the villagers were invited to guess the animal's weight. Nearly 800 participated, but not one person hit the exact mark. Astonishingly enough he found out that the mean of those 800 guesses was the exact weight of the Ox. This insight presages the idea of crowd sourcing and the wisdom of the crowd.

Now let's get back to the idea for my presentation. Take a deep breath...

I want to recreate this experiment on stage, but this time instead of using pen and paper, crowd wisdom will be collected using smart phones.

To do that, I need an Ox on stage ! (It could be another big animal, but if we wish to be true to the story, we're talking about an Ox)

I need it for just 30 seconds in which I'll ask the audience (including everyone watching the live stream) to use their smart phones, enter a short url, and then enter their weight estimate.

After a few minutes, I'll show how the mean of their estimate is accurate. In order to have a backup plan, I'll start this process 24 hours ahead of time (using HD video of the Ox) so that I'll have a backup number just in case.

I know it might sound a bit crazy. But I feel that this demonstration will have a big impact on the audience and will also be so much fun...

So can I have an Ox please?...
Thanks, Lior

It's the last line of Lior's email that really counts here. He says, "So can I have an Ox please?" You might be surprised at what happened next. Not only did TED give Lior an ox, they gave him a famous ox, Teddy, sourced from a company that provides animals to movie studios. This ox was the Brad Pitt of oxen.

You may not need the Brad Pitt of oxen. But what you need is just as important, and just as essential to your success. Your hopes, dreams, wishes, and ox-like requests can get you exactly where Lior ended up—fulfilling his dreams on stage, at TED, with an ox.

I'm telling you Lior's story for a reason. He could have rambled on and on about the ox and the story of the ox, and the only thing that mattered is that last sentence: "Can I have an Ox please?" He made the ask, he made it clearly, and then he shut up! Now I'm not saying Lior is a better "asker" because he's a man, but I can tell you this is where most women go wrong. Either we don't make the ask at all, or when we do, we immediately retract it. We say, "I'll need to be paid $100,000." (loooooong pause) "But if that's too much I can definitely be flexible. How about $90,000?" (another looooooooong pause) "Or $80,000. $80,000 is good." Congratulations, lady, you've just given your new employer a $20,000 break. Take a cue from Lior here. Make the ask and then shut up.

You've crafted your elevator pitch and worked up the confidence to make a clear ask. You're ready. Now, let's dive deeper to find out what you're really asking *for!* What you need now is a networking "wish list." In the same way you'll know your elevator pitch up, down, forwards, and backwards, so you can break it up piece by piece and use it throughout a conversation, you will need to learn your wish list and be ready to deploy the right "wish" the moment someone says, "What can I do to help you?"

The idea of a "wish list" certainly isn't unique to networking situations. Amazon.com uses it to keep track of the things you want to buy but haven't yet. Children use them to give Santa Claus ideas on what they want for Christmas, and mobile apps are popping up everywhere to drop hints to husbands and parents on gift ideas. But the best example of wish lists as they are connected to networking comes from the nonprofit sector. Many nonprofit organizations, front and center on their websites, have a "wish list" link or tab. Here, they list the goods, services, and other specific needs they have at the time. Organizations supporting school-aged children might be in need of notebooks, pencils, or backpacks, while others supporting adults in career transition might be looking for business suits and volunteers to review resumes. It's common for someone to call a nonprofit organization saying they want to volunteer or give back, but the resources and staff time required to answer every inquiry directly can be taxing. The beauty of publishing a wish list, from a fundraising perspective, is allowing your website visitors, who are looking to give back, the opportunity to self-select and provide the goods and services you need specifically rather than broadly.

In the same way nonprofit organizations have a standard "wish list," you should as well. It shouldn't exist only in your head, either. Just like you did with your elevator pitch, to truly keep your wish list in your back pocket and be able to deploy it at any given time throughout a conversation, you have to go through the process of creating it. You have to become intimately familiar with what's on it.

To get your wish list started, every individual need on your wish list should line up directly with a goal or intention you've set for your life and career. To fill out the chart below, consider looking back on your intentions from Chapter 1 or creating new intentions and goals to work with here. Take time to list your intentions in the column on the left, and for each intention, list a few tangible things you'd need in order to see it manifested.

Your Clear Intentions or Goals	What Do You Need to Get There?
Example: To make a career transition in the next year from financial planning to personal coaching.	Example: 1. Connections to individuals who are experienced in personal coaching to provide insights and advice. 2. People who might be willing to participate in a practice coaching session with me. 3. A website designer to help me get my site up and running to generate business.

Everything you've listed in the column on the right is – ta-da! – your wish list. Type it out, keep it with your elevator pitch, learn it, memorize it, and take it with you wherever you go. You'll never again find yourself saying, "Let me get back to you." Instead, you'll know exactly what you need and be ready to ask for it. But be careful, because asking for help is an art, not a science, and if you ask in the wrong way at the wrong time, you might find yourself turning potential connections off instead of on.

I said at the beginning of this chapter that networking is largely a transactional process. For this reason, many of us start to think about networking in the mode of a sales person. We go to events and think, "How many cards can I get?" We turn LinkedIn into a game of numbers, collecting connections even when they're friends of siblings or long-lost college acquaintances. We rack up Rolodexes full of cards, databases full of email addresses, and ultimately we think we've won the networking game. But in the process of asking for help and developing your network, I want to encourage you to tweak your mentality just a bit. Instead of thinking like a sales person, let's take another cue from the nonprofit sector and think about networking as a fundraiser. Fundraisers are, without a doubt, transaction focused. But accompanying their need to close the deal is a drive to fulfill their organization's mission, exactly the kind of example we need in order to build a strong network, make meaningful connections, and ultimately, to make powerful asks of those connections as well.

There's an old saying in nonprofit fundraising: "Ask for money, get advice. Ask for advice, get money." Truly great fundraisers know this and live by it in everything they do. I spent nearly a decade in nonprofit fundraising before starting Career Girl Network, and whenever I would tell someone I was a fundraiser, I knew what was going through their minds: "You ask rich people for money." Technically, yes. Practically, no. Great fundraisers know that the basis of all giving is a comprehensive understanding of the organization the donor is giving to, the purpose of the gift, and the impact they can expect it to have. That's why most fundraisers enter a relationship with the "ask for advice" mantra. This engages potential donors in a conversation about what the organization needs, where it can improve, and finally, how they can be of service in making certain improvements.

Let's break down our example above into how we might take a powerful request and transform its tone from "Help me" to "Give me your best advice." The woman in the example above, let's call her Liz, is a seasoned financial planner. She's worked for a corporate financial services firm for 15 years and recently she's discovered that while she enjoys working with her clients, the number-crunching portion of her job is draining her more and more as the years go on. She wants the ability to counsel clients on the decisions they make in their life, without being their checking account accountability partner. She's enrolled in a nationally recognized training program for life coaching and wants to transition in the next year to providing coaching services full time. She's clear on what she needs now–mentors in the coaching sphere, practice clients, and a web designer to help her implement marketing initiatives and direct sales for her coaching. Let's assume Liz is meeting an acquaintance for coffee to talk about her new business. She's given her elevator speech and the woman across from her is interested, engaged, and asks the inevitable, "How I can help you?" question. Which of the following responses is more powerful?

> *Example A: Do you know any coaches? I need to meet with someone who is already practicing to get some advice.*
> *Example B: Actually, you might be able to help me. I'm hoping to connect directly with coaches who have been successful already in their businesses. I noticed you're connected to someone on LinkedIn who works for a coaching group with multiple programs and coaches. Do you think she might be a good resource for me?*

Notice that in the second request, Liz doesn't ask directly for the connection, but rather asks for the person's advice about the connection. Does the person think this might be a good connection to make? This gives him or her the opportunity to say no, that's not a good connection. Perhaps the person or the group you're talking about is no longer in business and the person you're speaking to knows that. Or maybe she's not close to that person and simply doesn't feel comfortable giving feedback. But as much as it gives her the opportunity to say no, it also gives her the opportunity to say yes, or to offer another piece of advice or an example to help you in your search.

Let's look at one more example that might be more applicable to talking with someone you're meeting for the first time. How might you respond to their "How can I help you?" question differently than you'd respond to one from a person you've had time to research or learn more about?

> *Example A: I'd be willing to give you a free coaching session if you'd let me practice on you!*
> *Example B: You might be the perfect person to help me launch my coaching business! I'm targeting women who are very much like you–young, successful, and great networkers. Would you be willing to sit down with me to talk through the way you're setting goals in your career? It would help me to tailor my services to women like you.*

In both examples, as different as they are, Liz is asking for the same thing–a practice coaching session. But in Example B, she frames it in a way that shows the person she's talking about how much she would be helping her by participating in this kind of meeting, and she's being a bit more vague about the fact that she wants to practice her coaching skills on her. Someone who isn't familiar with life coaching may respond very negatively to the first example, but respond positively to helping Liz develop a strong marketing plan and demographic study for her business, as she positions it in Example B.

Making powerful requests, whether it's the first time you've met someone or the tenth, is all about being specific and clear, while keeping in mind what their needs and wants might be as well. If networking is transactional, you can't always be the one selling, and you can't always be the one buying, either. You have to meet your network halfway: Be willing to both ask for help and open doors to ensure you're engaging in a mutually beneficial connection, one that keeps you both happy about the relationship you're creating.

You know how to make the ask now, but do you know how to keep the relationship going in order to continue making the right asks of the right people at the right times? Don't worry, because we're going to figure it out together right now.

We've talked a lot so far about topics that relate largely to new connections. You're not going to saddle up next to your best friend or someone you've known for 10 years at a networking event and rattle off your elevator pitch. But at times, even connections you've had for years may not be entirely aware of what's going on in your life or your career. How, then, do you keep people in the loop and connected to what you need without being the constant "asker"? The answer: You have to "date" your network.

Here's another old fundraising adage for you: "You don't kiss on the first date, and you don't make the ask in the first meeting." That doesn't mean you don't make *any* ask. It means you don't make *the* ask. Go with me here, and let's consider our friend Liz from the example above once again. In the second example, she's networking with a woman she's hoping will become a practice client for her, and asking her very specifically to engage in a single meeting sit-down to talk through her career goals and desires. But let's be honest, what does Liz *really* want from this woman? She wants a client! Liz is becoming a life coach, and while she has to practice with a certain number of clients, surely the goal for those individuals is to transition into paying clients. Why would she be starting this business if she didn't want to make money? But Liz isn't going to say, "Hey, lady, do you want to have a couple of free practice sessions with me, and then I'll hit you with a bill?" No way! Instead, she's going to "date" her new acquaintance and continue to build the relationship.

Let's say they sit down for that first one-on-one session, and have a great time. They hit it off, it turns into a full-blown coaching session, and Liz really feels like she's helping her client set goals and get to the root of the actions she needs to take to be successful. At the end of the session, Liz will need to practice her "second date ask" and say something like, "I really feel like we're getting somewhere here. I feel like I'm growing as a coach, and I hope I'm helping you as well. Would you be willing to continue with another 1-2 sessions to help me gain experience as I'm growing my coaching business? These sessions would be at no charge to you." Liz is giving this woman a few more free "dates" to test the waters. Let's fast forward, then, and assume the next two sessions continue being productive and mutually beneficial. That's the point where Liz may say, "I'd love to continue working with you. I'm at a point in my business where I'm implementing packages and pricing and would love to discuss a coaching package with you to continue into the future." She might offer a discount or special rate to thank this client for being one of her first test subjects as well, but ultimately her goal is to transition this woman to a paying client.

The process Liz took is the same process all of us should take when we're hoping to make "big asks" of someone in our network. Here are a couple of examples of common big asks you might want to make and ways to romance your connections over time to get them done:

What You Really Want	Sample Process to Get There
You're in charge of business development in your company, and are hoping to land a deal with the company of a woman you recently met at a networking event.	1. Follow up after the networking event and ask her to coffee or lunch. 2. Keep your initial coffee or lunch meeting friendly and conversational. Learn about her background, her role in her company, and her life outside work. Close by inviting her to an industry event. 3. Attend the industry event with her and get to know her better. If it feels natural, find time to talk shop and tell her more about what you do during the event. 4. Reach out and invite her to meet you and a colleague and talk more about how you might be able to do business together.
You'd just LOVE to work for Calvin Klein and you just met their Director of HR at a friend's birthday party. You're fighting the urge to send him your resume and cover letter and beg for a job.	1. Ask your friend to connect you directly. Then, introduce yourself with a short and sweet email about how you're interested in what he does and would like to learn more about his work. 2. Schedule a phone call or meet for coffee, and come prepared with specific questions. With this kind of meeting, it's good to be clear you're looking for a professional connection and keep it focused on your career. 3. Connect on LinkedIn, follow on Twitter, etc. and begin to get a sense for what he's posting/talking about. Take this opportunity to connect via email about an industry issue or send a relevant article. 4. Keep watching for jobs available within Calvin Klein. When you find one, reach out to him directly and ask not for a recommendation, but for advice. "This looks like a fantastic opportunity. Do you think it's something I might be a good fit for?"

Even if you're meeting someone for the first time, you can generally size them up into one of three categories: 1) probably can't help me, 2) might be able to help me, and 3) definitely can help me. We'll talk more in *You Know Everybody!* about how to handle the first category, and we've already talked about how to make good asks of people in the second category. It's the third category where you absolutely must employ this strategy of "dating" your network. Why? Because if you're jumping up and down inside about meeting this person, chances are other people are as well. Chances are, they're one of the "hard to gets" that we'll talk about in Chapter 6. So take your time and let them get to know you. The more someone knows and likes you, the more willing they'll be to help you get ahead. And in that time, you'll get to know them and be able to better assess how you might be able to help them or their business as well.

Finally, in this "dating" process, there are a few land mines you should be painfully aware of avoiding in your interactions, especially when it comes to the big fish in your networking pool. Do your best not to make these common mistakes:

- **DON'T ask for something every time you connect.**
  If every connection you make with an individual in your network includes "Can you connect me to...?" or "Would you mind?" or "Do you have time?" you're asking for too much. There has to be room in your networking schedule for every person you're connecting with just to build a relationship. Reach out when you don't need something as much as you do when you need something. Whether it's a congratulations on a big deal they made that recently appeared in the local paper, or a Happy Birthday email, making connections for the sake of connection, and connection only, will build relationships far beyond what transactional networking can. And when you do reach out for a specific ask, they'll remember that the last email you sent or phone call you made was not an ask, and perhaps be more willing to provide their guidance or connections.

- **DON'T give up when someone says no.**

  I told you earlier in this chapter to be a fundraiser, not a sales person. But in some instances, you have to go back to the tricks of the trade when it comes to sales, one of which is "No is just the next step to a YES!" And while I don't advocate you hound anyone to get what you want, if someone refuses a request, consider the reason for the refusal. If you request a meeting with someone and they don't respond, try again, and try in a different way this time. If you emailed before, call the second time. If someone ultimately says no to meeting with you, rather than tucking your tail between your legs and running away, go back to the source and do what great fundraisers do: Ask for advice. If they said no to your meeting request, respond with, "I'm very interested in learning more about your business, and I understand your schedule is very busy. Is there someone within your company you might recommend I reach out to instead?" This kind of perseverance might turn someone off, but what's the worst that happens then? You're in the same place you were a moment ago–with a no. But the best-case scenario is they do provide a connection and that relationship blossoms into a mutually beneficial one.

- **DON'T assume anything.**

  When it comes to networking, especially for women, it's so easy to get caught up in our own insecurities. When someone doesn't return our emails, it's common to go into a tailspin of "She doesn't like me, she thinks I'm a moron, blah, blah, blah." Stop that. You can't assume anyone's intentions in this world, especially when it comes to networking. And you know as well as anyone how your email can fill up in an hour, you forget to respond to someone you want to respond to, and suddenly it's been a month with an unreturned phone call to your best friend, let alone someone you've just met or never met. Give the people you're connecting with and yourself a great big break and stop assuming anyone's intentions. Then, refer back to the second DON'T in this list, and try another tactic. Your insecurities will kill your networking more than anyone else's actions will.

At the beginning of this chapter, Elizabeth Gilbert painted a pretty dismal picture of what it looks like when you don't ask. She cautions us to be careful to craft clear intentions lest we end up with goals that are "boneless, floppy, inert; they swirl at your feet in a cold fog and never lift." You've set your intentions and created your asks in this chapter. With them, consider that picture for a moment. Looking down at your feet, you see all of the actions you hope to take, all of the asks you hope to powerfully make, and all of the amazing things that could come of them swirling at your feet in a fog. It's not a fun image, is it? So let's replace it with a more powerful one.

For a moment, think of all the intentions and goals you set earlier in this chapter. Then, think of every single thing you'd need to get there, everything on the list you made. It might seem daunting. If you're going to move across the country, you need recommendations for everything from a moving company to a realtor to a new hair stylist. When you pile on top of that a new job, a paycheck, insurance decisions, and the other "big stuff," you have one hell of a list of asks for those you're about to meet. But before you get bogged down in the behemoth of that list, take a breath and fill it with a photo to replace the one of swirling fog. Fill it with the image of what your life would look like if every one of the asks you'd need to make to get all of those things was fulfilled, and everything you needed to accomplish your goals were sitting in front of you, right at eye level. There it is for the taking. Choose your adventure. This image, one of abundance and strength and the gifts given to you by hundreds of people in your network, is more powerful than any I can imagine, and it should give you power as well. To lift the fog in your life and your career, to shine a light on what you truly want and deserve, you're going to have to first be bothered to articulate it, which I hope you've already done in this chapter. Then, you have to go out and ask for it with every ounce of professionalism, authenticity, and grace you can muster. Then, and only then, will you find the table full of opportunity sitting in front of you.

She Knows Everybody! Narrative: Chapter 2
Powerful Requests: Making "The Ask"

Cindy McLaughlin
Co-Founder, Chairman and CEO, Style for Hire

Find Cindy Online
Twitter: @cindymclaughlin
LinkedIn: linkedin.com/in/cindymclaughlin

If anyone is truly skilled at making asks, it's an entrepreneur. As you build a business, you'll find yourself asking for help, asking for partners, asking for money, and much more. Together with Stacy London, her longtime friend and the star of TLC's "What Not To Wear," Cindy McLaughlin launched the innovative fashion-meets-tech startup, Style for Hire. As CEO, Cindy McLaughlin is no stranger to making the ask on behalf of Style for Hire. Though the business is truly taking off in 2013, Cindy and Stacy have been working diligently on Style for Hire for more than five years. In 2011, Cindy's expertise in making the ask paid off handsomely as the company raised over $1 million in Series A funding.

Transitioning from a long career in fashion sales and buying to becoming the CEO of a startup makes Cindy the perfect person to tell us about the ways making the ask can be most effective in our careers. Listen up. This lady knows the drill!

Don't Sell, Partner!

Prior to joining Style for Hire, Cindy was the CEO of another startup and no stranger to the fashion industry. She penned deals and made sales with giants of the fashion world including Barneys and on behalf of Federated Department Stores early in her career. I asked Cindy about her experience selling to the "big dogs" in the fashion industry. Her response surprised me. In the shrewd and cutthroat world of fashion, Cindy's advice is that hard selling simply doesn't work. She says, "My strength has always been in creative partnerships. I spend a lot of time thinking about how one company can team up with another so that both companies benefit." Cindy advocates that in any ask you're making—whether in a job search or an entrepreneurship venture—to look for mutually beneficial options in the relationship you're creating.

You can't create partnerships, though, without truly knowing the person or company you want to partner with. Cindy says, "The longer you're in an industry, you start to understand the keys to language in the industry and the big issues businesses are facing. To approach business development in a partnership-driven way, you really have to understand the other partner's business and its need."

When you make an ask in your career, approach it by asking a few questions:

1. Do I fully understand the needs and current priorities of the person I'm approaching?
2. What benefit can this person receive from becoming my partner?
3. Am I looking for a win-win situation? Or is this ask all about me?

Partnership isn't important only in big businesses like Barneys. It's also important in building networks for business development with small businesses and for general networking. Cindy's company, Style for Hire, is educating stylists on this very partnership mentality. The strength Cindy brings to the table in creating partnerships in the fashion business has allowed Style for Hire to create corporate partnerships for their stylists. This model ultimately teaches Style for Hire stylists to build their business effectively with a partnership model that works just as well for individuals as it does for corporations.

Style for Hire's place in the market today is one that is big enough and strong enough to be sure they're being seen, but small enough to ensure the quality of their work and the partnerships they create. Take that notion and apply it to your own networking, and you'll never go wrong. Keep your network big enough to ensure you're being seen, and serving all interests in your career, but small enough to ensure your relationships are strong, your partnerships are meaningful, and the asks you make of those partners are strategic and professionally made.

Paint the Picture

If you've done the research and you're ready to make an ask, how do you do it in a way that makes the best impression on the individual you're asking? Cindy contends it requires just two things – passion and vision. "Paint the picture of what the world could look like 'if.' With that kind of passion, you can convince the people around you that you have the key to that vision and the ability to execute it." When you paint that picture, the picture of what your partnership would look like "if," your energy will be infectious, your excitement clear, and ultimately you'll be poised to receive a more positive reaction.

Often, when asking for a partnership to begin, someone might see only the hard work, the time, and the dedication involved in building a relationship. It's your job to paint a picture of collaboration that will show someone it's possible to do something revolutionary together. The idea of building something new, making a difference, changing something, or revolutionizing something will excite anyone!

Practice Makes Perfect

People say timing is everything. Cindy McLaughlin and her partner at Style for Hire, Stacy London, admittedly found themselves in the midst of some very bad timing at the beginning of their journey with Style for Hire. The company began in 2008 in the middle of the worst financial recession in recent memory. "This was not the ideal time," Cindy said, "to pursue funding for a new business." But between 2008 and 2011, when the company raised more than $1 million, Cindy became an expert at making the ask, specifically for funding.

Cindy told me, "I asked thousands of people for advice and funding in the beginning of Style for Hire, and I got much better at it over time." Cindy even noted that the process of making many, many asks was incredibly helpful to the business, as it gave Cindy and Stacy the opportunity to think through critical questions about building Style for Hire. Cindy said, "When making asks, every now and then someone asks you a question you haven't considered. If the answer to those questions isn't clear, you know it's time to go back to the drawing board."

If you're actively searching for a mentor or a sponsor, practice can make perfect when it comes to making those asks. Cindy recommends practicing on what she calls "low-risk friends." These individuals might be mid-level colleagues or current mentors who are willing to hear your pitch and give honest, but caring, feedback to help you get better. It's now your job to take their feedback seriously and implement it into planning your next asks.

Cindy said, "In 2008, nobody was investing in anything, much less in the services business or personal styling industry. Every single person we pitched taught us something. We spent a lot of time going back to the drawing board and rethinking the business. We made great headway by having coffee with people, listening carefully to them, and eventually, even if they didn't invest, they offered up ideas, connections, and resources that fed our process." You have to do the same in your career. Be willing to listen carefully and change your path if the ideas are good ones.

Women Helping Women

It's natural that people want to invest in things that resonate with them emotionally. In Cindy's journey asking for funding for Style for Hire, she found that men often didn't "get it" as quickly as women did. Most of them understood the business fundamentally, but simply didn't feel it for themselves. Things were different with women. When it came to Style for Hire, "They could see it. They understood the struggles in themselves and their family members. They were much more able to dig deep than men, who could intellectually appreciate the business model, but not connect to the outcome."

While networking with men should most definitely be a part of your strategy, the truth about asking for funding in a business geared towards women is the same truth of networking for women. Other women will sometimes just "get" your needs and desires more quickly than men will. If you're nervous about the idea of making an ask, no matter what it might be, it may be more comfortable for you to start by asking women you trust, then move on to asking women you want to meet, and only then consider asking men for their assistance in your career. Your comfort level is important in being successful in your asks, and often the notion of women helping women can aid in your success level.

The "Best of the Best" in Networking Advice

I ended each of the interviews completed for You Know Everybody! by asking each woman to provide to this book's readers her best networking tips and advice. Here are Cindy's tips and tricks.

- **Matchmaker, Matchmaker!** It's not the same as setting your best friend up with a guy you think might be her future husband, but being a matchmaker can be incredibly influential in your career. You might not end up making the maid of honor speech, but it counts nonetheless. Cindy says, "I love playing matchmaker and getting people together who might like one another and be able to help each other." Cindy recommends focusing your matchmaking on promoting women. When you matchmake with a person you truly want to help get ahead, your intentions will be pure and your results will be more successful.

- **Practice facial recognition.** Cindy says, "One of things I'm just terrible at is face and name recognition. So I try to remember stories about those people, and emotions associated with them, and that makes it easier to remember faces as well." If this is something you're not great at, work hard at honing your expertise. When you can look at someone and immediately remember her, it presents you in a more favorable light. People like to be remembered.

- **Remind me!** Even if you're doing exactly the same thing today you were doing last year, remind your network you're there. Send Christmas cards, quick hellos online, and update your social media regularly. You can't always remind people only when you need a change in your career. Sometimes saying hello when everything is the same is even more important.

three

The Who! Getting the Right People on Your Side

You need at least one friend who will help you move a body.
No judgment. There in a second. No explanation.

–Dr. Brene Brown

Hanging on the racks at your favorite high-end department store, be it Bloomingdale's or Nordstrom or Neiman Marcus, is a long sparkly gown that fits you like a glove. And if you're anything like me, once or twice a year, you find yourself wandering through that sparkly area of the store, trying on a few things. And as you stand in the dressing room thinking, "Damn, this dress makes my butt look good," you're also thinking, "I wish I had somewhere to wear it!" Unfortunately, our wallets can't always justify being all dressed up with nowhere to go.

The same notion is true for networking. Why have a sparkly shiny elevator pitch if there's no one there to hear it? Why should you set big goals if there's no one in your life to support you in them? The nature of a network, friends, is just like that elegant gown in the department store. The gown is justifiable to your bank account only if there's someone to see you in it. And a network is powerful only if it's full of people who want to see you succeed!

Building a network, though, isn't as easy as playing the numbers. Someone who has 1,000+ Facebook friends and hundreds of LinkedIn connections might seem well networked, but the truth is, they might not be. Building a network isn't just about collecting trophies in the form of business cards and online contacts: It's about strategically determining who you need in your network and the types of people you want in your network, and finding the right way to go after those targets to get them on your side, in your pocket, and fighting for your success. Your network should be exclusive, strategic, and intentional. Sure, this book is called *You Know Everybody!*, but the "everybody" in question should be the everybody you choose, not the everybody that's most convenient.

Take a moment to think of two or three people in your life who have massive networks. You know who I'm talking about. They're the kind of people you'd turn to and say, "*You Know Everybody!*" Maybe it's a boss who is well-connected in your industry or a friend who always has the skinny on the best after parties and VIP events. Chances are the people you're thinking of fit into one of two categories of networkers. Try these on for size:

Type of Networker	Characteristics
The *"Nobody Gets In to See the Wizard"* Networker	• *Trustworthy and loyal.* • *Comfortable networking mostly in her current industry, age group, and sector.* • *Fiercely guarded about her contacts, and will rarely if ever provide someone's email or phone number.* • *Hesitant to recommend someone she's just met without developing a strong relationship.* • *Would never connect with someone on LinkedIn if she didn't know her personally and for an extended period of time.* • *Boasts relationships that have lasted decades.*
The *"Everybody's Welcome"* Networker	• *Considers herself a social butterfly.* • *Immediately adds people to LinkedIn, Twitter, and Facebook after meeting them.* • *Calls someone her "friend" even if she's known her only a few days.* • *Always willing to make connections and ask for help on another's behalf of those in her network.* • *Always the hostess, she's constantly inviting you to events and telling you about new groups to join.*

If the great networkers in your life fall into one of the two characterizations above, you know some fantastic networkers. Both approaches can build strong and long-lasting networks for a multitude of purposes. Your goal in this process shouldn't be to become or avoid either of these types of networkers. Rather, it should be to combine the two strategically and become what I'm, of course, calling the *You Know Everybody!* Networker. Wouldn't it be amazing if, at the end of this process, you embodied all of the characteristics in the following chart?

Type of Networker	Characteristics
The *"You Know Everybody!"* Networker	• *Trusted by those she meets and loyal to those in her network, but always willing to add individuals to her circle.* • *Loves meeting people of all ages and industries, and is intensely curious about how other people work and succeed.* • *Willing to make connections within her network that will help those connecting and create mutually beneficial partnerships.* • *Commonly introduces friends she's known 10+ years to friends she met just recently.* • *Knows which events are the most valuable and which members of her network might be interested in specific opportunities.*

I bring up these types of networkers in this chapter because the key word in becoming the best kind of networker and building the most incredible network to get you ahead is this: Strategy. You want to build a network that has a plan and a purpose, one that supports you in the right ways, and supports your goals and intentions. You have to strike a cool balance. To ensure you're building the right kind of network, it is important to note that while not everyone should get in to see the Wizard, adding people to your network for reasons both substantive and shallow is not only acceptable, it's encouraged. Why? Because your network, when strategically built, should also be well balanced. To give you an idea of the balance you're looking for, I've created the "Seven Layers of Your Personal Network" to help you evaluate your current network and determine where you might need to add a few people here and there.

The Seven Layers of Your Personal Network, An Overview

1. The "Move a Body" Friend
2. Cheerleaders and Shoulders to Cry On
3. Cheers to You!
4. Coffee Mates and Lunch Dates
5. Conjunction Connections
6. Stand Still, Look Pretty
7. What's Your Name Again?

The Seven Layers of Your Personal Network, Deep Dive

1. The "Move a Body" Friend

I started this chapter with a quote from Brene Brown, famed TED speaker and author of the 2012 Best Seller *Daring Greatly*. She tells us we should all have at least one friend who would, without hesitation, "help you move a body." Now, let's hope you never call anyone looking for a shovel. But if you did, ask yourself this: Who would you call? These kinds of friends are few and far between, but hopefully we all have one or two of them in our crew.

I highlight this kind of friend as the first layer of your personal network for a reason. Often, we forget about them. When we think about networking, we think about connections we've made at work, at events, and through acquaintances. We sometimes forget to include our best friend from high school or college, or the next-door neighbor we've raised our children with. We get into a trap of separating personal and professional, and being unable to merge them back together. But when it comes to your network, personal connections can be just as powerful as professional connections, and their purpose can shapeshift throughout our relationships. So keep these "Move a Body" friends at the top of your networking list and don't count them out when you need help with smaller, less intense tasks than burial and general crime cover-ups.

To start to get a picture of who exists in your network, list a few "Move a Body" friends below:

_____

_____

_____

_____

2. **Cheerleaders and Shoulders to Cry On**
    While in your life you might only encounter a small number of "move a body" friends, hopefully you've collected quite a few who rest in this second layer of your personal network. They're the kind of friends you'd call if you went through a break-up, needed help moving across town, or wanted someone to look over a cover letter before you apply for a job. They're what I call both your "Cheerleaders" and your "Shoulders to Cry On." They're the first people you'd call when you need a boost or had a bad day, and the easiest people in your life to show your true feelings to.

It's easy to confuse these individuals with your "move a body" friends, but often those in your first layer don't fit into the second. And that's OK. I have a dear friend from college who I would literally lay down on a train track for. She is, without a doubt, my "Move a Body" friend. But when it comes to day-to-day hardships, she's not always my first call. That doesn't diminish the way she exists in my life or my network, and it doesn't mean she can't be a cheerleader or a shoulder to cry on. But for now, let's distinguish these two types of connections to make room for some analysis later on.

To continue painting an accurate photo of your network, list your "Cheerleaders and Shoulders to Cry On" below:

_____

_____

_____

_____

3. **Cheers to You!**
    The next layer of your personal network consists of connections I call "Cheers to You!" They're the people you'd invite to your birthday party at the hot new restaurant, the people you'd call when you're in the mood for a Wednesday night happy hour, and generally fall more into the "friend" category than the "business connection" category. They're an important part of your network because their relationship with you is largely personal, but they're usually willing to act as a reference, connect you to someone they know at a company you might be interested in, and if they're a social butterfly, even better!

    When you think of these kinds of connections, think of the "it girls" in your community, the ones who always have reservations at the best restaurants and whose wardrobes you'd love to steal. They're not always full of substance, but if they're having a martini with you once every month or two, it's a safe bet that their happy hour list is as long as their credit card bill, which can come in handy for you in the future.

Keep building on your network picture, and list some of your best "Cheers to You!" connections below:

_____

_____

_____

_____

4. Coffee Mates and Lunch Dates

At this layer of your network, we begin to cross over from those in the friend zone to people who are more specifically professional connections. When you're thinking about the kinds of people who reside in this layer, you'll think about former coworkers you continue to keep in touch with, individuals you may have met at a professional luncheon or event, potential employers you're networking with intentionally, and others you'd consider close to you, but in a professional capacity only.

At this layer, you might meet them for coffee every other month, or grab lunch together a few times a year. You catch up quickly, updating one another on the goings on in your career and your office, and spend much of your time "talking shop." What is your boss doing that's driving you crazy? Are you thinking about leaving for another position? Have you met anyone lately you'd want to connect them to? These are all the kinds of questions you save for these infrequent but enjoyable lunches. You help each other, you make connections for one another, but your conversations don't tend to overlap into the personal, intentionally.

Who, in your network, resides in this "Coffee Mates and Lunch Dates" layer? List a few of them below:

_____

_____

_____

_____

5. **Conjunction Connections**

Any child of the 1970s or 1980s will remember School House Rock. One of its most famous ditties went like this, "Conjunction junction, what's your function? Hooking up words and phrases and clauses." It's exactly that reason that the fifth layer of your personal network is labeled "Conjunction Connections." The people in this layer aren't "hooking up words and phrases and clauses" but they are hooking up people and information and opportunities.

One morning, you get an email from a colleague about a new position opening in your company's advertising department. They're looking for some great talent and ask that you forward the job opening to anyone who might be interested. The first person who comes to mind when you're deciding who to send the email to is 100% a "Conjunction Connection." This is the kind of person who knows which jobs are open, knows people looking for jobs, and knows how to get to them. Without fail, whenever you see these people, they're saying things like, "You know who you should meet?" or "I just ran into that woman you know from college, Debra. Isn't she awesome?" They don't know everybody, but the people they do know, they're always linking to one another. They're the perfect conjunctions, and they're usually fun to be around. This layer of your network should be full if you truly want to create your own *You Know Everybody!* plan.

Your network is probably filled with these "Conjunction Connections." List a handful of them below:

_____

_____

_____

_____

6. Stand Still, Look Pretty

We don't always want to admit it, but we all have these people in our networks. They're, for lack of a better word, decorative. You know who I'm talking about. At nonprofit galas, they're the people who dressed just a bit too flashy. You've done work with them, and they tend to have a good name in their field, but you know and so does everyone else that they're all talk, little substance.

The best example I have in my own network of a person like this is someone I might call a "friend," but who I quickly realized has a work ethic that is about 10% the size of her ego – not even a fraction of what she promises ever gets done. But somehow she's still become quite a big name in the world of public relations, even landing some national clients. The thing is, though, she's always landing clients and very rarely keeping them. She's good at the sell, not so good at the delivery. But because her name is so big and she shows up at every event, even her past clients won't speak negatively about her. Instead, they practice the double cheek kiss whenever they see her and say things like "lovely" and "fabulous" to mask their annoyance.

You might be thinking, "Marcy! Why in the world would you want someone like this in your network? Wouldn't this be the kind of person you'd cut out immediately?" No way. The truth about these people is that they mean no harm. They're good people who certainly don't want to do bad work or lose clients. And that's usually the reason they're not publicly chided. For this reason, it's good to keep them in your network, not as trusted friends or advisors, but as the kind of people in your life who simply "Stand Still, Look Pretty." You'd be happy to stand alongside their gorgeous Versace dresses in a magazine photo, but not so willing to recommend them to a friend. Why is this person valuable to your network? Because she knows everybody! Usually, these "Stand Still, Look Pretty" types are also pretty big gossips, and you don't want to be on her bad side. We've all heard the saying "Keep your friends close and your enemies closer," and while this isn't quite as dramatic, when someone knows everybody, despite the depth of her relationship with those individuals, you want to be sure she's on your side.

Take a few minutes and start to round out that networking picture. List a few "Stand Still, Look Pretty" connections below:

_____

_____

_____

_____

7. What's Your Name Again?

The seventh layer of your personal network is pretty self-explanatory. You met them, you took their business card, and maybe you even added them as a LinkedIn connection or followed them on Twitter. But the truth is, you would struggle to remember their name or their face if casually asked.

Someone asks you, "Have you ever met Judy Smith?" You think for a moment and search your brain. The person you're talking to sees you're struggling to find her in your mental contact list and says something like, "She's at Citi Bank." You say something like, "Oh, of course, I'm sure we've met. I just can't seem to connect where." Judy Smith is a perfect example of a seventh layer connection. She's the "What's Your Name Again?" person. If you wanted to get in touch with her, you'd begin your email by reminding her where you met or a little about yourself because you know that, for her, you're likely a seventh layer connection as well.

It would be foolish of me to ask you to name this layer of your network, wouldn't it? But when you get a moment, look at your Rolodex, your computer's contact list, or your LinkedIn connections, and evaluate honestly how many of them you really know and how many fit into this seventh layer. We'll talk more about the perfect network's ratio of each layer, including Layer 7, below.

You've hopefully taken the time to both think through and list out a number of your connections in each of the seven layers of your personal network. Take a few minutes to map your network. Which layers are you heavy in and which have fewer connections? None of these results is good or bad. It simply helps you to see the current diversity of your network specifically related to their proximity to you and your ability to immediately connect with them on certain issues and needs. To help you complete this exercise, I've given you an example.

Sample Network Level Map

Emily recently made a huge change in her career. After 15 years in advertising agencies in Chicago, she's moved to New York City to accept a leadership position in advertising and public relations within a large financial services firm. Emily grew up in Southern California and went to school at USC, where she was recruited to her first advertising position and moved to Chicago. In Chicago, she served on multiple Boards of Directors for local nonprofit organizations, was well known in the advertising industry, and has nationwide connections. In Manhattan just a few months, she is building her network slowly and strategically. Here's what her level map currently looks like:

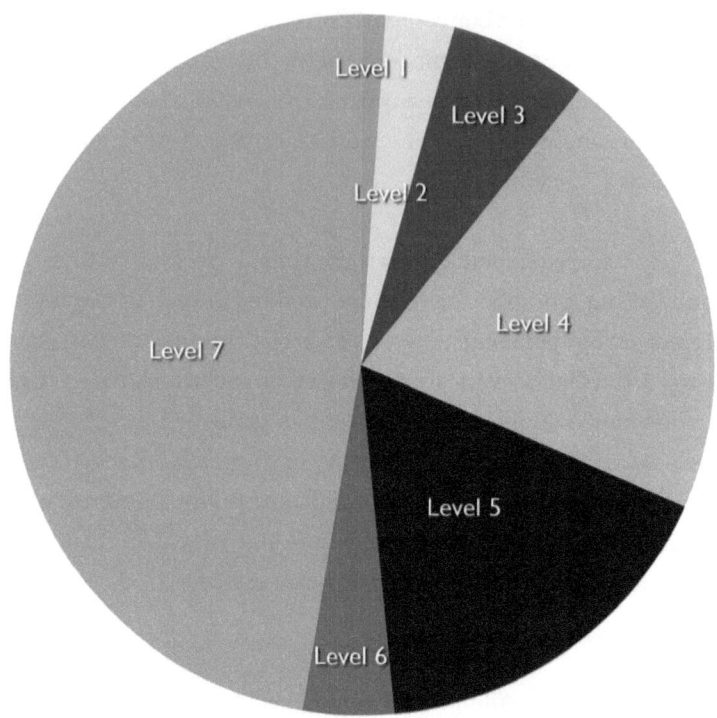

Because Emily is new to her city, she's networking a lot and carries a great deal of Layer 7 connections right now. That doesn't mean she won't turn those connections into higher level networking connections in the future, but this is the way her split looks now. She also boasts a great number of Layer 4 and 5 connections as well, close colleagues and professional connections nationwide who will no doubt help her to meet new people and introduce her to the right groups in NYC to expand her network. She carries with her a small long-term base in Layers 1-3, but from this analysis may want to add to her circle more friends and connections that are more personal than professional.

With Emily's example in mind, in the space below estimate how your pie chart network would break out today:

Finally, draw a few conclusions from the way you've constructed your networking circle. Where could you add more connections? In which layers are you heavy on people? Here, you simply want to consider how you might strategically change these ratios. It could be you're entirely comfortable with the structure, but simply want to add connections overall. We'll explore all of that as we move on.

The purpose of this exercise is to examine your network's diversity. But it's important to look at your network traditionally when it comes to diversity as well, instead of just looking at our seven layers above. First and foremost, think of your network in terms of a/s/l. If you lived through the 1990s and online chat rooms, you'll recognize this short code as the question most chatters asked the moment they first "met" someone in a chat room. It stands for age/sex/location. Even online, we were qualifying our network immediately upon meeting them. Are they in our age range or the range we were comfortable talking with? Are they male or female (this is usually a no brainer when it comes to in-person networking)? And finally, where are they located? In addition, you'll want to add some key demographic information as you examine the diversity of your network.

If you're already a LinkedIn user, one great way to do this is to use a LinkedIn plugin called InMaps. To access this app, visit http://inmaps.linkedinlabs.com/. InMaps will use your existing LinkedIn connections list to create an interactive color-coded map of all your connections. It's a phenomenal tool to use to understand completely, looking at one image, where your network resides both geographically and company-specific and, more importantly, how they are connected to one another. I highly recommend its use.

Another option is to think through the questions below and fill out this form. It will help you to connect the dots similar to the way InMaps would.

Consider this...	Observations
What age are most of your connections?	
What is the mix of men and women in your network?	
Where are the majority of your connections located, geographically?	
Are your connections concentrated in a single sector (corporate, government, nonprofit, etc.)?	
What kind of companies do your networks represent (consumer packaged goods, retail, media, etc.)?	
What leadership layers does your network span (entry level to the C-suite)?	
What are the main fields or industries represented in your closest network connections (marketing, science and technology, etc.)?	

The reason I recommend completing this kind of network analysis in the process of creating your *You Know Everybody!* Network is the same reason a personal shopper or stylist will always recommend completing a closet review before they take you shopping. It's impossible for a stylist to advise you on the purchase of anything from a necklace to a little black dress if she doesn't have an accurate portrayal of what exists already in your wardrobe. In the same way, it's impossible for you to strategically network to add to your circle without first knowing which industries, companies, and types of people exist in your network currently. This kind of analysis and strategic choosing of networking connections may seem brash or unfeeling. But to create the kind of network that will help you succeed, support you in your goals and intentions, and ultimately become the trusted advisors you need to rise to the top of your career, you must be intentional and strategic in creating these relationships.

The first season of *Sex and the City* contains an episode called "Bay of Married Pigs." In it, we get to know Miranda Hobbes, the high-powered attorney of the group, for the first time. Miranda attends her law firm's annual softball game, and agrees to let a colleague set her up on a date for the day. The only problem is that the date turns out to be a woman, and Miranda is not gay. Making the best of it, she spends the day with her date, Sid, and the two are a hit with the firm's partners. For the first time ever, one of the partners asks Miranda to attend dinner at his home with Sid at her side. She agrees and Sid, being a continued good sport, plays along. After the dinner, Miranda comes clean to the partner that she's not gay, at which point the funniest line of the episode comes from the male partner. He says, "My wife will be disappointed. She was looking to add a lesbian couple to our circle."

Hilarious as that line is coming from Miranda's uppercrust Manhattan boss, it's also a simple example of strategic networking. The man's wife wanted to add to their "circle." And while sexual preference is a controversial reason to network with anyone, you should look for the right members to join your circle, just like this couple was. When you look at the way your network splits out, choose to seek out connections in new industries, sectors, locations, ages, etc. These kinds of strategic additions to your circle could contribute to more meaningful relationships with a more diverse group of people, and ultimately a more diverse set of opportunities and connections to enhance your career and your life.

I highlight the Miranda Hobbes story here not to make an example of befriending a lesbian couple, but to illustrate the point of adding strategically to your network, and to explain to you one other important point: To build your network, you're eventually going to need to step outside of your networking comfort zone.

Women, much more so than men, stay in a very specific

comfort zone when it comes to networking. Take my husband, for example. He is, regrettably, a huge Minnesota Vikings fan. Shortly after we moved to Chicago in 2010, he discovered his beloved Vikings simply don't play on Chicago TV channels. They're bumped in favor of local teams. Quickly, he found a bar in Chicago's River North neighborhood that boasts the full NFL ticket television package, making it his regular Sunday afternoon watering hole. Every Sunday, he comes home with a new story of someone he met watching football. Ask any man in your life, and they'll tell you that shaking the hand of the guy on the barstool next to them is a regular occurrence. For most women, though, our networking comfort zone usually doesn't extend to sitting alone in a bar and introducing ourselves to the person sitting next to us.

While writing this book, I've spoken to hundreds of women about how they network and what struggles they have, and the answer is universal: Women tend to stay within a very specific networking comfort zone, and it's the same short code we talked about above: a/s/l. Women network mostly with women, largely in a similar age group, and local to their current home. To truly become *You Know Everybody!* Networkers, you must get out of that comfort zone and extend your network to include more diversity in all of the areas we've discussed above. We'll talk more in Chapter 9 about truly innovative networking techniques and really challenging yourself to get out of your comfort zone. But for the purpose of this chapter, to truly know who you need on your side, you'll need to expand your views to begin to build coalitions around your goals and propel your career to its greatest heights.

Just like you did in Chapter 2, you'll need to create the same kind of strategic plan based on not *what* you need, but *who* you need in order to reach your goals and manifest your intentions. Imagine this kind of networking strategy as a "perfect storm" to create your next step and you'll see your long-term goals come to fruition. You created in Chapter 2 a list of the resources you need. Now, get specific when it comes to people. How you work through this exercise is up to you. Perhaps list your perfect types of connections, but also consider listing specific people if there are clear connections you hope to make to be successful in your goals. Consider, again, the example of our financial-planner-turned-personal-coach below:

Your Clear Intentions or Goals	Who Do You Need to Get There?
Example: To make a career transition in the next year from financial planning to personal coaching.	Example: 1. An amazing personal coach for me. I've heard my friend Linda has a great coach. 2. I would love to be able to coach high powered women in C-level positions. I'd love to network with a female CEO to learn how I might engage this group. 3. Friends and personal connections who will review my business plan and act as a sounding board for ideas.

If you find yourself a bit lost in generating specific ideas of who to connect with in the list above and real names to add to your hopeful connections list, let me guide you through a few ideas of how to get a hopeful connections list going and to track that list and its successes over time.

- **Use your universe . . . specifically your university!**
  Alumni networks are some of the friendliest to connect with and the easiest to find direct connections to in

your life. Saying, "I'm an alum of X College" can get you in the door with a powerful business mogul much faster than any job application, interest connection, or "Conjunction Connector." To start developing your list of potential alumni to connect with, start with your college or university's alumni services website. Many schools have searchable databases where you can narrow your field by current location, field of interest, field of university study, years of experience, and more. Create a list as long as possible of potential connections from your alma mater.

- **Use LinkedIn as a "House of Cards"**
  When you pull one card out of a house of cards, the rest come tumbling down. It's the same way with LinkedIn when it comes to finding a connection. Surely, you have at least one connection already who is exactly the kind of person who can help you get ahead. Certainly, connect with them, but also use the tools LinkedIn provides to find additional potential connections. When you're viewing an individual's profile on LinkedIn, scroll down and look to the right where you'll find "Viewers of this profile also viewed..." These individuals are powerful prospects for your networking list. Also, with those you're already connected to, their profile lists the number of connections they currently have. Click on that number and you'll see a full list of that connection's connections. These can be powerful prospects, as they're already closely connected to you through at least one person on your list.

- **Friends and Family: It's Not Just for Sales!**
Stores like Ulta, Sephora, Macy's, and GAP regularly conduct what they call "friends and family" sales, when their sales associates are given a limited number of discount codes or special shopping hours to give to their close friends and family. Take this to heart and don't count out your friends and family—who are often in the first two layers of your personal network—when you're looking for good connections. Don't be ashamed to ask your parents or your aunts and uncles, friends from high school or college, or even your friends' parents for help in connecting to powerful people. Those who are closest to you personally know you on a deeper level than most of those who know you professionally. Though they may not be able to recommend the work you do at your desk every day, they can speak openly and honestly about your integrity and general character, which can provide powerful connections.

- **Walk Back Across the Bridges of the Past**
My father is notorious for saying, "Don't burn bridges," and we all know why. Every bridge you burn in your life is one you won't be able to walk back across later. And while you may not want to walk backwards to take that job again or work for that horrible boss a second time, the connections you've made in your past companies can be powerful connections to keep you moving ahead in your industry, even when you move on from a company. Take time to reconnect with those you've left behind in old positions. Ask for their advice to get ahead and thank them for the guidance they may have provided earlier in your life.

As you think through these kinds of groups, and peruse LinkedIn and other social networking sites, your Rolodex or online address book, and more, continue to add to your list above and create your hopeful networking connections list. In subsequent chapters, we'll tackle how to get in the door with the names you're generating here, and how to keep a constant pipeline continuing to fuel networking meetings, new connections, and long-term and short-term relationships that will be key in hearing the words *"You Know Everybody!"* in your networking. What you're setting up here are lists of the kinds of networking coalitions you'll need to build in order to create that perfect storm of people + resources = goals met and intentions manifested.

Now that you know both what you need in the way of resources, and who you need to connect with to become successful, let's get on with it and tackle the great big HOW of marketing yourself, getting in the door, and nailing those meetings. You're on your way, Career Girls. Let's keep moving…

She Knows Everybody! Narrative: Chapter 3
The Who! Getting the Right People on Your Side

Mary Blegen
Executive Vice President, Employee Engagement
and Leadership Development, U.S. Bank

Throughout this book I talk about the importance of asking for what you want and being able to articulate effectively what you need to those around you, including new connections, mentors, and trusted advisors. In that advice, though, there is a vocabulary word every Career Girl must learn to truly become a *You Know Everybody!* Networker: Sponsorship. I'm not talking about the kind of sponsorship you see on the sides of sports stadiums. I'm talking about the kind of sponsorship that gets you ahead in your career and brings you to the next level in your life.

There could be no better woman to speak about sponsorship than one who is championing the idea of sponsorship within her own organization and has been my sponsor over the course of my career, even though we've never worked in the same company. Mary Blegen is Executive Vice President and Director of Employee Engagement at U.S. Bancorp. She is a 40-year member of the U.S. Bank staff and has been instrumental in hiring and developing the careers of countless women within the company. Outside her work at U.S. Bank, she has been a key leader in numerous local and national nonprofit organizations, including WomenVenture, where Mary and I met, and United Way Twin Cities, among many others. I asked Mary to share with us her wisdom on sponsorship. You're about to get a great lesson in what it means and how to use it to your advantage.

What is Sponsorship?

Mary's definition of sponsorship is this: A practice in which any person (and it doesn't have to be a leader) sponsors another individual for an assignment, a position within the company, a graduate program, or another opportunity that can enhance that individual's career. She says, "It's really beyond being a mentor. Mentors give advice and ideas. Sponsors are actively engaged in moving that person forward."

Sex and Sponsorship: Does Gender Matter?

Sponsorship might be a new concept to you, but believe Mary Blegen and me when we tell you it's a centuries-old concept for men. Men have been naturally sponsoring one another for generations. They are incredibly willing to say, "Hey, this guy's got potential." That's all they need. And frankly, it's not just in the sponsors that men have it easy, it's also with the individuals being sponsored. Younger men are much more willing to go out on a limb and ask for help (or for a job) than young women are. Mary told me, "When a man sees a job description with a list of five things and he has two, he applies. When a woman sees a job description with a list of five things and she has four, she decides she's not ready yet."

Women, stereotypical or not, have a tendency to be very comfortable in mentoring relationships. Why? Because we always start from the idea of forming a meaningful relationship. That's OK, but it doesn't always progress to solid sponsorship naturally. It's not a part of our regular thought pattern to ask someone to help us get from Point A to Point B. Instead, we ask for advice and thoughts and ultimately end up well armed with information, but not with action. Mary tells me there is a common notion that "women mentor, men sponsor."

Powerful women tend to be afraid that the failure of someone she sponsors will reflect badly on them. Men don't. It's the old adage, "Men are hired based on potential, women based on performance." These tendencies are not listed here to discourage you. In fact, it's just the opposite! Women like Mary have had to fight for their place in business over time, even with so many doors closed to them in the process of fighting for equality. We talk openly here about these tendencies because by writing about sponsorship and examining its place in your networking journey, you can learn to overcome what might be a female tendency to focus more on mentorship than sponsorship.

Alright, Then...If I Need a Sponsor, How Do I Get One?

Just like you heard in Chapter 2, you have to ASK! When I asked Mary Blegen how a woman can effectively ask for a sponsor, she said emphatically, "Women have to GET BOLD! Women tend to be 'beat around the bush' kind of people. They think, 'I really want Mary to sponsor me, but I don't want to risk being rejected, so I'll just ask her to mentor me and I'll hope she'll decide to sponsor me.' When we, as women, are ready to be sponsored, we have to feel confident in asking."

Consequently, you also have to be open to the answer you might receive, and willing to react appropriately and with respect in any situation. For example:

- If a potential sponsor is too busy or uncomfortable becoming your sponsor for any reason, you must be gracious and accept her decision. However, you can ask for her advice in approaching another sponsor or inquire as to what circumstances would need to change to make her answer different.

- When you ask someone to become your sponsor, you might be asking about a specific position or department and hear something like, "I don't think that's the right role for you." In this instance, again, ask for explanation. A more seasoned woman's approach to a specific position could certainly help you to better understand your strengths and the way they might fit into a position in your company.

- You may also find someone who is willing to sponsor you but wants you to try something else before they're willing to open a specific door. Mary's advice here is to be intentionally transparent in your conversation. What are you willing or unwilling to do? If a potential sponsor, for instance, thinks you need an MBA to get ahead and you disagree entirely, it's up to you to draw that line in the sand and be clear in your intentions.

No matter the answer you receive when asking someone to become your sponsor, you have to be honest about what you want and need, and the person you're asking has to feel confident that if she can't sponsor you, she can be free to tell you why.

Mary asks us all to remember that while sponsorship is a powerful tool within your organization and to enhance your career, this person isn't your fairy godmother. She says, "Just because you come to me to be your sponsor doesn't mean I'm guaranteeing anything. You still have to earn your way, but sponsorship can pave the way." When Mary sponsors a woman at U.S. Bank, she becomes cognizant of getting that woman on the radar of other powerful people in the organization. She keeps that person's name on the tip of her tongue and isn't afraid to say, "I think she's fabulous. Next time you have a position open, she is worth taking a look at." It isn't about ushering you into a high-powered job. It's about making you a good candidate by putting your name in the wind (more about that in Chapter 8).

A few other tips from Mary for finding the right sponsor:

- **Getting to Know You.** Mary says before she agrees to sponsor someone, she really does want to get to know that person. She may schedule two or three meetings to learn about that individual's background, educational process, previous job experience, and what she's doing today in order to glean whether or not that individual is the right kind of candidate to sponsor within the company. You must be comfortable with this kind of information gathering. Sponsoring can be powerful but it can also be a slow process, as your sponsor will want to develop a strong relationship before she recommends you for a job or strategic connection.

- **Use Social Networking Opportunities.** Take advantage of every internal networking activity you can. In her role, Mary sees firsthand that "A lot of people bypass company picnics, internal volunteer opportunities, and other chances to connect with coworkers. Don't! These can be valuable activities for making connections within the company. If you skip these things, you're losing huge opportunities to network and eventually find a sponsor." When you show up to social activities, you have a unique opportunity to build much tighter relationships than you can in the office.

- **Informational Interviewing Works!** If you're actively searching for a sponsor, start with conducting a few informational interviews around the company. This can lead you to the right area for you within a company, and a more targeted sponsorship ask. Mary says, "Women need to feel comfortable being bolder in our asks – whether they're for jobs, sponsorships, or salaries!"

Sponsorship: It's Not "One Size Fits All"

While there are key differences between mentors and sponsors, there are also different kinds of sponsorships. Here are two key types of sponsorship Mary recommends you become willing to ask for and be open to:

1. **Position Sponsors** Someone who is a position sponsor is exactly as it might seem, sponsoring you to get a higher or better position within your company. These individuals will be helping you get a leg up with executives, get introduced to key players in the hiring process, and perhaps even help you to scout a specific position, apply, interview, and land the job.

2. **Network Sponsors** Sometimes, even though a woman wants to be your sponsor, she's unsure about whether or not you're right for a specific department or position. You have to accept that she may not feel comfortable recommending you for something specific. However, she can become your network sponsor, making available to you the people in her network so that she can help you discover the right place for you and explore your role within the company.

To wrap up on sponsorship, I want to add a quote from Mary Blegen, not in reference to this book, but one that shaped me more than five years ago. Women like Mary spent the last 30 or more years fighting tooth and nail for the successes they've achieved. At an event in 2008, Mary said, "This generation kicked down many a door." She's right, and she recognizes there are more doors to be kicked down in order for women to achieve equality in the workplace. Sponsorship is just one of the ways to make that happen. A point of caution when asking for sponsorship, though, is to remember that women like Mary can be phenomenally helpful in your career, but they also deserve a phenomenal amount of respect. It is our job to show the individuals we humbly ask for sponsorship how deeply grateful we are for the work they've done to get women to the next level. Together, across generations and through sponsorship, we can finally achieve parity for women.

The "Best of the Best" in Networking Advice

I ended each of the interviews completed for You Know Everybody!
by asking each woman to provide to this book's readers her best
networking tips and advice. Here are Mary's tips and tricks.

1. **Get the List!** Being a volunteer on a committee for an organization or a Board member gives you special perks, and sometimes that means you can get the list of who's who at a networking event before you attend. Mary does this frequently, and goes to every event with a clear, targeted approach to who she wants to meet and talk to and what she wants to talk about. She carries that mission throughout the event.

2. **Take a Risk!** Mary says, "I'm an introvert in many ways, but I've worked hard at developing this specific skill: walk in, scan the room, and look for the group of women who truly seem to know each other well. Then go jump right in with that group." Those kinds of groups can be incredibly intimidating, but because they have already developed camaraderie, they may be a fun group to jump into, and one

you can ask good questions of and learn about quickly.

3. **If you feel left out, it's because you left yourself out!** Sure, you can stand in a corner at a networking event and say there were no good people to talk to there, but the truth is, your networking is up to you. If you leave an event feeling empty and like a failure, it's because you allowed yourself to feel that way. It's up to you to take the reigns and jump into a conversation.

four

You're the Brand: Creating a Personal Marketing Plan

You become a brand as soon as you sell one thing.
So you can either recognize it and embrace it,
or you can deny it and pretend it's not happening.

–Taylor Swift

Have you ever had someone say to you, "I have good news and bad news, which do you want to hear first?" What a stupid question! Always hear the bad news first, Career Girls, because at least then the good news can cheer you up, right? In the spirit of that notion, I have good news and bad news for you, and I'll start with the bad news. The bad news is, your pitch is not enough. It will never be enough. You can be completely engaging for the 60 seconds you're making your pitch and make the person you're talking to think, "I LOVE THIS WOMAN!" But first impressions, as important as they are, cannot sustain you through the relationship building process and the ultimate delivery of your products, services, and self to the people you want to buy it all.

Standing behind your elevator pitch must be a real

person with real experience, and a plan to get your story heard and your message out there. In essence, you must have a pitch to start, a brand to sustain, a marketing plan to convey your message, and the goods (in the world of corporations, it's a business plan) to back it up. All over the world, there are individuals who are great at interviewing but terrible at getting things done. Every hiring manager in the world has had the experience of hiring someone who was great in the interview and simply bombed at the job. In this chapter, we're going to tackle the broad and difficult subject of branding on the whole, but more importantly, I'm going to teach you point by point to write an incredible personal marketing plan that will take you from pitch to sale. It will give you the tools to support your needs and wants with competencies and planning that will prove you're not just a great pitch-gal, but a fantastic all around Career Girl!

The biggest mistake you can make in branding and marketing specifically is to be all talk and no action, or attractive with no real substance. It's the mistake many companies make when they spend months and months deciding colors and logos, but never actually work on a business model and revenue strategy to sustain the growth that could naturally develop with a great brand and marketing plan.

Some of you may remember Pets.com, a company whose rise and fall spanned a mere 28 months. If you don't recall the name, perhaps you'll recall the company's ridiculous sock puppet mascot, which was positioned front and center at the Macy's Thanksgiving Day Parade in 1999 and at the 2000 Super Bowl with an ad that cost the company a whopping $2 million. Pets. com closed its doors in November 2000, just nine months after its Super Bowl commercial ran, costing various dot-com investors upwards of $300 million. Entire books could be written on the problems Pets.com encountered and the reasons for its complete and total failure, but for my money, it boils down to one big thing –

bad planning. Pets.com had the elevator pitch mastered. Millions of people around the world knew it and could regurgitate it at will – a must for any big brand to succeed. For all intents and purposes, it had a strong brand and clear marketing strategy. Strategy and planning, though, are two different animals (or pets, if you will). Leadership at Pets.com made clear their intentions – to get the Pets.com brand in front of as many people as possible, as many times as possible, for as much money as it took. Unfortunately, the company lacked the resources, distribution channels, and a solid business plan needed to sufficiently support the claims made by its marketing and advertising worldwide. Pets.com neglected to take the time to evaluate its brand, plan its marketing based on brand loyalty, and create a product or service that proved its brand statements. It cost investors millions and the company an incredible amount of embarrassment in what was, at that time, the beginning of a volatile tech market.

Of course, none of you Career Girls want to make the same mistake Pets.com made. You want to have a great pitch (as good as a Super Bowl commercial, even), a strong brand, and the skill set and experience to prove that your brand isn't just about a sock puppet or a $2 million commercial. It's about a real and honest portrayal of who you really are, what you truly want, and the way you can (not wish for, but *can*) achieve your goals.

You might be saying to yourself, "Marcy, I'm not a brand. I'm just a person." Unfortunately, for professional women, that's just not the case any more. You are a brand. From the moment you apply for your first job out of college to the legacy you'll eventually leave in your career, your brand is evident from start to finish. It isn't static or something you create and walk away from. It evolves over time and is part of your growth and development.

I started this chapter with a quote from Taylor Swift. Whether you love her or hate her, the fact is, she's a branding genius. Her unique combination of humble, girlish, and doe-eyed, as well as her music's ballsy and irreverent cross-genre appeal has made her one of the biggest stars of her generation, appealing to both kids and parents alike. The quote at the beginning of this chapter came from Taylor's Fall 2012 interview with Katie Couric on 20/20. Katie asked her if it was possible for her to "just" be a singer/songwriter. Could she be that without being a brand? Taylor's maturity and business savvy shined when she admitted, "You become a brand as soon as you sell one thing." The same goes for each and every professional woman reading this book. You may not be in sales, but you are always selling something – yourself! Take Taylor's advice here: You can either "recognize it and embrace it, or you can deny it and pretend it's not happening." Pretending, though, doesn't mean it isn't happening. You are branding yourself. It's up to you whether you do it intentionally or unintentionally.

The age of remaining anonymous and brandless and still achieving success is over. To rise to the top of your field, your brand must be front and center, and your marketing plan must support your brand fully and strategically. More and more, you will begin to see non-celebrities on the pages of magazines and television. Why? Because today, branding is easier than ever. A "no-name" person with a great social media strategy, a huge network, and a bang-up marketing plan can become a pseudo-celebrity.

In 2012, you may have caught the short run of a Bravo show called "Miss Advised." This reality-style show followed the lives and loves of three love and sex experts who themselves had difficulty finding and sustaining romantic relationships. One of these so-called experts was a woman named Julia Allison. Prior to her time on "Miss Advised," she was well known for being named by Gawker.com as one of the "Most Hated People on the Internet." Formerly a shock-value writer for publications like *Star* and *Cosmopolitan*, she became an Internet sensation for her big opinions and lack of filter. This reputation for not only being famous, but somewhat infamous, as well, is what led Bravo to give her an opportunity on this show. Her articles became fodder for bloggers, her social media persona became comment-worthy and controversial, and ultimately her brand brought her more traditional fame in the form of a television show. These kinds of stories will continue to become more common over time. We'll see non-celebrities developing larger personas and often becoming celebrities themselves. Bravo is notorious for its ability to make a star out of a seemingly normal individual on shows like "The Real Housewives" and "Miss Advised."

The difference between Julia Allison or the members of "The Real Housewives" cast and everyday women is these women's inherent ability to take a normal opportunity and use it to market themselves strategically. Julia Allison could have crawled under a rock, embarrassed by being called "most hated" by a well-known website. Instead, she used it to get ahead and capitalized on her newfound fame, whether good or bad. If all press is good press, then all marketing is great marketing when it comes to your brand and your professional persona.

Like the women of Bravo, your brand exists in everything you do. From the coffee you drink to the television you watch to what you post on Facebook and what you say in the midst of an important networking meeting, you are conveying your brand and executing your marketing initiatives as a professional. Sure, you might not be famous enough to get an endorsement deal with the clothing line you wear, but you never know what might happen in the future. If women like Julia Allison are offered television series, maybe the next wave of celebrity will come from hardworking middle managers in cubicles. It could happen to you!

I hope by this point, you've got it. You're a brand, you must strategically develop your brand, and you can't become wildly successful without knowing how to brand yourself. The key, though, isn't just knowing your brand, but being prepared, willing, and able to speak eloquently and with enthusiasm about your brand at any time. In Chapter 5, we'll talk about getting your foot in the door, and in Chapter 6, I'll lead you through the key steps in learning to nail a meeting. To truly nail that meeting and get what you want from your network, you will need to learn to effectively convey your brand statements and describe your marketing plan. It's only when the individuals you're networking with can understand what you want and how you want to get it that they can truly see themselves fitting into that plan and lending their hand to your cause.

Take a moment now and think about where your brand is currently represented in your professional life. If someone wanted to identify and describe your brand, what documents or concrete examples might they find or look for surrounding your professional brand persona? You might currently have:

- A resume that represents your brand.
- Personal business cards.
- An awesome cover letter format you can tailor to every job application.
- Social media profiles.
- A personal website or online portfolio.

Take some time in the next few days to look at all of these components of your persona professionally, both online and off, and ask yourself some hard questions:

- If you took your name off the top of your resume and LinkedIn pages, would you be able to easily identify that they were written by the same person and have the same brand concept?
- Is your Facebook profile vastly different from your LinkedIn or Twitter profile? Can you tell you're the same

person from one social media platform to the next?

- Is your brand easily accessible online, or is it captured only offline in business cards and resumes?
- Without getting crazy with resume design, does your resume truly "look like you"? Does it feel like your personality or is it the black Times New Roman 12 point font that any stuffy businessman would use?

You might have any combination of the resources above at the ready. If you've made the effort to create your online portfolio or a personal website, you rock! You might be thinking, "What? I need a website?" Don't worry, it's not a requirement. Your brand can be conveyed in your resume alone or in conjunction with your social media profiles. There's no requirement to have any of the sophisticated personal branding tools some people might recommend. One tool, though, that I believe is essential in building both your personal brand and your network is what I commonly refer to as a PMP (Personal Marketing Plan). Before we get started on the components of a PMP, let me say for the sake of transparency that I did not personally invent nor develop the concept of a PMP. It has come to me through multiple channels, and it's used frequently by recruiters, companies offering outplacement services, and job search professionals around the world in some form. What I'm about to give you in this format combines countless types of PMPs I've seen over the years, and tweaks I've made to market myself personally in my own networking meetings.

The bottom line, though, is not the format of the marketing plan (although I think mine is pretty good), but the fact that you've taken the time to completely develop and work through the marketing plan before doing any strategic networking or job searching. Adjust this to fit your needs and the needs of your networking strategies as you see fit.

The Personal Marketing Plan: Format and Components

Section 1: Professional Objective

Ask a group of hiring managers or human resources professionals their thoughts on including the standard "Objective" on a resume today, and you'll inevitably receive a different opinion from every individual. Some love objectives, some hate them, and some have a newfangled approach to writing one, or a section you should include instead. I'm personally not a big fan of objectives on resumes, but I am a huge proponent of including one as the first section of your PMP. Though I'm using the term objective, I want you to divorce yourself from the kind of objective you might include on a resume. This is not about the kind of position you want or the goal of your job search. It's a much broader objective that will help the reader of your PMP understand fully your career objectives, both long-term and short, and to quickly identify what you desire.

Consider the following examples (note that for the purposes of this chapter, I'll provide an example for the PMP as written by a job seeker, and another for someone who is not actively job seeking but networking for other purposes):

Example A (Job Seeker):
Transition from the financial direct service industry to a position directly related to marketing and public relations in an agency setting. Seeking responsibilities that will combine my experience with client service and my passion for direct marketing and public relations, utilizing a skill set in relationship building, customer visibility campaigns, and strategies to reach target markets and potential clients/consumers. Strong desire to work for a company that specializes in working with financial and professional service firm clients.

Example B (Networking Only):
To build a network in the field of financial services that is both broad

and deep, and expands nationwide. Seeking a mentor who is skilled in developing strong marketing pipelines to develop clientele, and guiding women in financial services who are entrepreneurial and have been successful at building a sustainable client-based business model. Strong desire to connect with networking organizations catering to women in finance and other industries.

Section 2: Function

Again, when we're talking about function in resumes, you'll find varying opinions on the subject. Many hiring managers prefer a chronological resume, while others are fond of a functional format emphasizing the kinds of areas you have developed expertise in throughout your career. While you might leave the functional format behind in a traditional resume, it's important to the development of your PMP, as it's the clearest way to convey to a reader what kinds of positions you're looking for or the key skill sets you're seeking to develop through networking.

This section will be vastly different for those who are networking to build strategic connections vs. those who are networking specifically to complete a career transition or job search. For job seekers, you'll want to use a heading like "Preferred Position Functions Include" and for networking specific connections, you could consider a heading of "Developing Professional Expertise In."

Example A (Job Seeker):
Preferred Position Functions Include:

- *Client Relations*
- *Direct Marketing*
- *Public Relations, including direct press pitching*
- *Business Development*
- *Financial Writing and Blogging*

Example B (Networking Only):
Developing Professional Expertise In:

- *Business Development*
- *Client Relations*
- *Estate Planning*
- *Long-Term Care Planning and Insurance*

Section 3: Positioning Statement

Your positioning statement is different than your objective and your functions in that it's all about who you are today and what you've done in the past. It's similar to your elevator speech, but in this case smaller and more to the point. If someone asked you to give a 15-second, two- to three-sentence pitch about who you are, why you're great at what you do, and why people respect you in your field, your answer would be your positioning statement. The reason you want to include this in your PMP is to give your reader an opportunity to learn quickly how they might help sell you as well. If someone said to a person in your network, "Tell me about Charlotte," are you confident that individual could effectively portray both your experience and your unique attributes to sell your brand? The positioning statement in your PMP gives those you're networking with the exact tool they need to be your second-best sales person (only you can be the best!).

Example A (Job Seeker):
Financial services marketing professional with a knack for selling financial products with an innovative and fresh approach. Ten years in direct sales with one of the nation's leading financial services firms. Experience in client relations and creative marketing campaigns appealing to consumers and corporate clients alike. Excels in 1:1 relationship building and finding the right pitch for any potential client. Known for outstanding work ethic, positive attitude, and consistently diligent follow-through.

Example B (Networking Only):
Financial services professional actively building a sustainable client docket and the opportunity to serve a wide array of high net worth individuals to ensure financial security. Experienced in tax planning for small business owners, and consistently developing additional resources for estate planning and long-term care initiatives. Known in the industry as a strong networker with a passion for helping women in financial services connect and succeed together.

Section 4: Competencies and Skills

Similar to your resume, you'll want to be sure to include in your PMP a clear picture of the skill set you bring to any new position or networking relationship. Listing your skill sets and key competencies in your PMP gives you an opportunity to convey, in your own words, the skills that build your reputation in your field and to articulate your history (whether short or long) as a professional.

Like you would on a functional resume, consider keeping this section of your PMP to two or three key skills or competencies, followed by three to four bullet points regarding each area of expertise. Unlike most resumes, you can feel free to write the bullets for this section in first person, if that feels most comfortable for you. This is your opportunity to promote yourself. I'll provide you with one example of this section of the PMP, since it is the same whether or not you're job seeking.

Example:
Client Relations and Partnership Development

- *Experience in the financial services industry provides a unique skill set to marketing agencies specializing in professional services firms – combining the knowledge of financial sales with an understanding of the marketing necessary to create successful pipelines for client engagement.*

- *Focused on results-oriented partnerships. My work in the financial services industry has focused heavily on work with individuals and families, ensuring my clients have direct access to the best financial resources on the market.*
- *Extensive experience developing both internal and external partnerships with individual and corporate clients.*

Direct Sales

- *Broad knowledge of the products available to my clients, and the ability to effectively convey the benefits of key product lines to individual clients.*
- *Collaboration with local experts in various fields to create additional opportunities for clients to receive resources outside the financial services field and develop an additional touchpoint with my firm.*
- *High-volume event sales experience and the development of innovative sales techniques, including trade show and event-focused sales.*

Branding and Messaging:
Strategic Planning and Implementation

- *Creation of marketing plans incorporating print, sales, events, and media to sell financial services to individuals and organizations.*
- *Campaign and messaging development centered on consistent brand visibility for my firm and partners within it.*
- *Target marketing to increase client satisfaction and brand awareness.*
- *Results analysis and extensive tracking of metrics.*

Section 5: Personal Attributes

This section of the PMP is one that would not appear on a resume. In job interviews, you're focused heavily on your skill set and ability to excel in the job at hand. In networking, you're focused on both your skill set in your industry and on developing a personal relationship, which is based on the individual attributes that make you valuable to your networking target. Your charming disposition may seem unimportant if you can sell hundreds of thousands a year in product for a new company, but it is important to the person you want to recommend you, introduce you to others, and become a close networking contact. Those individuals want to get to know your personality and important personal attributes as much as, if not more than, your skills and competencies.

This list will remain the same for job seekers and non-job seekers alike. All of the traits should be professional in nature, but should also showcase your personality. This isn't the place to display your incredible knitting skills, but it might be the time to show your passions and values in a way you can't with skill sets.

Example:
Personal Attributes:

- *Strong work ethic*
- *Positive attitude*
- *Strong internal motivator*
- *Pride in building teams*
- *Passion for excellence in my work*
- *Dedication to volunteer work and cause-related marketing*

Section 6: Target Market

If you're job seeking, this is a clear target not for the kind of position you want, but for additional details about the things that are important to you surrounding the job. If you're not job seeking, this can still be a powerful section: It's your chance to tell your network what kind of networking targets you're seeking. Check out the two examples below for ways you might write this section based on your goals as a networker.

Example A (Job Seeker):
Target Market:

Geographic Location:
New York, NY or Washington, DC
Open to a position requiring travel.

Types of Industries:
Focused on industries that incorporate my background in financial services and desired change in focus to marketing and public relations. Prefer a marketing agency with clients in professional services. Also open to national/multinational financial services corporations with an interest in building marketing departments with financial services professionals.

Size of Organization:
100-500 employees

Example B (Networking Only):
Target Market:

Geographic Location:
Atlanta, GA
Open to networking nationwide
Accepting clients in the Greater Atlanta area

Types of Industries:
Interested in networking with individuals with strong backgrounds in the financial services industry, accounting, and insurance sales.

Next, you'll find a full PMP that is different from the examples used above. I want to ensure you're receiving as many concrete examples as possible in varying industries and job functions. The example below profiles an individual with experience in marketing and a passion for nonprofit work and community relations.

Complete Example: Personal Marketing Plan, Marketing-Related Job Seeker

Professional Objective:
Transition from the nonprofit sector to the for-profit or foundation sector to create results in community relations, corporate responsibility, or events marketing strategies. Seeking responsibilities specifically in the development of partnerships, visibility campaigns, employee engagement, and strategies to reach target markets and potential clients/consumers. Strong desire for a position incorporating partnership and relationship building, both internally and externally.

Preferred Position Functions Include:

- Community Relations
- Events
- Business Development
- Corporate Communications
- Partnership Marketing

Positioning Statement:
Communications and events professional with experience in partnership marketing, events management, sales, corporate relations, and strategic development/implementation. Excels in

both strategic and creative marketing, partnership, and relationship development, both internally and externally. Known for work ethic, positive attitude, and consistent, diligent follow-through.

Competencies and Skills:
Community Relations and Sponsorship Sales

- Experience in the nonprofit and public sector provides a unique skill set for effective community relations, combining the knowledge of the good a corporation can do with the understanding of the strategic planning surrounding philanthropy and engagement for corporations.
- Focused on results-oriented partnerships.
- Extensive experience developing both internal and external partnerships with corporate clients.
- Passion for the philanthropic and volunteer engagement work of corporations and foundations – direct experience with the positive effect corporations and foundations can have on the work of a nonprofit.

Events Management and Marketing

- Production of events ranging in size from 3 to 3,000; from galas to meetings to professional conferences.
- Strategic event marketing to ensure high levels of brand presence.
- Collaboration to create event partnerships including monetary and in-kind sponsorships, as well as client and community partnerships.
- High volume event sales experience and the development of innovative sales techniques, including trade show, event ticket, and sponsorship sales.

Branding and Messaging: Strategic Planning and Implementation

- Creation of marketing plans incorporating print, sales, events, and media.
- Campaign and messaging development centered on consistent brand visibility.
- Target marketing to increase client satisfaction and brand awareness.
- Results analysis and extensive tracking of metrics.

Personal Attributes:

- Strong work-ethic
- Positive attitude
- Strong internal motivator
- Pride in building team morale
- Effective oral and written communication skills
- Passion for excellence in my work

Target Market:
Geographic Location

> Chicago, Illinois
> Open to a position requiring extensive travel

Types of Industries

Focused on industries with multiple business units and a diverse range of brand awareness and marketing needs. Prefer national/multinational corporations or large foundations with commitment to corporate responsibility and employee engagement through community relations.

Size of Organization

- 1,000+ employees
- Fortune 500 preferable

When formatting your own PMP, I want you to ask yourself a few questions:

1. **What is your real purpose for networking?** Dig deep when asking this question. You might say you're networking to build your network, and not for job seeking. Make sure that's true before you say it out loud. Do you really want a job, and you're disguising that desire? If so, be honest with those you're networking with, if possible, about what you really want.

2. **Does the plan you're developing support the brand you're building?** Can the individual reading your PMP at least begin to understand your brand and the way you plan to market yourself as a professional? Like your resume, your business cards, and your website, if you have one, your PMP should fall in line with the look, feel, and emotional connection you want readers to develop with your brand.

3. **What questions might someone ask if reading your PMP?** Are you leaving something out that could help you land the next big meeting or the job you've always dreamed of? The PMP is not the time to hold back or veil your real desires. This is your marketing plan, not your pitch. Don't disguise what you're really looking for and the path to get it. With this plan, you're giving the individuals you're networking with a clear opportunity to step up to the plate and help you get ahead.

This document gives you an opportunity to leave your networking connections with a concrete piece of collateral to display your strengths and abilities, without the sometimes awkward process of shoving a resume in someone's hands. Resumes scream, "give me a job," and there's nothing that will ever change that fact. A PMP can be easily presented and even more easily explained. You'll simply say to the individual you're meeting with, "Because I'm strategically building my network, I've put together a personal marketing plan that explains in detail more about me, professionally, and details about what I'm looking for in my networking." This opens the door for you to walk your connection through your marketing plan, if appropriate, and introduce them to your goals, skills, and achievements in a natural way. If you're the kind of person who finds networking conversations awkward, a PMP will help you frame your conversations. If you're a natural networker, a PMP can take your networking connections to a more strategic level and provide an important framework to show your target that you're not just networking for free coffee, but to strategically build your relationships and overarching network.

What you are creating when you introduce your PMP to a connection is an ambassador for your network and, ultimately, for your career. You are developing, with great intention, brand ambassadors who will understand your marketing plan, understand your brand and, most importantly, understand you as a professional and as a person.

Experts in corporate branding will tell you that ambassadors for brands are key to distilling the brand's message around the world. Employees are ambassadors, customers are ambassadors, and everyone who has ever touched the company or its brand can easily be an ambassador for the brand. Even the most remote areas of the world have access to powerful brands and the ability to become brand ambassadors. It's American corporate behemoth Coca-Cola that has most effectively implemented the notion of brand ambassadors in growing its business worldwide.

Travel to any remote village in the world, and though you might not find cellular phones or credit cards, you will almost always find a bottle of Coca-Cola – so much so that it will surprise even travelers to small villages in Africa and India accessible only on two wheels instead of four. How does Coke get its product to these remote areas? They use the assistance of powerful brand ambassadors. These individuals are not employed by Coca-Cola. On the contrary, they actually pay Coca Cola for its product. Individuals who have transportation travel to the closest larger village with access to Coca-Cola's mainstream distribution and pay for crates full of Coke. These individuals strap crates to bicycles and other small vehicles and bring them, sometimes hundreds of miles, to sell in their own remote villages. Here, Coca-Cola is creating not only entrepreneurs in their own right, but brand ambassadors where brands can almost never go. These small shop distributors are ambassadors for Coca-Cola's brand, and so are the young children who taste Coke for the first time and the men and women in these small villages who wait for the distributor to arrive each week.

You may not have the ability to distill your personal brand to the kind of mass worldwide market a company like Coca-Cola can. You can, however, use the model they've developed to set your brand on fire and ensure it reaches as many key targets as possible. By providing to one connection, in one meeting, on one day, a beautifully prepared marketing plan, connecting directly to the brand you want to build, you are ensuring that individual will, at some point, strap your proverbial brand to the back of their bicycle and bring it to another person on their journey. If you've done your job correctly, somewhere at a luncheon or a networking event, there is a member of your networking saying to a person they've just met or a long-time friend, "You simply have to meet this incredible woman" – YOU! Don't sit back and let the branding opportunity of a lifetime pass you by. You might not have a fragrance line to go along with your breakup song like Taylor Swift, an infamous and controversial column in *Cosmopolitan* like Julia Allison, or the worldwide distribution of a Coca-Cola. What you do have, though, is something no one else ever will. Y.O.U. That, in building both your network and your brand, is all that matters.

She Knows Everybody! Narrative: Chapter 4
You're the Brand: Creating a Personal Marketing Plan

Julie Cottineau
CEO, BrandTwist

Find Julie Online
Website and Blog: www.BrandTwist.com
Twitter: @jcottin
Facebook: facebook.com/BrandTwist

It's one of the biggest misconceptions forced upon us by the corporate world that big ideas, great ideas, business and career changing ideas, come to us while we are at the conference table, brainstorming with a group of like-minded corporate employees. We are taught, not just in a corporate environment, but at a young age, that T.E.A.M. (Together Everyone Achieves More) and the art of the brainstorm are the ways to get great ideas. While these are certainly valid ways to come up with ideas, I think if you ask some of the great idea generators of our time where they came up with their genius products or businesses, it would be somewhere like the shower or the car or (as it was with the woman we're talking about in this narrative) at the airport.

Before we get to Julie Cottineau's brilliant idea inspired by an airport terminal, though, let me tell you a little about this accomplished and amazing woman. Like the rest of the women profiled in my *She Knows Everybody!* narratives, Julie Cottinneau is an expert in the field of branding. She began her brand consultancy, BrandTwist, to help entrepreneurs and corporations build their brands and leverage them as actionable business assets after serving as the VP of Branding at Richard Branson's Virgin Group. Her resume continues to include brand strategy executive positions at Interbrand and Grey Worldwide in both the U.S. and France. She's been an adjunct professor at Columbia and Cornell, and she continually teaches the world about branding on her blog at www.BrandTwist.com every day. That's a mouthful, right? You can imagine how excited I was to talk to Julie about personal marketing and the ways it can connect to your brand. After all, she's been the voice behind some pretty big brands, Career Girls. Let's go!

The Brand Twist: Inspired by an Airport Mirage

Julie left her position at Virgin in 2011 not only to become an entrepreneur, but also to help other entrepreneurs. She realized that the kind of branding expertise she could cultivate and access at Virgin simply wasn't available to small business owners and others who couldn't afford massive branding and marketing teams. Frankly, she knew so many people were just getting branding wrong. When it comes to branding and marketing, Julie told me, "Even people in the industry don't get that there is a difference! Branding is about understanding the core promise of your product or service. Marketing is the next step. Marketing without branding may work for a short while, but if the fundamentals of the brand aren't there, the marketing dollars are wasted." Julie knew that with her new company she could give the kind of brand strategy she developed at Virgin to companies struggling to find just that branding and marketing balance.

The idea for BrandTwist came to Julie in an airport terminal (for my money, a much better place to brainstorm than a conference table). In the distance, Julie saw the McDonald's golden arches on the tail fin of an airplane while she was running from gate to gate. She wondered, "What would it look like if an airline took on the brand persona of McDonalds?" Simple, right? She told me it would be "consistent, would provide good value, be family friendly" and all of the other brand traits we might associate with the golden arches. The golden arches and the plane turned out to be just a mirrored reflection of an airport McDonalds, but this "brand mirage" gave Julie the idea for her company and the signature twist she provides to her clients.

Julie said of this "a-ha moment," "It got me thinking about the companies I represented. They were confining themselves specifically to their category and drawing comparisons only from those in their area. To get inspired and break that mold, they had to start thinking about other companies." She pushed herself to think outside her category strategically when considering brand problems. Imagine an airline or a hotel chain, instead of comparing itself to another airline or hotel chain, comparing its brand to IKEA or Starbucks or Whole Foods. Julie pushes her clients to ask, "If an aspirational brand outside your category came to spend a day with you, how would its lens change your business?"

You can begin to practice the BrandTwist as you look at corporations you easily interact with every day. What would happen if Walmart adopted some of the brand persona of Google? Would products be easier to find? Cataloged based on what you regularly buy there? Perhaps you'd find free products that bring you in the door more often. What would it look like if Best Buy adopted some of the brand persona of Starbucks? Stores might get smaller, and production would get faster. They might consider being less sales oriented and more process oriented. Where Starbucks greets you with a big smile and a quick "get you through the line and out the door" mentality, Best Buy takes a longer sales process and browsing time into account. Could you fundamentally change its success by applying a completely different twist to its brand? Julie thinks so! And I agree.

It's All About YOU!
The BrandTwist Concept in Your Own Career

In our conversation about this narrative, I asked Julie to help me teach you all how to apply the concept of BrandTwist to individuals. Could I really create "Marcy Twete + Meg Whitman" and get something great? I may be the CEO of a tech startup, but I'm no eBay! Could it work person to person? Her answer was a resounding "YES!" Even better, she shared with me her own experience in building a personal brand and a brand for her business using an individual, person-to-person BrandTwist.

Julie knew when she launched her business she couldn't simply differentiate herself within the field of branding experts – there are just too many. Worrying about what someone else is doing in her own field and trying to compete would be a daunting task. Developing her own brand and focusing on being herself, though, seemed like a fun and digestible task. Julie looked not to her own field, but to one far away from hers for inspiration – cooking. Her personal BrandTwist became Julie Cottineau + Rachel Ray. Why? Julie told me, "Rachel Ray makes cooking fun. She stands out against all the other chefs because she's accessible. She's not too serious. She's colorful. She's fun. She has long hair! And above all, she has a 'make it work' mentality. Don't have shallots? No big deal. Grab an onion!" Julie's model of Rachel Ray's brand inspired her to launch her business with a full infusion of fun and a dedication to accessibility. She's launching "Brand School" this year and realized she can be the "Rachel Ray" of branding consultants – someone everyone can understand and afford.

The fact of the matter here is that you don't have to try to emulate Starbucks or Apple or McDonalds. You can get incredible brand inspiration from an individual whose brand truly shines – someone like Rachel Ray.

Julie also reminded me in our discussion of a celebrity who is already using the BrandTwist concept in her career. You may not know it based on her long history of performing, but Beyonce Knowles is deeply shy and has consistently dealt with bouts of stage fright. It's almost inconceivable after seeing Beyonce perform for decades, first with Destiny's Child and later as a solo artist. Her secret is a self-created alter ego named Sasha Fierce. In an interview with Allure Magazine in 2010, Beyonce spoke openly about creating Sasha Fierce early in her career to separate her own timid and shy self from the courageous and sexy stage self she had to cultivate to become successful. Each night, before she went on stage, she would "put on" her Sasha Fierce persona and leave Beyonce behind backstage. Her stage fright and shyness melted away and she became a fierce, fearless female.

You can apply both Julie and Beyonce's BrandTwists in your own career easily:

1. **Finding Your Own "Rachel Ray"**
    Close your eyes and walk yourself through the statements you'd make about the brand you want to cultivate. Think about the kinds of statements you made in creating your PMP. How are you positioning yourself? What are your key skills and personal attributes? Then, begin to think through a Rolodex full of celebrities, high-level women in business, authors, etc. Who pops into your head? Who might you want to twist your brand with to make you even more powerful? From there:

    - List the brand traits that represent that individual.
    - Make a second list next to that one of the ways you might incorporate those traits into your own brand.
    - Find commonalities. Even if you're a lawyer comparing your brand persona with Angelina Jolie, you might be able to find similarities between you

to make your brand even more powerful (maybe you both love giving back and volunteering or you have a strange affinity for bad boys). Note these commonalities.

2. **Create Your Own "Sasha Fierce"**

Perhaps you're just not finding the right aspirational person to twist your brand with. Consider using Beyonce's technique of developing your own personalized alter ego. Remember, it may not always be a tuned up version of you. It could be a tuned down version of you. I know in my own career and branding exercises, I'm high energy (one might even call me, dare I say it, loud!). In certain instances, I need to put on a more quiet or reserved persona to ensure I'm connecting my brand with good marketing. To create your alter ego, start with the following questions:

- What traits do you desire in your brand but currently feel are missing?
- Which of those traits is outside your comfort zone?
- Which of those traits do you currently have but perhaps need to amplify or diminish?

The great news about these exercises is that you won't need them forever. Julie Cottineau has created a brand phenomenally strong in itself, even without her Rachel Ray comparison. Before talking with Julie about this narrative, she and I had never met, but I've followed her BrandTwist blog for years. Before our conversation, I described Julie to my husband as someone who has a "fun approach to something that's normally difficult to understand" and even remarked to him that her brand was "colorful." Clearly, I hit the nail on the head with her branding promise and the persona she includes with it. I'd say

Julie has reached her aspirational branding platform!

The same goes for Beyonce. After titling an album *I Am... Sasha Fierce,* she told Allure Magazine that she felt she could finally leave behind her alter ego. She explained, "I don't need Sasha Fierce anymore, because I've grown now and I'm able to merge the two." You, too, will become comfortable enough in your brand persona in the future to let go of your alter ego and be confidently yourself in every situation. It takes time, though, so keep your own Sasha Fierces or Rachel Rays around for as long as you need them!

The "Best of the Best" in Networking Advice

I ended each of the interviews completed for You Know Everybody! by asking each woman to provide to this book's readers her best networking tips and advice. Here are Julie's tips and tricks.

- **Be incredibly specific in making any ask.** When you approach someone as follow-up or in a cold call or email, you want to get to know her. It's very important, though, that you be incredibly specific in your communication about what you want to talk about, what you want to get out of it, and most importantly what you can contribute. Have a specific task. Julie says the worst offenders are young women who say things like, "I've been reading about you, and would like your advice." As much as women like Julie would love to give advice to everyone who asks, there are only so many hours in the day. You're much more likely to get a response when your request is specific.
- **T.M.I. Don't Overshare!** Julie told me, "Women are *so guilty* of this. When you're telling a story, you need one headline, three bullet points. That's it! You have

to make it easy for people to 'get you.' Unfortunately, we're trained to overshare. That's what makes us fun girlfriends, but it doesn't make us great in a professional setting." In any first impression, you might have 20 seconds before someone stops listening or moves on in the conversation. Take Julie's advice and make them count. Edit! Edit! Edit! Is the information you're sharing really relevant? Or is it an overshare?

- **Refresh!** You're doing all the work in this book to position yourself, to learn to make great connections, to build the network of your dreams. But one of Julie's best pieces of networking advice is to "Be willing to refresh your approach when it doesn't work." You might think your elevator pitch is the perfect one for you, but if it consistently falls flat and turns people off, you've got to go back to the drawing board, not reluctantly, but willingly and with the excitement to make it better.

#

Getting Your Foot in the Door

She knocked and waited, because when the door was opened from within, it had the potential to lead someplace quite different.

—LAINI TAYLOR IN DAUGHTER OF SMOKE & BONE

If you're like me, you've likely seen the movie *Pretty Woman* several hundred times. And for that reason, I know you won't mind that I begin Chapter 5 with the second (and probably not the last) reference to this iconic film. Go with me, please, as we follow Julia Roberts' experience after her $3,000 negotiation with Edward. She sulks after being shunned by the evil shop girls of Rodeo Drive and as she's about to be shunned by hotel manager Barnard Thompson, she angrily and tearfully asks for his help. She pulls fists full of cash out of her tattered black purse and says, "I have all this money now and no dress! Not that I expect you to help me, but I have all of this, okay? I have to buy a dress for dinner tonight. And nobody will help me." In this moment, she is desperate. She wants to fit in, she wants to impress Edward, and she wants to be the woman he expects her to be.

As much as I'll try to avoid the comparison to a famous (albeit fictional) prostitute, this conundrum is actually a quite familiar one for women when it comes to strategic networking. It's as if you're sitting in Barnard Thompson's office at the Regent Beverly Wilshire and out of your proverbial big black bag, you're depositing on his desk fists full of knowledge and information. You have all of "this": Your elevator pitch, your wish list, your target list of individuals and companies. It is akin to a having wad of money and nowhere to spend it. What you have here is a plan full of strategy with no one to use it on.

What you need is exactly what Barnard Thompson gave to Julia Roberts' character in *Pretty Woman*. He picks up the phone, willingly and without reservation, at the pleas of this terribly dressed but inevitably lovable young woman, and calls his friend Bridget to help her. He opens a door for her that no one else would open. He gives her an opportunity no one else would have given her. What you need now—armed with your pitch, your lists, and your ideas—is an open door. And in Chapter 5, I'm going to teach you not only how to find it, but how to ensure it opens naturally for you. I can't guarantee a man will run up a fire escape for you at the end of the process, but hey, it's worth a shot.

At this point in the *You Know Everybody!* process, you've identified the right people to add to your network and in what areas you might need to strategically search for individuals to fill out your networking constituencies. Now is the time to discover how to get a foot in the door.

What was Julia Roberts' character missing the first time she trekked down to Rodeo Drive? It's pretty clear, right? She walked into those high-end shops looking like a prostitute. She was without connections, without references, and she didn't look the part. She had no credentials and she had no ability to "fake it till you make it," either. The next step in the process, though, was to walk into the department store with a reference. Next, Edward takes her shopping with him – another reference, another connection. And finally, when she's able to clean up and dress the part, she is free to shop Rodeo Drive all on her own without issues. We're going to teach you to amass these same kinds of connections and references, and ultimately to learn to look the part, fit in, and eventually become a part of that door-opening crowd you need to succeed in your networking endeavors.

When it comes to closed-door networking, there are generally two specific scenarios you might be facing:

1. You already have the name and the title of the person you want to contact. You may even have her email address or phone number. The problem isn't contact information; the problem is knowing how to connect appropriately to get a foot in the door.

2. You have a target company, department, or industry, but unfortunately not a specific person or name to connect with. The problem you need to solve is more than just getting in the door; it's finding out the names of the key players and where they're positioned in the hierarchy of the companies and industries you're interested in.

Let's work backwards in this "how to" and start with number two. You'll need to get names before you get noticed! Let's assume, then, that you're in scenario two and you have ideas about companies but not specific people to go after. Step by step, let's find the person you need to find.

Taking Names (and Email Addresses): 6 Easy Steps

Step 1: Choose a company and a specific department or business unit within that company you want to connect to. Don't worry about whether or not you'd want to work there. Sure, it might be the perfect employer for you. But if you're truly networking strategically, and considering all layers of your personal network, you'll want to target companies for connections as well as opportunities.

Example: Amy is currently in sales with a big box retailer. She's fallen in love with the cosmetics portion of the business and wants to transition to a high-end cosmetics company in direct-to-consumer marketing. She intends to live in the Chicagoland area and is targeting Chicago-based Ulta Beauty.

Step 2: Who is the tip-top guy or gal in the department you're targeting? Almost all large corporations list senior staff members (think C-suite) and members of their corporate governance boards on their websites. Take note that this portion of the website can be difficult to find. It's not always in the main menu or even in the footer. Try searching online for "Company Name Investor Relations" to find this page specifically. Once there, you'll likely be able to find someone who is the top person in the department you're looking for, be it finance, sales, marketing, public relations, etc. Usually this is not the perfect person to network with at the company; someone who works for that person will have more time and willingness to meet you. But that one name is a strong jumping off point.

Example: Searching Ulta Beauty's Investor Relations site produces names of the women who oversee both Merchandising and Marketing for the company, areas that are good matches for Amy's sales background during an interview process.

With this information, start a company map as I've laid it out below. This will help you develop a list of potential connections that is comprehensive of levels of leadership and potential connection strategies. We'll fill in the rest of the map as we go on. For now, fill in your target company, the leadership names, and positions you've found.

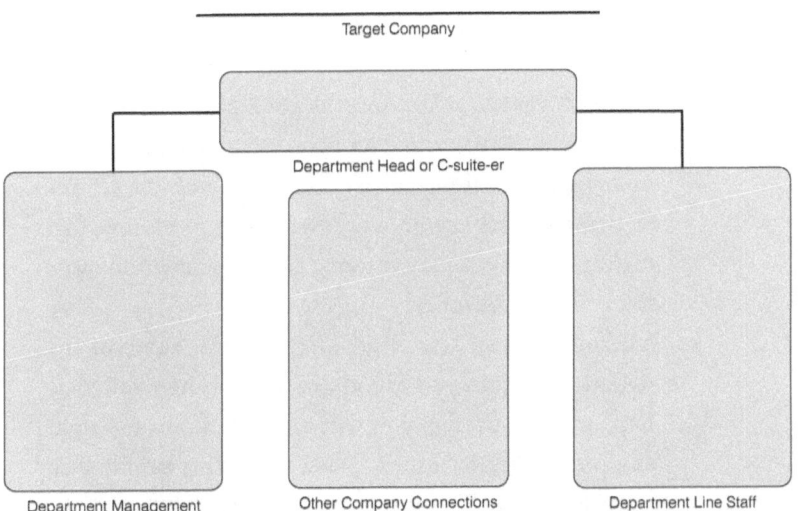

Target Company

Department Head or C-suite-er

Department Management   Other Company Connections   Department Line Staff

Step 3: Who works directly with the person at the top of your target department? There are multiple ways to find these kinds of connections. The people who work directly for or with the person at the top of the department are usually the right people to connect with at a company. They're not in the company's senior leadership team, but they are generally the hiring managers at the company, and those who supervise the most staff within the company. If you're looking for a director-level position within the company, you might report directly to one of these people. If you're looking for a coordinator or assistant-level position, you'd likely report to one of their direct reports, but new hires usually require their stamp of approval, making them key individuals to add to your network.

Let's look at a few ways you can find the names of these individuals:

- **Google:** As great as any other tool might be, Google is obviously your best option in finding any information about a company. Search (in quotes) the name of the department head you found in Step 2. Consider searching "FirstName LastName" CompanyName, as this will give you more direct search results. Here, you'll find a huge range of resources. You may locate a press release with the individual's name and it might also include the names of key players on her team. You might look for articles in *Business Week* or *Inc.* and other trade magazines that highlight the work they're doing and often mention more than one staff member.

- **LinkedIn.** First, search on LinkedIn the name of the department head you found in Step 2. When you view her LinkedIn profile, you will see a menu on the right side of the screen called "Viewers of this profile also viewed...." This information is incredibly valuable. Imagine, for a moment, you interviewed with the head of this department. Who else might you look at on LinkedIn? You'd search the other people you interviewed with, hiring managers, and other people who work directly with the department head. This list usually contains close colleagues within the company.

- **Job Postings.** Even if you're not looking for a specific job with the company you want to network with, sometimes its job postings can have valuable information, including names of HR professionals and hiring managers. But here's a tip: Don't rely on the job postings on the company's website for this information. Most of the time, web postings on the main site give you not names or departments but job numbers internal to the company. Instead, search for jobs with a simple Google search to find which other sites the company (or specific department) uses to post jobs. Often, on smaller, trade-specific job search sites, it's required to include a real email address or name in the contact information. Look on LinkedIn Jobs, small career boards specific to your industry, and Indeed. com for a wide array of job search sites.

This process should have produced a larger list of names within the target company who are potential hiring managers and networking connections. Use the chart above and fill these names in the left column labeled "Department Managers."

Example: Our friend Amy who wants to network into Ulta Beauty found great results using Step 3's tactics.

- *Google produced for her three separate press releases with the name of the department head and at least five names of individuals who work directly with that person. By searching these names on LinkedIn, Amy was able to find their exact titles and tenure with the company and add them to her list.*
- *LinkedIn also helped Amy to find not only the kind of connections she's looking for within the department, but also to discover a bit of information on the corporate structure. She noted that her top name was a Senior Vice President, but connected mostly to VPs. She didn't note the appearance of Associate Vice President or Director levels within any of the connections she searched, and concluded that VPs are likely the main hiring managers within the company.*
- *Job Postings were especially helpful to Amy. She found that a hiring manager had posted on a university's alumni jobs board*

a job posting that is exactly the kind of position she's hoping to get within Ulta. This yielded the name and email address of the hiring manager, a perfect person to add to her list.

Step 4: Can you find allies within the company who are on your level? You'll now want to follow a strategy similar to Step 3 to find "line staff" within the company. These individuals work within the department you're targeting and likely report to many of the department management individuals you've listed above. They can be valuable networking connections, as they're often more willing than leadership to meet for coffee with someone they don't know to build their own networks. These are the people who are doing the kinds of jobs you might be looking for within a company, if you're not yet at the level of a VP or SVP.

To search for these individuals' names, you'll want to employ the same strategies as above. Search the "Viewers of this profile also viewed..." section on LinkedIn, and search Google for specific leadership names to find their team members. But also consider a few more in-depth research tactics to get these names:

- **Industry Networking Groups.** If you're networking within a company that is a leader in its industry, it will often expect its young professional staff to be leaders in industry networking groups. Consider looking at young professionals groups on LinkedIn, in your city, and around the country that are specific to your industry. You may find that some of their leadership is from the company you're targeting or from peripheral companies that can help you get in the door.
- **Twitter.** If companies are smart, they'll view all of their staff as key ambassadors on Twitter. You'll find that many young professionals are retweeting and promot-

ing what their company is doing on their personal Twitter streams. Run a quick search on Twitter for the company's name and note who is tweeting on their behalf. Check personal profiles to find out if that individual might work for the company and in what department. Direct messages to these individuals can be lucrative for your search.

Example: *This portion of the process was especially successful for Amy. She found the names of more than ten "Senior Buyers" within Ulta. This is exactly the position she'd like to apply for. She can now reach out to these individuals for informational interviews, inquiring about their experiences with the company and asking for advice on how she might get ahead (we'll talk more about those kinds of strategies in Chapter 6).*

Add these "line staff" connections to your existing chart above in the column on the right.

Step 5: Don't forget "who you know" already. Networking within a specific department is certainly strategic when it comes to being an expert in your industry, but it's not always the most effective because, the truth of the matter is, you're cold calling (or emailing) these individuals. And while later in this chapter I'll teach you how to do that successfully, a warm lead is always preferable. So before we move on, make sure you've exhausted your resources in the realm of people you already know to ensure you haven't ignored the foot you might already have in the door. Consider these tactics:

- **LinkedIn.** At the top of LinkedIn is a Search bar. First, change the search type to "Companies." Search your target company and you'll immediately see a list of individuals on the right side of the screen called "How You're

Connected." These include existing first-degree and second-degree connections in your network within that company. You may already know someone who works there, or have a second-degree connection you can easily access through your network.

- **Glassdoor.com.** A company search on Glassdoor can produce similar results to LinkedIn, but rather than connecting to your LinkedIn profile to look for connections, Glassdoor connects to your Facebook profile, a valuable tool both professionally and personally. Check here if you have personal connections who might be able to make introductions within the company.

Example: Amy completed this kind of search and found that a close friend from college just started a new job at Ulta Beauty last year. She knew her friend worked in the beauty industry, but was unaware of her recent job transition. Here is a wide open door for Amy to walk through.

Step 6: You've completed your list of connections. **Now, you need to find their email addresses and phone numbers in order to contact them directly.** Finding email addresses and phone numbers is something of a puzzle. It can be easy once all the pieces look clear to you, but it takes time to get those pieces in place.

- **Personal Connections.** If, in the network you've identified above, you have any direct connections on LinkedIn or Facebook, they should be your first approach to finding emails and phone numbers. Ask them directly if they can get someone's specific email address or phone number.
- **Check Out the Website.** You've likely already familiarized yourself with the company's website. You might get lucky and find a company that lists the email addresses

of their staff. Many small companies or nonprofit organizations list email addresses of leadership, and sometimes for all staff, on their main site.

- **Finding Email Naming Conventions.** One of the easiest ways to identify email addresses is to identify the company's email naming convention, which will generally remain the same company-wide. Some companies use firstname.middleinitial.last name. Others use firstnamelastname, and some new companies are using firstname.lastnameinitial. The list goes on. Every company's naming convention is different. There are a number of ways to find this naming convention:

    □ **There is almost always an email address listed in a company press release.** Visit the company's press page on its website or Google "Company Name" "Press Release" to find a sample. This will often include an individual's email address. You can likely assume that the naming convention of her email is also the naming convention of the email of the person you're looking for.

    □ **Google can be powerful in finding naming conventions.** Type into Google "@ companyname.com" and you'll find at least one or two company emails. If this doesn't work, try a common name like "Johnson" "@ companyname.com" or a department name like "Marketing" "@companyname.com."

- If you're still not sure of an individual's email after taking these steps, you'll want to **harness the power of Google** once again and remember to always use quotation marks in searches. You already know the company's web URL, so try a few different naming conventions with the name of the person you're searching for included. If you're search-ing someone named Constance Hyerdahl, you could try searching "hyerdahl@companyurl.com" or "constance" "@companyurl.com" or "chyerdahl@companyurl.com." Keep playing with these kinds of searches.

- **Phone numbers** can be either much easier or much harder. Try one of these tactics.
  - ◻ **Call the company's main phone number.** Advising you to lie might be controversial, but in this case, I'm going to advise you to stretch the truth a bit. When you call the main line say something like, "Hello. I'm sorry to bother you, but I'm trying to connect to (Target Name Here), and it seems that I have the wrong phone number. Could you possibly tell me what her correct extension is?" Sometimes they'll say no and sometimes they'll give it to you. It's worth a shot.
  - ◻ **Again, use Google strategically.** Try the person's name plus "ext" or "phone." You might be surprised to find something specific.

The six steps above will help you to identify key players and potential connections, and they'll connect you to an email address. It's a perfect process to find information for those you don't know directly and can't yet identify contact information for. But recall that these kinds of networking targets are the second kind of target. The first is someone whose name you know and whose contact information you have, and you just need to get your foot in the door. If you've completed the five-step process above, not all of your targets will fit into the first kind of target category. Let's move on and discover how to open the door with someone whose contact information you already have.

Getting the Door Open: 3 Challenges to Overcome

Challenge #1:
Get Through the Gatekeepers

Every powerful person is inevitably surrounded by a group, either large or small, of "gatekeepers," those who are employed largely to protect the individual's schedule, act as a buffer for potential annoyances, and ensure that only VIPs are added to her calendar. The President of the United States, for example, has hundreds of gatekeepers. The Secret Service surrounds him at all times with three rings of security. The first ring protects the President's person, the second ring controls the area immediately surrounding the President, and the third, ring works to secure the building he's in and the streets surrounding. These teams are working around the clock to ensure that the President is secure at every moment, planning weeks and months in advance of important travel and appearances. And while corporate Senior VPs may not have three rings of security, you should consider their gatekeepers in the same way you might the Secret Service. So, how can you penetrate each of these three levels of gatekeepers?

- **First Level – Personal Assistants:** This level is the toughest. They are the immediate gatekeeper to the high-level individuals you want to network with. And the only way to get through them is to kill 'em with kindness. To get through a truly great assistant, you have to strike a balance between selling yourself and becoming their friend. One of my favorite mentors is a high-level banking executive with an assistant who, at first glance, seems like an easy-going, happy woman. But she's had decades of learning to protect her boss' schedule and says no forcefully but cordially. Being blown off by this woman will actually feel nice! She's the hardest assistant to get through, and you need to show your value immediately. To get in, follow these directions:

- □ Explain concisely and quickly your purpose for wanting to meet her boss.
- □ Ask for a small, but specific amount of time (20 or 30 minutes is usually quite appropriate). Immediately emphasize your flexibility, but try not to sound too desperate. Something like, "I'm able to accommodate her schedule if she'd be willing to schedule some time to meet with me."
- □ Always, always, always thank the assistant profusely. Thank her when she schedules the meeting, thank her when you confirm the meeting, and thank her after the meeting. Thank her, specifically, and do not just give a blanket thanks to her boss. Address her by name—it will go very far.

- **Second Level – Internal Company Contacts:** If you already have connections within the company, they may also act as gatekeepers to the individuals you really want to connect with. Perhaps they offer to recommend you for a job themselves rather than introducing you to the hiring manager, or hesitate about how well they really know the person you want to connect with. Finessing this situation requires a strange combination of being direct and delicate.
  - □ Consider sending an already prepared email introduction for the individual you want to connect with and an email to your contact saying, "I've drafted the email below for (Person A). Would you mind forwarding with a quick note that I'm a friend of yours?"
  - □ Use LinkedIn. Asking someone to connect you directly to a colleague through company email could be uncomfortable, but LinkedIn

can give some much needed distance. At the bottom of the LinkedIn profile of a person you aren't connected with, there is a link called "Get introduced through a connection." When you click this link, you'll have the opportunity to send a request to your current connection asking for a LinkedIn hook-up to that individual. It's easy to say "yes" to a request like this one.

◻ Finally, if the person isn't comfortable providing the connection, ask simply if it's okay to use their name when you introduce yourself to the person in question. They may be more comfortable with a name-drop than a personal recommendation.

- **Third Level – External Company Contacts:** You may find that you're connected to one of your target individuals through friends or colleagues who do not currently work with the individual. They could be personal friends, former coworkers, or passing connections from a networking event. For these types of connections, you'll want to follow the same protocol as the Second Level, but with one additional step.

  ◻ Before you do anything, connect with your connection directly and ask them specifically A) if they know the person you want to connect with and B) if they might be willing to make an introduction. Though they might be connected on LinkedIn or have worked for the same company, unfortunately they may not really know the person well. You have to respect that someone might not want to open a door for you when the door belongs to someone they don't actually know.

Challenge #2:
The Art of the Cold Contact

You have an email address or phone number or both but, unfortunately, no other connections. To get your foot in the door, you'll have to make a cold call or send a cold email and cross your fingers for a response. However, there are tactics you can employ in order to ensure your voicemail is returned and to increase the likelihood of your email receiving a response.

Whether you're calling or emailing, ultimately what you'll rely on is a version of the elevator pitch you crafted in Chapter 1. To keep your call script simple, follow the formula G.I.R.L.S.

- **G – Greet Your Target**
- **I – Identify Yourself**
- **R – Make Your Request**
- **L – Link Your Need to Their Work**
- **S – Suggest a Next Step**

Consider our friend Amy as an example. She's found the perfect contact within Ulta Beauty, and she's ready to make the call and get in the door. How will she position her ask?

Example A – Voicemail:

Good morning, Patty. My name is Amy Mancini. I'm interested in learning more about what you do and your work at Ulta, and I would love to meet you for coffee. I have a long history in retail sales with Target Corporation and currently manage relationships with cosmetics companies on behalf of Target. I'm interested learning more about companies focused directly on beauty. You can return my call at 555-555-5555. I'd be happy to meet you for coffee before your workday begins anytime in the next two weeks.

Example B – Email:
Subject: Coffee with a Connection in the Beauty Industry?

Ms. Smith,

Good morning! I hope this email finds you well. I'm Amy Mancini, and I'm currently in cosmetics sales with Target Corporation. I would like to meet you to learn more about your career path and your work at Ulta. I have a long history in big box retail sales and have recently considered transitioning to working inside a cosmetics company.

Could we schedule a phone call or perhaps a coffee meeting in the next few weeks? I know your expertise in the industry and your experience at Ulta could be incredibly valuable as I begin to make decisions about the types of positions I'm looking for and which companies might be the best fit for me. I have a passion for cosmetics and retail sales and, with so many avenues within the industry, I know the next step for me is to focus my search strategically. Could I suggest meeting for coffee near your office next week? My schedule is flexible and I look forward to meeting you.
Thanks so much!
Amy

In these examples, Amy has made her request clear, she's been both respectful and complimentary to the receiver, and to close, she has made a request that lives appropriately between too vague and too specific. Just remember, G.I.R.L.S.—Greet. Identify. Request. Link. Suggest.—and you'll never be afraid of a cold contact again.

Challenge #3:

Using LinkedIn to Make Strategic "I Don't Know You Yet" Connections

Let's assume you've found yourself in the undesirable situation where you have a target networking connection and cannot find a single common connection. You've struck out on her email address and phone number, and you're still dying to meet this person. Your last resort, assuming they have a LinkedIn profile, is a direct LinkedIn connection. For the purposes of *You Know Everbody!*, we're going to assume you have a free LinkedIn account, and not a premium one. With a free account, you have only one option to connect directly with someone who is not your connection, and that is through a LinkedIn connection request. Unfortunately, within these requests, you have only 200 characters to get to the point and make your ask. It is possible, though, and can be effective.

To achieve your desired results (acceptance of your invitation first, and a response to your message second), follow the G.I.R.L.S. formula in a similar but shorter manner than you would in an email. It may be appropriate to remove a formal greeting in lieu of getting to the "what you want" point.

Example:

As a fellow beauty industry professional, I'm interested in learning more about the work you do and your career path at Ulta. Could we connect in person for coffee or schedule a short phone call?

If you've done the right things, and all of the pieces have been put in place using the process above, you should be happily sitting in the waiting room of the person you want to meet, ready to wow them with your talents and experience. But I know what you're thinking: "Marcy, what if I've done all of that and I'm still not in the door?" This will happen. You'll do everything right, you'll have the best channels available to you, and somehow still the door remains closed. Does this mean you give up? No. It does, however, present another challenge to overcome.

There's a reason I wrote this book for women. Sure, men can read it and I hope any member of the male gender who does is able to build a network that works for him with the help of the concepts in this book. The truth, though, is that men and women are different. Men think differently, act differently, and network differently than women. This scenario is a perfect example of the often opposite ways men and women network. You've done everything right, you've networked strategically, used LinkedIn when necessary, sent the perfectly crafted email or left an impeccably delivered voicemail message, and still...nothing. In this situation, I can tell you exactly what a man usually does: He knocks harder. He stands at the door as long as he can and he knocks harder and louder until someone either opens the door or calls the police to have him removed. Women, in this situation, react entirely in the opposite manner. When a door won't open, women tend to walk away. We internalize the reasoning behind receiving no response: "I'm not a good enough candidate" or "Why would someone like that ever want to meet with someone like me?" or "It probably wouldn't have worked out anyway." Neither the male or female instinct here is correct, so don't worry, I'm not going to tell you that you need to be more male and less female or vice versa. Instead, there's a better way for all of us.

My former boss and past President of WomenVenture, a nonprofit organization that helps women expand their careers and start small businesses in Minnesota, once said, "The only difference between a good job market and a bad job market is that you have to be willing to get in through the back door instead of the front." Simple, yes, but true nonetheless. When the market is down, when your luck is out, when you've run out of options even if you've seemingly done everything right, you can't just walk away and you can't always stand at the door and pound harder. You have to be willing to step back and ask yourself, "Am I standing in front of the right entrance?" It may be that too many other people are knocking at the front door or that the main entrance is blocked by politicking or bureaucracy.

How do you get in the back door when it comes to big names in your field? Think like an investigator. If you can't get to someone through traditional channels – 9 to 5, phone, email, LinkedIn, etc., you're going to need to get creative. Consider these ideas:

- **Time (on the clock, I mean) is of the essence.** Most people make key phone calls between the hours of 9:00 a.m. and 5:00 p.m. Consider extending those hours just a bit, and you may find more success. Many executives are in their office as early at 7:00 a.m. and after 6:00 p.m. Calling at 7:45 a.m. or 5:45 p.m. could mean an individual is more likely to pick up their phone rather than letting it go to voicemail, giving you the opportunity to show that you are not only willing to be flexible with your time, but you're savvy and ready to do business, even after hours.

- **Location, location, location.** I'm not going to give you advice on becoming a stalker, but this piece of knowledge is key to getting a back door entrance to someone at the top of your field. Most people with busy lives and busy jobs also tend to have rigid schedules. They follow a similar pattern daily. Perhaps it's the same gym, the same parking garage and walk to work, the same lunch or coffee shop in the afternoon. There are ways of finding this information that doesn't involve following a person around. Get to know their assistants, the line staff in their company, and casually ask questions. If you know that the

CEO of a boutique firm you want to get to know better works out every day at the same gym you do and loves green juice from the juice bar there, you might be able to get an introduction through a personal trainer or gym employee. This knowledge may be useful even in your G.I.R.L.S. process from earlier in this chapter, especially when it comes to the "S." If you know that the Director of Marketing for your target company eats lunch every day at a certain booth in a certain restaurant, you can use your "Suggest" portion of G.I.R.L.S. to suggest that very restaurant. The introduction of a place that's convenient and already familiar to them might make them more apt to reply in the affirmative to your request.

- **Use the seven layers concept.** You've mapped out the seven layers of your personal network, but it's easy to forget that you're not the only person who has those seven layers surrounding them. The person you're connecting with also has seven layers of a personal network, and chances are, you're only connecting with one or two of them. To get to the person you want to network with, you're likely looking at only professional connections to them. Think about finding personal connections as well. Is it possible that you have a common friend on Facebook or follow the same people on Twitter? Who is in their circle of friends and family?

- **Cocktails connect!** If you're looking to connect with industry leaders, consider going to events they're likely to attend. A CEO at a conference or a cocktail party will be much more willing to talk to someone she don't know than she would via direct call or email, because a social occasion is the right time to show her willingness to meet new people and network on behalf of her company. Search industry publications and websites for event calendars. Google search the name of the person you want to connect with and "speakers" to find out if they might be sitting on a panel discussion or speaking at an event in the near future. Introduce yourself at the event and employ the G.I.R.L.S. concept to immediately ask for a meeting and suggest a time.

These concepts will help you to identify the right door to enter and exhaust all options, but there's one more piece of the puzzle we haven't yet covered: When is a door opening most powerful and effective for you? Our instincts are to put our foot in the door the moment it opens, ready to hold it open and fight our way in, if necessary.

I opened this chapter with a powerful quote from fiction writer Laini Taylor. Ms. Taylor says that when a door is "opened from within" it has "the potential to lead someplace quite different." It's a simple concept, but an important one. If you kick down a door or pound on it long enough for someone to open, the person on the other side will never be receptive to what you're saying. To truly see results in the opening of a door, the person behind it must be able, willing, and ready to give you the opportunity to succeed in your interaction. There is not only great power in a door being opened readily for you, but great grace as well. This kind of open-armed, receptive willingness to help comes only to those who show that grace and ease in their approach to knocking on the door.

Know in your pursuit of networking with the targets you've listed in this chapter that, in time, with the right tactics, your doors will open not forcefully, but gracefully. You must be willing to recognize the difference between aggression and perseverance, between relentless ambition and annoyance. It's a delicate line to walk, but I know you can do it. Avoid being overly male or overly female in your approach. Don't shove yourself into a doorway, but also avoid walking away willingly because you're afraid.

A few final notes before we move on to Chapter 6:

- **Being difficult to reach doesn't necessarily mean unwilling.** Some of the greatest mentors I've ever had are notorious for being impossible to reach via email, and always having full voicemail boxes. These traits might mean unavailable, but they don't always mean unwilling. Keep trying, go through all of the doors, and always think about how to get the door to open gracefully from within.
- **Start with willing, then move to difficult to reach.** We all want to get in the door with the C-suiters. But they aren't always the most practical networking buddies. Start your networking journey with those on the right and left side of the chart you filled in earlier. Networking with these individuals will make the higher level contacts you'll target more accessible.
- **Keep your eyes open for "movers and shakers."** Forgive using a term my grandmother might use, but "movers and shakers" are exactly the kind of people we all need in our networking journeys. When you're looking into a specific industry or company, you'll begin to see some of the same names over and over again. You'll see them at events, at conferences, online, in social media, and more. Watch for them, recognize them, and reach out to them. These kinds of individuals are "Cheers to That!" and "Conjunction Connectors" in your seven layers, and they are incredibly powerful to your process. Getting to the top of your industry requires the knowledge and recognition of these kinds of leaders.

You're ready, Career Girls! Don't go emailing and calling away just yet, though. We have more work to do. This chapter taught you how to get in the door. What's next? Ladies, you need to know how to walk in the room like you own it and nail that meeting. Let's go!

She Knows Everybody! Narrative: Chapter 5
Getting Your Foot in the Door

Aleen Bayard
Principal, Aleen Bayard Transformative Consulting

Find Aleen Online
Website: www.AleenBayard.com
Twitter: @AleenBayard
LinkedIn: linkedin.com/in/aleenbayard

When I thought about women I wanted to interview to include in these "She Knows Everybody!" narratives, I thought of women who had mastered each of the skills in the chapter at hand. When it comes to this chapter, though, rather than finding someone who was skilled as "getting in the door," I opted to interview a woman who is skilled at opening doors. There could be no better person for this task than Aleen Bayard. You'll recall the story I told you at the beginning of this book about my first networking event after moving to Chicago, a luncheon with Professional Women's Club of Chicago (PWCC). That day, frightened out of my tree, I met a lot of women, passed out a plethora of business cards, and did something I'm not good at doing: I asked for help. That day was also the day I met Aleen Bayard. Sitting around my first PWCC table, the task at hand was to introduce myself in a quick one-minute pitch. I did so, with all the gusto I had, and Aleen leaned across the table to me and quietly said, "I have tons of connections for you. Call me and we'll have coffee." In that moment, I saw a woman who did not know me, but was willing to immediately extend her hand to help a new Chicagoan.

Aleen and I met for that coffee a few days later, and she gave me both good connections and incredible advice. Her thoughtful words on my career path ultimately shaped my decision to pursue consulting, which in turn influenced my decision to start Career Girl Network. She has remained a favorite connection of mine and continues to open doors for me and countless others, selflessly and with grace and ease. So let's talk to Aleen about her experience in those door-opening moments.

The Two E's: Expertise and Excellence

I asked Aleen, "How do you know who to call when you need to open those big doors, either for yourself or for another person?" Her answer was simple and poignant: expertise and excellence. Whenever someone with an existing *You Know Everybody!* Network is looking for a connection within it, she should ask herself two questions:

1. Who has the most expertise on the subject I'm looking for?
2. Where can I find uncompromised quality and excellence in my pursuit?

By searching first for these two qualities, it's almost certain that the connections you make will be welcomed and quality ones. Aleen works largely today as a consultant, and says of that role, "When you're a consultant, the client is counting on you as an extension of them. They're using you because they don't have the bandwidth. There's something they need that they don't have. You have to think as if you were the client. Who is your arsenal of talent and how can you bring them to the table for your client?" After she spent decades building a network that works, Aleen's arsenal of talent includes phenomenal numbers of both excellent and expert individuals. But parts of your network are both expert and excellent already, right? When you scroll through your LinkedIn connections or thumb through the business cards in your desk, you already know who those excellent and expert individuals are. Make them the ones you connect to, with, and for others, and the rest of your network will thank you.

Opening Doors: It's About Being Fearless

The day before Aleen and I met for this interview, I spoke in an online webinar for the Levo League and a young woman asked me about confidence...and fear. She talked openly about being afraid of making a "cold call" and said (exact quote), "I don't want to be that annoying girl." It seemed the perfect subject to ask Aleen to comment on, as she is someone who is not afraid to make those door opening calls and requests. We talked about how young women, especially, are often too afraid to be persistent, and lose business and opportunities as a result. Aleen attributes much of her success to being unafraid and willing to take big risks. She told me, "I'm not afraid to call anybody and be persistent about it. I'd get on the phone and call Michelle Obama right now if I needed to and not hesitate a moment. People just give up too easily! Even successful people are shy. Believe it or not, I'm a shy person. But it's not about me. It's about the need I have to fill."

Aleen wants all of you to become what she calls "just in time" networkers. Sure, you want to be proactively networking, but you also have to be comfortable with the fact that sometimes networking is a "just in time" proposition. Aleen says, "If someone I know has a particular need, I rev that up." When your best friend loses her job, you're going to rev up your networking to help her, aren't you? That kind of networking might be more "just in time" than it is strategic but it's valid nonetheless, because when you harness the power of "just in time," you're also giving yourself permission to be ballsy! You're giving yourself permission to make a confident and clear ask. Why, though, is that so much easier to do when we're in distress (or more likely a friend is in distress) than it is when we're just curious and interested in networking?

Aleen talks about being persistent, but she also had some great insights about balancing persistence with appropriate amounts of follow-up as well (more about that in Chapter 10, too). Aleen follows what she calls the "Rule of Two"—two follow-ups, that is. The first contact might be via email; therefore, a follow-up might be appropriate via phone. That's the connection. The second follow-up is all about trying again. If it doesn't work at that point, you may need to sit back and let both the individual you're connecting with and yourself off the hook. You might hear from that person months or weeks later, and you might not. With a great piece of outreach, though, and two follow-ups, you know you've done what you can and it gives you permission to move on. There's always another option. Find it, and start again with confidence. Aleen's "Rule of Two" doesn't mean giving up forever after two follow-ups. You might look for the person at an event or keep her email fresh in your mind for an upcoming invitation to an event. You're simply not hounding the individual on the same topic multiple times.

Everybody? It's MY Everybody!

Let's not get into delusions of grandeur. This book is called *You Know Everybody!*, but of course that doesn't mean everybody literally. Hell, you're not Santa Claus. There's no master naughty or network list to check twice. The key to being a *You Know Everybody!* Networker is to know the *right* "everybodys." Aleen Bayard said it best in my interview with her: "I don't think about this as my network. I think about this as the people I have met that would be value-adds to one another. **I know everybody that**

my everybodys want to know."

Take that advice with you wherever you go in your networking journey. You want to know everybody that your everybodys want to know. This line of thinking might just make networking easier for those who are truly nervous about networking. Why? It takes you, personally, out of the equation. What if you don't go to that networking event to better your own career (though you should) or learn something new (though you should do that, too)? Instead, you could say to yourself, "Tonight, I'm going to this networking event to get some contacts that will help someone else in my network." Go for your best friend who just lost her job, or your cousin who started a new business and wants referrals. Assume the intentions of another person and be the person who just wants to connect your everybodys to everybody. In that moment, you've freed yourself from the confines of asks and pitches, and you've just become what every great *You Know Everybody!* Networker is at her core – a connector!

Kindness Is Networking in Disguise

Connection: It's not always about what you get from people or who you connect them to, either. Sometimes it's just about the pure sense of that word – connection. Sometimes it's doing something for another person with no agenda, with no requirements, and without hope of follow-up. Aleen is a door opener not just because she has a massive network, but also because she is kind in situations where networking would never work. Let me tell you two quick stories to illustrate my point.

When Aleen and I met, she told me a story about meeting a sharply dressed New York woman on a street corner in Chicago. Aleen was out walking her dog in her Michigan Avenue neighborhood when the woman stopped her and commented,

"What a nice neighborhood." The woman asked Aleen if she lived nearby, and she did. Aleen stopped to chat with the woman, not out of expectation or politeness, but truly to be kind and friendly. The woman herself looked friendly and warm, and put Aleen at ease in the question she asked. The woman was interested in moving to Chicago and intrigued about the neighborhood. And in that moment, Aleen did something very few of us would do. She took the woman up to her apartment to show her the view. Aleen tells me she keeps in touch with that New York woman and was glad to open her home to show someone from Manhattan the kindness of a Chicago stranger.

Finally, one of my favorite Aleen Bayard stories is one many Chicagoans heard a while back. In early 2011, Chicago was buried in a snowstorm deemed "Snowmageddon" by the news media. For days before, radio and TV stations urged drivers to stay off of Lakeshore Drive during the upcoming storm. Few listened, of course, and on the day of Chicago's biggest storm in years, countless cars became trapped in snowbanks on Lakeshore Drive (for non-Chicagoans, Lakeshore Drive is immediately adjacent to Lake Michigan and is piled full of snow whenever there's a storm in Chicago). Anyone who knew Aleen Bayard heard about her the next day when the Chicago Tribune reported her name as someone who, during the blizzard, was passing out granola bars and Diet Cokes to stranded drivers on Lakeshore. It just so happens that Aleen lives right next to Lakeshore Drive and saw the opportunity to be kind to people suffering in an annoying twist of traffic fate that day. I tell you this story not because it's a networking story, but because it's a kindness story. Many of Aleen's established networking connections saw that news story and thought, "Yes, that's Aleen."

Moments of kindness like Aleen inviting a lovely New Yorker into her home and passing out treats to stranded drivers are what make her such an incredible networker, because she doesn't think about herself or her needs. She thinks about the needs of others first, and literally opens doors (and her own door in this instance) to friends old and new. Here's an insider piece of knowledge, too: The woman from New York turned out to be a Managing Director for one of the largest consulting firms in the country. A good connection for Aleen? You bet! Networking from kindness can be so powerful, and establish long-term patterns that will change you for the better.

The "Best of the Best" in Networking Advice

I ended each of the interviews completed for You Know Everybody! by asking each woman to provide to this book's readers her best networking tips and advice. Here are Aleen's tips and tricks.

- **Find connections EVERYWHERE!** You've heard about Aleen making connections on the street in Chicago, but she also finds them in negative places in her life. Aleen told me about another woman she met during a fender bender. The woman didn't want to go through insurance and instead offered to pay for the small damages on Aleen's car. As a trade for the $1,100 in damages she paid for, Aleen provided the woman's large financial services firm with the same amount of money in free consulting, which resulted in a lucrative long-term relationship. It might be in a traffic accident rather than at a networking event, but see everyone as a potential connection!

- **Be generous, both with your time and your connections.** Giving back to your network is the best way to build connections. Don't guard the people in your network, and don't guard the time you have to give. Give freely and with excitement for those around you.

- **Facilitate "turnkey" referrals.** Too often, people make connections, but they don't make it easy for one another. "I think you should meet so-and-so" isn't enough! You have to make it easy for the person to connect, give her the tools she needs to succeed, and set her up for success. Perhaps you invite both individuals to an event where you can facilitate the conversation, or offer to join the two for coffee. At the very least, you'll want to be sure you're providing contact information and setting realistic expectations for each party. If, for instance, you know that one of the individuals you're connecting has a schedule difficult to nail down, you'll want to inform the other individual of that fact to manage expectations of setting a meeting. There's a lot of good will out there, Aleen says, "But you have to be strategic about the way you use it. Make it easy for me to help you!"

Knowing How to Nail the Meeting

It occurs to me, Jim, that you spend too much time trying to be interesting. Why don't you invest more time in being interested?

–John Gardner's advice to Jim Collins
from Good to Great

There comes a time in every career when networking becomes annoying and mundane. You might be thinking, "Really, Marcy? You're calling networking annoying and mundane...in a book about networking?" Yes, I am. Networking is hard. It takes dedication and hard work to build a network, and even more dedication and a strong work ethic to maintain one. If you've created a stellar network, though, there will be a point at which you'll ask yourself, "Do I really need to keep building this thing?" The answer is a resounding YES! Unfortunately, most people don't get that message. Which, for you, means you'll inevitably be attempting to network with some people who have gotten to a point where networking, for them, has become annoying and mundane. Many of your industry's high level players will fit into this category—people who have just stopped networking with anyone who isn't already a connection.

If you've followed the steps I've outlined in this book, you'll find that even those with the most rigid "I don't network" mentalities will kindly open an office door to you and give you an opportunity to make a phenomenal first impression. Because even though the big dogs sometimes hate networking, they can usually inherently see its value, and if not for themselves, then for the people who want to meet with them. From there, the rest is up to you. For a powerful individual to want to add you to the inner circle of her network, you have to show her how you can bring value to the table. The onus is on you to effectively convey your value to the people you meet, both broadly as a professional and specifically as a connection to that individual.

Whether you're having coffee with someone who is a potential administrative-level hire in your own company or networking with a C-suiter from a potential client or company you want to work for, you'll all be asking yourselves, "Why is this person valuable to my career? Should I add her to my network?" The task of conveying your value is harder as you move up the ladder. With already expansive networks, high-level individuals will absolutely be asking why you might fit into their already stocked-full network. It's up to you to convey your value strongly enough to prove your worth.

I've already taught you to convey your value properly in your elevator pitch and ultimately in the ask you make of an individual. You've gotten your foot in the door with the power of that ask and your clear value proposition, but it can't end there. You must be able to coherently and persuasively convey your value during an in-person meeting as well. You want to walk out of every meeting you have and be able to high-five your proverbial self and say, "You nailed that!" Hopefully you already know that feeling and have had it before in your career. You can harness the drive to get there again, and have those kinds of meetings where everything flows perfectly from beginning to end. But it's not without preparation and hard work that those kinds of meetings occur.

That's why we're going to move methodically through the process of nailing a meeting with a networking connection in two phases: Before the meeting and during the meeting. We'll get to the "after" part in Chapter 9.

Before the Meeting:
There's No Such Thing as Over-Prepared

When you're meeting with someone you haven't met before and don't have a strong personal connection to, the brutal truth is, you have one shot. You don't get a second chance to make a first impression, and you don't get a second chance to make a good networking connection, either. Within the first few minutes of meeting you, the person across the table from you has already made up her mind about who you are, what you do, and whether or not she wants to have a relationship with you. In short, don't blow it. The only way to ensure you've set yourself up for a successful encounter, though, is to prepare, prepare, prepare, and after that, prepare more! There are ways to reverse a bad first impression, but none of us want to be in that position, so it's best to prepare in order to do it right the first time.

The first key to effectively prepping for a meeting is research. Sure, we've all run a quick Google search before our next coffee meeting, but if you're like most people, you're running that search ten minutes prior to the meeting, maybe even while you're sitting in the parking lot waiting to walk in the door. Simply put, that's not good enough. To be prepared to nail a meeting, you must have a wide range of knowledge about the person you're meeting, the company you're targeting, the individual's background, and current events that could steer your conversation.

Consider the following tools when conducting pre-meeting research:

Researching an Individual

You'll want to find as much information as you can about the person you're meeting with. How long has she been with the company? What is her background? Is she involved in industry groups or clubs you might need to know about? What school(s) did she attend (which might show you where she's from originally)? Has she received any awards lately? All of these points will help you to connect personally with your target connection and engage in a robust conversation about her personal experiences and knowledge.

- Of course, a **Google search** is a necessary first step. To ensure you're searching for the right person, use search terms like "First Name Last Name" + Company Name or "First Name Last Name" + City or State.
- There's a fantastic new service called **Newsle.com** that allows you to directly search for news (articles, industry periodicals, guest TV appearances, etc.) on a specific person and add alerts to send you updates when that person is featured in the future. This tool can be useful not only in preparing for a meeting, but in long-term follow-up as well.
- Hopefully your target has a **LinkedIn** profile, which will provide you with key information about her background, education, and tenure with the company.
- Spend time searching common social media sites like **Twitter** and **Facebook**, but also include lesser-used sites like **Pinterest** or **Instagram**. These more personal

social media channels can provide insight into an individual's hobbies and interests that you wouldn't find on LinkedIn or Google. You might find that someone is an avid knitter or planning a wedding in the next few months, which may help steer your conversation.

Researching a Company

You may be engaging in meetings where you have no interest in the company for whom the person you're meeting works, and conversely, you may be interested more in working for the company than you are networking with the individual. In either case, though, a thorough knowledge of the company, its recent happenings, and history may aid in your networking connections.

- When it comes to researching companies, **Google Alerts** is a powerful tool. In the days or weeks leading up to your meeting, set a Google Alert within Google News to email you automatically when the company of your target contact is mentioned. If the company announces a large merger or a cutback during the time leading up to your meeting, you'll be sure to be aware of it with this service.
- If you're interested in working for a specific company, spend time on **Salary.com, Glassdoor.com,** and **Indeed.com.** Along with pertinent information about the company's current openings and expected salaries, on all three of these sites you'll find reviews of the corporate culture from past and current employees, and information about the company's current priorities.
- Depending on which sector the company represents, find more information on websites that offer financial records and information. For nonprofit organizations, **Guidestar.org**, and for corporations, **Hoovers.com**, are great resources.

- Companies often keep a **press/media page** available on their websites. Check it often leading up to your meeting. Bring yourself up to speed with their current releases, and, if available, consider watching any videos or listening to podcasts with C-level employees. Many corporate CEOs record quarterly reviews of their companies' financial statements for their stakeholders, which are usually public and included on a press/media page.

Researching Existing Connections

In your research to develop this meeting, you should already have a working list of connections you might have in common with the individual or company you're targeting. You'll want to take the time to research these connections as thoroughly as you do the individual you're meeting with. Do any of these individuals have a new job, or has anyone moved away from the company? The last thing you want to do is drop a name in the middle of a meeting and flub the person's current workplace or position while doing so.

- Consider making a few phone calls to the individuals who are direct connections between you and the person you're meeting. Ask specifically for advice on the meeting you're having. You may find that your contacts have insider knowledge you won't find anywhere else.
- Also utilize the same tools in this search you would use when researching the individual you're meeting with.

Now that you've done your research and are ready to go, the next step is to plan, plan, plan, and when you're sick of planning, plan some more! I want you to think of every meeting you have just as you would think of going on a European vacation. You'll never hear someone say, "Oh, no big deal, just heading to Paris this weekend. I'll throw some stuff in a bag on Thursday night." Why? Because a trip to Europe requires careful planning, thinking ahead, and a logistics timeline that will ensure a seamless trip through the airport, navigating through a country you've never visited before, and a relaxing departure that doesn't make you regret taking a vacation in the first place. An important meeting is no different and, with these vacation-like considerations, you'll never end up stranded without your passport.

Let's organize your perfect "networking vacation" with these step-by-step travel plans:

The Art of Wardrobe Planning

If you're planning a huge vacation, you're going to want to plan out full outfits for a variety of purposes. Perhaps you're going to see a show and a nice dinner one evening, and the next day hike a mountain. You can't bring the same pair of shoes for both excursions, and you can't get up a mountain trail in a little black dress. The same logic goes for planning your wardrobe for an important meeting.

It would be very easy for me to give you the traditional "wear a suit" advice when it comes to networking interviews, but unfortunately it's just not that easy. A suit speaks volumes, and sometimes not the kind of volumes you want to shout in a first meeting. Black suit, black pumps, button down shirt screams "job interview" more than any other outfit can. If you're meeting someone for the first time who may or may not be a job prospect for you, it might be wise to consider another option. You want to look polished and professional without being presumptuous or overly eager. A few options that work (nearly) all the time:

- **The Dress.** Walk into any Macy's, Nordstrom, or Bloomingdales and make a beeline straight to these brands: Calvin Klein, Ralph Lauren, Anne Klein, or

Tahari. Certainly there are additional amazing brands to add to this list. But if you get yourself to the dress section that carries those four, you'll find you're in the right ballpark for others as well. If you're going to wear a dress and not a jacket covering it, find something with sleeves (long or short, it doesn't matter) that falls at a flattering place on your leg (just above the knee is the most universally professional length).

- **The Slacks/Blazer Combo.** It's not quite a suit if you buy coordinating separates, and it can be a perfect "in between" look that is both professional and approachable. To add a more feminine look, consider pairing a great pair of slacks and a jacket with a knit top rather than a traditional button down.

- **The Skirt/Cardigan Sweater Combo.** A cardigan sweater has become the universal half-step-down-from-a-jacket uniform for women across the country in business or business casual settings. If you know you're headed into a more casual environment, but still want to look well put together, channel the Mad Men look and button up that cardigan with a great pencil skirt (J. Crew's No. 2 Pencil Skirt is a great fit in almost every size and shape).

But don't just stop at the outfit itself. You'll want to take time to plan ahead the jewelry you'll be wearing, your shoe choices, and put some thought into the way you wear your hair.

- **Jewelry.** Keep your jewelry understated, but showing your personality. If you love and regularly wear chunky earrings, wear them! My husband jokes often that if an earring is huge and dangly, I will love it, and it's entirely true. I'm not going to put in a pair of diamond studs just to impress someone if I usually wear something bigger. Whatever you wear, be sure it's something you've worn before and know you'll be comfortable with. Nothing is more annoying than sitting in a meeting realizing your earrings are catching on your scarf or your bracelet is clanking every time you move.

- **Shoes.** This is important, Career Girls, and not just because you want your feet to look good. You also have to take into consideration the many possibilities of what you'll be doing during your meeting. If you're meeting someone at Starbucks, it's safe to say you can rock those "Jay Leno Shoes" (you know, the ones even celebrities can only stand to wear from the green room to the chair on the Jay Leno show) and never worry about tripping over your clumsy left foot. If you're meeting at a corporate campus, though, keep in mind how massive office layouts can be. You might be walking quite a distance from check-in to the individual's office. Early in my career, I interviewed for a job with a big box retailer in a distribution center (why I thought this was a good idea is an entirely different book). I wore a great looking skirt suit and my favorite 4" Stuart Weitzman pumps and felt confident and ready to rock the interview. Little did I know, there was a 60-minute tour of the distribution facilities on the agenda. After 30 minutes of walking on hard concrete in stilettos, my feet hurt so badly I could barely think about the job. To be certain you won't end up in the same situation I did, wear shoes that you'll be able to stand and walk in comfortably to accommodate any kind of tour or walking conversation you might have.

- **Hair.** I cannot stress this enough, you must (I repeat, you MUST) wear your hair for big meetings the same way you normally wear your hair. A friend of mine has naturally curly hair with beautiful ringlets, but insists that it's "more professional" to straighten it for things like interviews. This same friend has, countless times, been caught in the rain or hit by a humid day and seen her perfectly straightened hair become a crazy, poufy mess on her way to a big meeting. If only she would wear her hair the way she normally does, she'd find herself less self-conscious than she is when she's expecting her strands to stay perfect all day. If you always wear a ponytail or a bun, you'll never feel comfortable with your hair down for an important meeting, and you'll likely spend far too much time fidgeting with it and allowing it to become a distraction. When it comes to your locks, keep it as normal as you can and show them the hair you really have on a daily basis, not the hair you wish you'd have if Ken Paves came to your house every morning like he does with Jessica Simpson.

Once you've decided what you're wearing from head to toe, the key is to bring it all together. How you do this is as different for each of us as the contents of our closets. We all have a process for planning a vacation wardrobe, and your process for planning an outfit for a key encounter will be similar. You might lay everything out on the bed, adding jewelry and shoes to every outfit. You could use the "plan around your shoes" method and stack like-colored items with the shoes that work for them. Whatever method works for you when it comes to vacation wardrobe planning, use it to ensure you've planned the appropriate wardrobe ahead of time for a big meeting. I personally use the hanger method. Every outfit goes on its own hanger with everything included for the outfit. If I were preparing for a big meeting tomorrow, for instance, you'd find the following hanging on my closet door:

- My favorite "go-to" red dress from Ralph Lauren
- Chocolate brown tights
- A brassiere that is comfortable and non-fidget inducing
- A stylish green plaid blazer on top of the dress
- Earrings and bracelet tucked in the pocket of the blazer
- Comfortable but stylish loafers on the floor ready for my walk to the meeting
- My most comfortable pair of Cole Haan pumps tucked in my bag for the next day

Planning a full outfit ahead of time in the process I've just described might seem like overkill for some, but it's a key step in your journey to nail the meeting. If you've ever been freezing cold on vacation, wishing you had thought more strategically about packing sweaters and scarves, you'll realize how important it is to avoid the same feelings at a business meeting.

- **Passports and Papers**
  When you're planning for a vacation, you likely have a stack full of paperwork needed to get you from Point A to Point B. You'll need to be certain you have photo identification, boarding passes, passports (if you're traveling internationally), and confirmation numbers for everything from your airline tickets to your rental car and hotel. The same paperwork prep goes for networking meetings. Err on the side of having too much paper versus not enough. Even though you may not need all of this, take it with you to every networking meeting:

◊　Photo identification (In many buildings, getting through security requires it.)

◊　Copies of your resume (Even if you're not looking for a job, a networking connection may ask for your resume to better understand your background.)

◊　Copies of your personal marketing plan (These documents can be even more useful than a resume when you're networking specifically for a job search.)

◊　Directions to your meeting location (These don't necessarily need to be paper copies since most of us have GPS on our phones these days, but make sure you've at least taken a look at the directions prior to your meeting, mapped out a path, and calculated the time it will take you to get there.)

◊　Business cards

- **Perfect Packing**

  The key to success in any vacation travel is packing efficiently and keeping in mind what you'll need on each leg of your trip. Which items are you checking and which are you carrying on? The same process will give you a leg up in your networking meetings. We've come a long way from the Judith Lieber clutches Jackie O. carried around. These days, the bags we carry as professional women are more like suitcases readied for a long trip than what you might call purses. If you've ever stood in line at a coffee shop, you've seen women in line ahead of you rifling panicked through their massive bags looking for exact change, a pen to sign the receipt, and their ringing phones among other things. This kind of Mary Poppins bag search will not bode well for you while sitting in front of a powerful potential pal, which is why perfect packing matters.

A great investment for any Career Girl is a fabulous leather portfolio. Here, you can keep your important paperwork, a notebook, and a pen at the ready for any meeting. Slip this in an outer pocket of your bag, and you'll never have to unzip the rest of the suitcase while you're en route to or introducing yourself at your meeting. If you do need to change shoes or give your hair a quick brush, pack your bag to make these essentials easily accessible as well.

The night before any big meeting, you should (just like you would if you were flying out the next morning) be finalizing your wardrobe and paperwork, and zipping up that bag so it's ready to go the next morning.

- **Checking In**
  This step in the process is one many Career Girls forget, both in the airport and in networking. Most airlines now allow check-ins up to 24 hours in advance, and for some airlines, checking in advance of your flight might even mean being awarded with an upgrade or a better seat. For this reason, a 24-hour check-in rule is key in both travel and networking. When you add a meeting to your calendar, set a reminder to buzz you either on your phone or your computer 24 hours in advance of the meeting. This is your reminder to check in.

When you receive this reminder, send an email to the individual you're meeting or her personal assistant to confirm the next day's meeting. This doesn't need to be long or highly thought through. The subject line: *Confirming Our Meeting: 2:00pm Tuesday* and a quick email something like, *"Hi Mary, Looking forward to meeting you tomorrow at 2:00pm at your office. Thanks so much for taking the time. See you tomorrow."* Don't over think it. The important thing here is that you checked in and confirmed the meeting, not necessarily the content of the message. Simply use it as an opportunity to confirm and to say thank you in advance for her time and willingness to meet with you.

- **Getting to the Airport**
  As I mentioned before, hopefully at this point you've already planned your route to the location of the meeting and estimated the amount of time it will take you to get there. Add at least 20 minutes to that time, and give yourself ample amounts of time to arrive without being flustered and worried about being late. Traffic, detours, and even changed bus routes (if you're not driving), can add to your transportation time, and being late can adversely affect a first impression.

- **Making it Through Security**
  When it comes to job interviews, my advice is always to consider the interview starting the moment you walk into the building. The same rules apply to other networking meetings. The way you interact with "security" (usually the receptionist, the individual's administrative assistant, etc.) can speak volumes to the company or individual with whom you're meeting about your manners, poise, and ability to create relationships. Say hello, ask for a name if you're dealing with a company

representative, and be sure to thank her for her help. Just like airport security workers, these individuals often have thankless jobs and deal with people all day long who are in bad moods and wish they were somewhere else. Do your best to put on the happiest face you can, say hello, and treat them like real people. Too often, we gloss over administrators and receptionists, avoid eye contact, and just try to get where we're going. A little polite banter goes a long way.

- **Boarding the Aircraft**
  Think about the sights and sounds and your own actions when you're boarding an aircraft. You likely don't notice the people around you, the goings on of the flight crew, or anything else for that matter, because you're just trying to look for your seat and get settled in. This might work on an aircraft, but when it comes to a networking meeting, the little details matter. Pay attention to where you're being led in the building so you can find your way back. Shake hands with the person you're meeting and look her in the eye. Do more than just worry about where you're going to sit or how you look or whether or not sweat is dripping from your brow. Look around and admire the office, or notice a photo on the desk of her children or a particular piece of art. The meeting starts and first impressions are made long before you ask the first question. Use this "boarding time" wisely.

- **Spacing Your Connections**
  Finally, and most importantly, you'll want to make sure you keep your meetings far enough apart to accommodate travel and breathing room, just as you would with flights. While no one wants to be stuck in

an airport for hours waiting, and no one wants to kill hours in a Starbucks between every meeting, you'll be more relaxed moving from space to space and person to person if you carefully schedule meetings far enough apart to allow for travel time and rest. If you must schedule important meetings on the same day, think carefully through your schedule before offering someone a 2:30 p.m. meeting when you already have a 1:00 p.m. lunch scheduled.

We'll dive deep into the final step in your before-the-meeting process in Chapter 7 – put your name in the wind. You've mapped out your relationship with the individual you're meeting, and you should already know which connections you might have in common with her. Don't stop using these connections the moment you've landed the meeting, as they can be incredibly helpful leading up to the meeting as well. In the research phase of preparing for the meeting, you may have already contacted your connections to ask for advice on the meeting you're having. This is, of course, helpful in learning more about your target contact, but it's also helpful in potentially preparing that contact for your meeting. If your connection, Marianne, runs into your upcoming meeting contact, Deborah, at an event in the next week, she might say, "Oh, I hear you're meeting with Amanda! Isn't she fantastic? You're going to love her." Your friend might even take the opportunity to talk about your skill set and position you perfectly for a potential interview or job offer.

This is the beauty of great networking. It's never about one thing. Your research isn't just research, it's connection. Your connection isn't just connection, it's relationship building. Your relationship building isn't just relationship building, it's friendship. You'll find that as you take all of the steps in this book, you'll find new steps appear before you again and again, getting you ready to nail the meeting first and to build strong relationships and a *You Know Everybody!* Network in time.

Now that you know how to set yourself up for success *before* the meeting, let's move on and tackle the time *during* the meeting – from "Nice to meet you" to "Thanks for coming."

During the Meeting: Somewhere Between Plan B and Plan X

The annoying part of any meeting is that humans are involved. By our nature, we are unpredictable, varying our moods, likes, and dislikes day by day, and we are at times difficult to read. If there's one absolute I can give you regarding networking meetings, it's that they'll never go exactly as planned. You can strategize until the wee hours of the morning before your meeting, plan everything you're going to say ahead of time, and be 100% prepared to make the right kind of asks and ask the right kind of questions. Very infrequently will your meeting follow the path you originally set for it. This is why it's important to not only anticipate having to move to a Plan B, but also to a C, D, E, and all the way to Z. The truth is that the meeting you're about to have is probably going to fall somewhere between Plan B and Plan X, and that's not always a bad thing. A meeting you thought would be boring and uneventful could turn into an interview for your dream job. Vice versa, an interview for your dream job could turn out to be boring and uneventful. You must be prepared for all scenarios. That's what I'm about to teach you.

First things first, though, no matter how the meeting goes in the long run, you have to make a great first impression and introduction. Thankfully, this part of the meeting process is more science than art. A great first impression is easy to make if you can harness your own confidence to provide:

- A strong, confident handshake.
- A warm smile.
- Say thank you right away – after all, time is money, right?
- Convey confident body language. In two words: Stop fidgeting. Nothing can cap off a great first impression better than sitting up straight, looking your meeting partner in the eye, and planting your feet on the floor as if to say, "I'm here. I believe in myself. I'm ready to do business!"

After this, things get a little more complicated. There are countless variables to consider when navigating the conversation, especially with the relationship building that occurs in a first meeting. I've narrowed the field to just four key variables you need to be aware of and prepared to navigate.

1. **Type of Conversation**

   There are two basic types of conversations you could have with a new connection – one that you drive or one that is driven by the other party. One of the most common mistakes in networking meetings is assuming that the meeting and the conversation within it will be driven largely by the individual you're meeting with. You requested the meeting, it's your network you're building, and you can't simply sit back and rely on someone else to start, lead, and drive the conversation. That's your job. You should prepare to be the conversation leader in every meeting. You should also be prepared for the fact that, although you want to control the meeting, your meeting partner may be the kind of person who takes charge. Come to the meeting with questions and important statements ready in order to steer the conversation if you feel it's being commandeered.

2. **Type of Connection**

Three types of potential connections exist in networking – personal, professional (general), and professional (employment related). At any time, a meeting can transition from one to another. You may think you're meeting someone to discuss a potential position with her company and within a few minutes realize you're much more likely to connect with this individual as a friend than as a boss. Conversely, you may think you're meeting your friend Emily's friend Paige for coffee but discover that Paige has an opening in her company and you might just be the perfect fit. These kinds of connection changes are common and, to be truly successful in any networking meeting, you must be able to keep an open mind, recognizing that any or all of the types of connections here are valid and can add to your network and enhance your career.

3. **Length of the Meeting**

Knowing how long a meeting will be can be either cut-and-dry or tricky, depending on the organization level of the person you're meeting with. If someone's personal assistant sends you a calendar invite that expressly states your 1:00 p.m. meeting ends at 1:45 p.m., you know going into the meeting at least a general framework of the meeting length. But anything can happen in the moment of a meeting. You may find out that your contact has a hard stop time of just 30 minutes because another important meeting came up last minute. You could find that the individual you're meeting completely forgot you were coming (which she shouldn't, if you properly checked in the day before), and now can only spare 10 or 15 minutes. All of these time scenarios drastically change the kind of meeting you're able to have. You cannot make the same kind of connection in 5 minutes that you can in 55, but you can make a connection, and a powerful one at that. It's all in how you play the game.

4. The Meeting's "Flow"

Finally, there are three general ways a meeting can flow. I call them Q&A, Grill Session, and Workshop. In a Q&A flow, you're generally asking your meeting partner thoughtful questions about her job and experience, and advice on your own career. She's answering your questions and the meeting flows in a sort of ping-pong, back and forth, conversational way. In a Grill Session, the conversation is often led by the other party, who may ask you question after question, rapid fire in many cases, to find out as much about you as she can. This kind of meeting style is most likely to occur when a meeting is employment related. The third kind of flow is the Workshop meeting, where a connection works with you very much in the style of a career coach. In this kind of meeting, you might find someone who wants to mark up your resume or marketing plan, dig into their Rolodex in front of you, or work to "get something done" for you in the time allotted.

To give you a visual representation of the kinds of meeting scenarios you might encounter with these four variables, take a look at the chart below:

Meeting Scenarios			
Conversation	**Type of Connection**	**Length of Time**	**Flow**
Driven by You	Personal	Less Than 30 Minutes	Q&A
Driven by Them	Professional (General or Employment Related)	30 Minutes	Grill Session
Alternating Drivers	Professional (Employment Related)	60 Minutes	Workshop

As you can imagine, it would be next to impossible for me to prepare you for every scenario combination you might encounter using the variables listed above. What I can do, though, is share with you a few stories from building my own network to help you to see how meetings can turn on a dime and how connections can be entirely different from what you thought they might be when you shook hands and sat down.

Meeting #1: Driven by Them, Professional (General), 60 Minutes, Workshop

In September 2010, my husband (then boyfriend) and I prepared to travel from Minneapolis to Chicago as he interviewed for his dream job. With an impending move, I also began applying for jobs and quickly became excited about a position with a Chicago-based nonprofit theater group. I wrote my cover letter and resume and applied online, but knowing I'd be in Chicago for Charlie's interview, I took the leap and reached out to ask the hiring manager for a meeting as well. I was transparent in the fact that I'd applied for the job, but requested a meet and greet for general networking purposes. She responded quickly and confirmed our meeting for that Friday. So while Charlie interviewed for the dream job, I navigated Chicago's Red Line train to meet with a potential employer as well.

Though I'd applied for a position with this specific hiring manager, the meeting description was unclear. Was I entering the conversation as a job seeker? Or as a new Chicagoan seeking connections? I didn't know. I had to be prepared for both scenarios. I wore a suit, as I would for a job interview, and came equipped with my resume. I also brought copies of my personal marketing plan and prepared to have a more networking-focused conversation. Immediately upon introducing myself to the woman I was meeting, she launched the conversation saying, "Usually, I start informational interviews by giving the person I'm meeting some feedback about their resume and LinkedIn profile." This statement made it immediately clear to me that this connection would be professional, but not specifically regarding employment. The fact that she dove head first into my resume and LinkedIn profile also meant I could be prepared for a conversation driven by her and conducted in a workshop style.

In the moments I made these realizations, I had to change my expectations for the meeting entirely. Rather than asking questions about the job, I had to ask her advice as a new Chicagoan, and steer my questions toward learning more about her and the industry in which she worked in a city I wasn't familiar with yet.

Ultimately, this conversation shaped my job search in Chicago immensely. I learned, through my questioning related specifically to the nonprofit sector in Chicago, that my experience in Minneapolis might be difficult to translate to Chicago-based nonprofit organizations. I also learned about a number of the key players in the consulting and community relations industries in Chicago I should be networking with to build relationships that would ultimately help me to land a job. Years later, I keep in regular contact with this incredible woman, who has since moved on and upward from the position she was in when I met her, and has helped me in numerous ways both personally and professionally. In the moments at the beginning of my meeting, I could have pounded through and focused on the job, but by being flexible and listening to key cues, I gained a valuable relationship and insight I wouldn't find elsewhere about industries of interest for me in a new city.

Meeting #2: Driven by Me, Personal, 60 Minutes+, Q&A

In October 2012, an acquaintance contacted me to tell me she'd recently met an "incredible woman" and I simply had to meet her as well. She had a consulting background (like me), was a writer (like me), and apparently had a great personality (I hope, like me). Despite all of these commonalities, I was not entirely excited to meet her. I knew, based on her LinkedIn profile, that she was in direct sales, and I worried she'd try to sell me something I certainly didn't want to buy. Nonetheless, we agreed to meet to talk about our respective businesses at a local Starbucks. It was raining that day in Chicago, and not a seat could be found in the coffee shop, so we decided to walk down the street to a wine bar and grab a glass of wine. This (along with her fabulous bright orange handbag) was a key indicator to me that I would, in fact, like this person.

I started the conversation and drove the opening portion of our meeting together by telling her about Career Girl Network, my journey as an entrepreneur, and essentially the parts of my elevator speech that I thought might appeal to her. Within a few minutes, though, our conversation turned intensely personal. Over a bottle of wine and quite a number of hours that evening, we became fast friends and talked about everything from divorce to personal finance to PMS! Hours later, we left one another with a warm hug and a promise to continue our conversation at a later date.

Since that first meeting, this individual has become one of Career Girl Network's most popular writers, has been instrumental in helping me to plan for the future of my business, and we continue to share bottles of wine over countless hours of conversation that bridge the huge gap of personal, professional, childhood, adulthood, and everything else under the sun.

I could have easily kept this woman at an arm's length. I could have talked about my business, given her my card, and sent her on her way. But on that day in October, I allowed my networking meeting to take the kind of scenario it was meant to. I adjusted my expectations in the moment to open myself up to a powerful personal connection, rather than simply a professional one.

Meeting #3: Driven by Them, Employment Related, 30 Minutes, Grill Session

Everyone who has ever interviewed for a job has one of those standard "bad interview" stories. This is one of those stories. As I mentioned above, most job interviews are inherently "driven by them" kinds of conversations. At an interview in Spring 2011, however, my conversation wasn't just driven by the interviewer, but driven at 100 mph down what felt like the autobahn of job interviews. It was the final interview in a series of interviews I'd done with a corporation in Chicago. All I had left was to meet a member of the C-suite, and the job was mine. I prepared beautifully, I researched the company, and more than any interview before, I was ready to nail this meeting.

From the moment I entered his office, the questions were rapid fire. One after the next, barely waiting for me to answer each question, he interrogated me about everything from my employment background to my upbringing and my relationship with my then fiancé. At one point in the interview, he even asked me about the professions of my parents and my grandparents. When I responded that I was the granddaughter of two North Dakota farmers, he launched into a lengthy line of questioning about farm acreage, cattle, and soy beans that left me feeling like the world's worst Midwestern farm kid ever raised. The question peppering stopped only for a moment, at which point he looked at me quizzically, paused for approximately 30 seconds and then said, "Are you intimidated by me?"

Naturally, I was intimidated. Anyone would have been. But I held my own, content to know that I had prepared for every scenario and could easily adapt my expectations to the one at hand. I left the interview feeling good about what I'd said, even though I didn't remember most of it, and confident I'd be offered the position (I was, and it ultimately didn't work out, but that's another story).

It's these kinds of surprising scenarios that can make for incredibly awkward networking situations, whether in the form of a job interview or simply a meet and greet. If I had tried to control the conversation, move it into a Q&A flow, or had expected to be given more than 30 minutes, I would have been flustered and frustrated rather than willing and able to answer questions.

This kind of scenario will also teach you something about the person you're networking with. If, in this case, he's the kind of person who likes to put people on the spot, make potential hires uncomfortable, and really see what you're made of, there are huge red flags to be seen about whether or not that individual would also be a good mentor or boss. In the case of the job at hand for me, meeting an eccentric C-level employee and coming face-to-face with what I'd inevitably be dealing with every day was enough of a red flag to give me pause about taking the job.

Meeting #4: Driven by Me,
Professional (General),
Fewer Than 30 Minutes, Grill Session

When it comes to scheduling networking meetings, there's a very fine line between someone being difficult to pin down and being blown off. I walked the center of this line in 2007 when I was working for a nonprofit organization in Minneapolis selling sponsorships for a large women's conference. In my sales process, I targeted a high level marketing executive at a large Minnesota-based corporation, and played a long and tedious game of phone tag with her assistant. Repeatedly, her incredibly pleasant assistant reassured me that her boss was, indeed, interested in learning about sponsorship opportunities and definitely didn't want to walk away from the chance to meet me and learn more about our organization and the event, but she simply couldn't find time in her schedule to meet with me.

Over and over during the course of weeks and leading into a month or so later, we would schedule a coffee or a lunch meeting and she would cancel at the last minute, pulled into a meeting or needed in last minute travel. My deadlines loomed and it was time to close the deal. I asked her assistant during one of our cordial cancellation chats what time her boss got to the office every morning. Seven o'clock, she told me. I took a leap and asked a little more about her morning routine and found that she frequented a downtown Minneapolis fitness center every morning at

5:15 a.m. and then walked the Minneapolis Skyway System three blocks to her office. I asked her assistant if I might be so bold as to meet her outside her gym and walk with her to her office one morning. Her response? "It's worth a shot!"

The next Wednesday morning, that's exactly what I did. Lingering strangely in a skyway, I waited and caught her quickly with a PowerPoint print out in my hand, ready to wheel and deal. We walked briskly while I gave her my best pitch. All in all, it took about five minutes. I'd like to tell you that quick jaunt to her office yielded a huge sponsorship for my event and the organization I worked for. It didn't. It did, over time, yield for me a strong relationship with this individual. Months later, she invited me to join her at an industry event. Years later, she recommended me for a job during my transition to Chicago. She remains a trusted connection, and with a new job in a new city herself, she's become much easier to get on the phone than she was in 2007.

I've told you each of these stories to illustrate the ways you might prepare for, position, and effectively utilize your own networking meetings in the future, whether or not they turn out as you expect. Consider the following points in your journey:

- Not everyone has 60 minutes to devote to your growth and development. Don't count someone out simply because she's strapped for time. While it does take time to develop relationships, it takes only seconds to make a first impression and minutes to make a great impression.

Take those minutes if you can get them because they may lead somewhere more powerful in the future.

- While we'd love for everyone to become powerful personal and professional connections, some will remain peripheral members of your network, and some will stand out as individuals you simply don't want to associate with.

- Harness the ability to immediately accept reality. You can pretend there's a six-figure paycheck waiting for you at the end of every networking meeting, but if you spend your time focusing on that outcome, you'll miss all of the wonderful opportunities the connection might present in between.

- Find a way to work in your elevator pitch, no matter how the meeting goes. Whether your connection is driving the conversation or you are, whether the meeting is 15 minutes or 50, and whether you're flowing through Q&A or a workshop of sorts, it's up to you to find the time within that framework to deliver your pitch and ask for the help you need from each individual you meet. The onus is on you to set the expectations at the end of the meeting, even if you're not the driver throughout.

When you've given yourself the benefit of good planning and preparation, and when you've let yourself off the hook from the expectations of a perfectly run meeting that goes exactly as you'd hoped, you're officially ready to go out there and nail that meeting! The best piece of advice, though, to nail any meeting, can't be found in your research or any amount of preparation. It's best found in the quote I started this chapter with from Jim Collins' book *Good to Great*. In it, Jim tells us of advice he received from a trusted mentor, John Gardner. John tells Jim he's spending too much time trying to be *interesting*, and wouldn't it be so much better to start trying to be *interested*. Think about that for a moment, and apply it to your own networking meetings.

Here you are, about to walk into a meeting with an amazing new contact and you're thinking, "Will she like me? Do I look OK? Do I have the right kind of experience to get into her inner circle?" Will she help me get a new job?" You're focused on being interesting, and with these kinds of self-doubts, concerns, and hopes/dreams, you may find that you are not, in fact, interesting. Turn those thoughts around, though, and you may find something entirely different. Start thinking, "What kinds of things got this person where she is today? What challenges did she face that I might be able to learn from? How does she go about building her own network and deciding who fits into her inner circle? How did she find her job?" These questions are the kind asked by a person who is *interested*, not trying to be interesting. Positioned in this way, I think what Jim Collins found, and you will, too, is that when someone is truly and authentically interested, they immediately become, to the person they're speaking, interesting in turn.

Chapter 6 Add-On: FAQs on Meeting Etiquette

While writing *You Know Everybody!*, I've had the occasion to talk to hundreds of women about the way they network and the difficulties they encounter in one-on-one networking, specifically. In all of my conversations, I've found the same sets of questions come up. To help you get to the next level in your meetings, I've added this section of frequently asked questions to make your meetings more meaningful and less stressful.

Q: **I'm meeting a networking connection for lunch.**
What do I order? And who pays for what?

A: You'd think evolution would give humans better
skills for eating and talking at the same time,
but this feat remains one of the most difficult to
accomplish not only in every day life, but especially
in business settings. When it comes to business
lunches, take the lead of the most senior person at
the table with you. If he or she orders a beverage
other than water, you can feel free to order a
similar beverage if you wish. If he or she orders an
appetizer, you may want to partake in one as well.
When it comes to entrees, order something that
is easy to eat and doesn't require the use of your
hands. A burger is probably not the most ladylike
or professional meal to eat in front of a potential
colleague or boss. Consider ordering a salad that
doesn't require extensive cutting (stay away from
the wedge salad), a simple chicken dish that's easy
to cut and eat, or pasta like tortellini or ravioli that
doesn't require noodles twisting around your fork.
Ease of eating is key. When the check comes to the
table, always reach for your wallet, even if you're on
a job interview. Though the person you're meeting
may pick up the tab, an offer to cover your cost is
always welcome. If the other party does offer to pay,
don't get into that "No, I've got it" back and forth
argument women tend to have. Graciously thank
your host and continue the conversation.

Q: **What are the networking and job interview rules on alcoholic beverages at events after normal workday hours?**

A: No one likes to hear this answer, but the truth is, it depends. Let's look at a few potential situations where you might be up against this decision and the right choice for each of them. If you're meeting a new connection for networking and you've specifically mapped out that you're going to meet "for drinks after work," by all means, order a drink. Note the use of "a" and not the use of "some" when describing the number of drinks you might have. One drink with a new connection is a great place to start…and stop. Another sticky situation might be a dinner interview for a job. A company who schedules an interview over dinner is likely trying to gauge your appropriateness in social business settings. Again, as at lunch, take the lead of the most senior person at the table. If that individual orders a bottle of wine for the table, you should certainly partake if you'd like. If that person orders a martini, consider ordering yourself a glass of wine or mixed drink as well. Don't feel the need, though, to match the individuals you're with drink for drink as if you were in college, though. You're more than equipped to show them your social side without losing your inhibitions. Finally, my favorite tip for women working in high alcohol content environments is this: If you're going out with connections who are known to over imbibe, the best thing you can do is get there early! Why? Take a few moments to introduce yourself to your server and your bartender. Tell those individuals that throughout the evening, you will be drinking sparkling water with a lime, and no matter what you order, to always bring you sparkling water with a lime. This little trick will allow you to go along with your colleagues' let's-have-another-drink mentality, while being careful to know your own limits. Go ahead and ask for that gin and tonic. The server and bartender, for the price of a generous early tip, will be happy to continue to serve you water with lime.

Q: **How do I address someone I'm meeting for the first time? My parents always told me to use Mr. and Mrs. when addressing those in authority. Is a first name too informal?**

A: In today's business world, nearly everyone in America is accustomed to being addressed by first name. We live in a society that is often comfortable with calling our Commander in Chief Barack rather than President Obama, so naturally there are very few people left out there who take offense at using a first name. But alas, they do exist. My advice is that when addressing anyone over the age of 40, anyone in governmental power, or high-level executives to err on the side of caution and use Mr. or Ms. in your initial meeting. A trick to avoid any awkward moments around this subject, though, is to allow the individual to introduce himself first. If someone says, "Nice to meet you, I'm John," you can feel quite secure in calling him "John" rather than "Mr. Smith."

Q: **I met someone for coffee hoping they would be a great connection for me, and unfortunately we had nothing to talk about once we both explained our current jobs. How do you break awkward silences with people you don't know personally?**

A: "Great weather we've been having, isn't it?" Not a sentence anyone wants to utter during a networking conversation. You want to have dozens of substantive things to say, but with some people, no matter how hard you try, conversation is like pulling teeth. In these awkward-silence moments, ask questions that are specific and cannot be answered with a yes or no. Try playing to the individual's passions with a question like, "What projects are you most excited about in your job right now?" Consider turning the conversation personal vs. professional by asking, "What do you like to do outside of work?" If you're speaking to a parent, consider asking, "How do you balance work and your personal life while raising a family?" Just like John Gardner suggested to Jim Collins, if there's an awkward silence, break it by being interested, not interesting.

She Knows Everybody! Narrative: Chapter 6
Knowing How to Nail the Meeting

Linda Descano
Former President and CEO, Citigroup Women & Co.

Find Linda Online
Twitter: @lindadescano
LinkedIn: linkedin.com/in/lindadescano

As the Y2K rumbles ended and the world moved into a new century in 2000, corporations around the globe began to see that there was a new day dawning in marketing. No longer were Americans willing to sit back on their couches and be sold to. We wanted real engagement and real interaction. We wanted for the first time to feel like the brands we loved involved us heavily in the creation of their work. Citigroup recognized that at the top of this pile of newly engaged consumers were women. Citi realized women wanted to engage with their bank, to be voices in the field of what products and services they would receive. This launched one of the largest women's initiatives in the American corporate landscape: Citigroup's Women & Co. At the helm of Women & Co. since 2003 is a dynamic woman named Linda Descano.

I know Linda won't mind when I tell you she's one of "those women." She ranks right up there with the Sheryl Sandbergs and the Marissa Mayers and the Meg Whitmans of the world. She is a female executive in a world largely dominated by men and it's safe to say for most women, regardless of age, Linda is a bit intimidating just by the nature of her position. Naturally, when thinking about the right person to profile for a chapter on nailing the meeting, I had to go straight to the top. Because if you can't nail a meeting with someone like Linda Descano, then Career Girls, I haven't done my job in this book!

I often ask women when they tell me they're struggling with networking, "Who are you reaching out to?" The answer I receive is almost always the same. You're calling friends of friends, friends of colleagues, and because you're on the ladder somewhere in the middle, you're probably reaching out to people who are also on the ladder somewhere in the middle. So I ask, "What's keeping you from calling the big names? The C-suiters?" The answer is almost always the same – some combination of "they're too busy" or "she'd never return my call," when what they really mean is, "What's the point?" So during our conversation I asked Linda Descano to tackle those kinds of fears in women, and I think you'll be surprised at her advice. Read on...

The Problem Isn't Time, It's Focus

Just like you heard Julie Cottineau say in Chapter 4's narrative, Linda acknowledged first that your fears are probably right in that executives only have so many lunches and coffee meetings to go around. Once they're done meeting with other executives, clients, and potential employees, there isn't much room for giving away time to a random gal who wants advice. Linda contends, though, that the problem of setting meetings with high-level executives isn't about their time, though. It's about your focus! She implores you all to think in terms of strategy when you're reaching out to anyone, but especially to high-level executives. When you're sending an email, LinkedIn connection request, LinkedIn InMail, or leaving a voicemail, you have to be very specific. Linda wants to know:

- What are you trying to do?
- Why is her skill set perfect to help you accomplish that task?
- Why should she give you 15-20 minutes of her time?

In this conversation, Linda said something to me that my own business coach tells me often. "Don't try to boil the ocean!" You have to be able to say, "I'm trying to get from X to Y, and this is exactly how I want you to be instrumental in that journey." The amount of focus and specificity you put into your request will directly correlate to the response you receive.

Linda also advocates (a woman after my own heart) dedicated research before any piece of outreach. She said, "Show me that you know my background and you've researched my skills, knowledge, and expertise. Show immediately that you are cognizant that my time is a finite resource and that you're being respectful of it."

Finally, and probably the most frustrating point for those of you reading this book is this: You have to be willing to wait. Linda said, "I'm sure I've missed requests here and there. I try to respond personally to every request, even if it's a polite no. Most people, even executives, do their best to make the same kind of effort." Wait it out. Follow up appropriately without becoming a pest (more on that in Chapter 10).

The Power of Predisposition

The dictionary defines being predisposed as being "susceptible to" something. Linda tells me that predisposition is one of the most powerful forces you can use in strategic networking. Linda and I, for instance, met through Step Up Women's Network, where we both serve on the organization's respective Boards (Linda in New York and me in Chicago). Linda told me, "Step Up and organizations like it are great vehicles for meeting women across generations, industries, and functions. If someone is involved in an organization I'm involved with, especially if I know they've devoted their time to serving on a committee or in another volunteer capacity, then I'm predisposed to put them on my calendar."

How else can you ensure your networking connections are predisposed to adding you to their list of "must connect with" people?

Take Linda's advice and **get involved!** Having an organization's interest or a nonprofit's cause in common can be powerful in ensuring someone has a predisposition to say yes.

Think about **your natural networks** – alumni, friends of friends, friends of parents, former colleagues, etc. These natural connectors could mean you're primed for someone to be predisposed to meeting with you.

Having real **knowledge of the background of the person you're reaching out to** can speak volumes to your intentions.

Preparation, Meet Style.

Having spent much of her career in banking, a notoriously male dominated industry, I asked Linda about her experience nailing meetings with men vs. women. How, I asked her, do you approach meetings with men differently than with women? Her answer surprised me. Linda said, "When I plan for a meeting, gender is not even in the top five things that come to mind." Instead, she suggests focusing on "style." How? Consider these things:

- What role does the individual have in her company?
- Can you predict the individual's leadership style?

- Do you know anything specific about the individual's communication style?
- What kind of meeting concept would this person respond to—a PowerPoint presentation? Is she a concept person or a numbers person?
- What kind of "business head" does she have? Heartstrings? Or logic?

After answering these kinds of questions to the best of your ability, you'll be much more prepared to enter a conversation with any person, admin or exec, male or female. Linda says, "Focus less on gender and more on style. Create your presentation or pitch based on factors surrounding style."

Finally, the Dos and Don'ts

If you're going to network with Linda or someone like her, one of the first questions you're going to ask yourself is all about the dos and don'ts. Are there absolute "no-nos" to nail the meeting and absolute "must dos"? Absolutely! I asked Linda to tell us some of her own deal makers and breakers, and she came up with an awesome list.

- **Linda's Deal Makers**
  - Displays passion, energy, and enthusiasm
  - Has a bright and genuine smile
  - It's clear she's excited about her work
  - Obviously smart with a can-do attitude
  - Ready to roll up her sleeves and work rather than just telling others what to do
  - Great attitude and work ethic
  - Likeable

- **Linda's Deal Breakers**
  - Anyone whose attitude screams "it's all about me"
  - They take credit for everything, never attributing things to a team effort
  - Anyone who is rude or negative
  - Playing the victim or the martyr when talking about past experience

The "Best of the Best" in Networking Advice

I ended each of the interviews completed for You Know Everybody! by asking each woman to provide to this book's readers her best networking tips and advice. Here are Linda's tips and tricks.

- **Get in a "networking state of mind."** If you walk into a room full of people and you know you're uncomfortable, everyone else does to. You have to radiate the kind of energy you need to be present and purposeful. The best way to do that is to see a purpose for every interaction or event. If you're headed to a huge networking event, be strategic and set your goals for quality, not quantity. Perhaps one evening you say to yourself, "Tonight, I'm going to find three people who work in content marketing, social media, or public relations." Ask for introductions to those people, seek them out, and create relationships.
- **Not all networking is created equal.** You have to weigh opportunities that will help you connect with the right people, not just people in general. Research and ask yourself what the caliber is of the people involved with the organization or group. Linda says she's a "big fan of networking opportunities where you can learn

something as well!" Seek out events where professional development is involved, where you can then meet interesting people. But go with a clear idea of what you're going to get out of that specific opportunity.

- **Put yourself second.** Linda told me, "When I started out networking, I thought it was all about me. I learned quickly it's really about what you can do to help someone else. Put yourself second. Be open to meeting people and developing a relationship where you can bring your network with you to help advance someone else." Think through the kinds of introductions you can make for people, insights you can offer, articles you can share, and other value adds you bring to the table. Putting the focus on giving instead of getting will get you far!

- **Practice random acts of networking kindness.** To build a *You Know Everybody!* Network, you must nurture and invest in your network, and that can't be just when you need something or when you're interested in someone's work. To be great at it, you have to be a bit random about it. Linda says she uses LinkedIn to stay in touch and sometimes finds great ways to incorporate her LinkedIn connections into Women & Co. articles and introduces friends randomly to one another. What can you do for a connection today that would put a great big networking smile on her face?

seven

Cocktails and Connections:
Networking with Strategic Events

I'm planning this great mixer. You have to help me.
I'm thinking like a luau or casino night.
It'll be just like senior year except funner!

–ELLE WOODS, *LEGALLY BLONDE*

She's what you might call an "it girl." Last month's big charity event, she's there. The random networking event last Tuesday, she's there. She fills your Facebook timeline with event invitations and posts about the newest store openings, art openings, fashion shows, and everything else under the sun. She's the person who works the room, who effortlessly plans dinner parties, and flawlessly stands for hours in the highest heels and the most uncomfortable dresses. She is, for lack of a better description, Elle Woods. Though, at the end of *Legally Blonde*, Ms. Woods becomes one heck of a lawyer, she will forever be known as someone who was more concerned with her sequined bikini and connection to Hollywood producers than her credentials, and upon arriving at Harvard Law, asked first for her social calendar and then for her class list. This Elle Woods-type character, one of whom we all know in our own lives, is the same kind of person who birthed the idea of the networking event. For her, Wednesday nights drinking bad Chardonnay and passed hors d'oeuvres is "just like senior year except funner."

I know, I know. You hate her. Don't worry, I hate her, too, and for most of my career, I've been her! I'm the person who <u>loves</u> networking events and is excited to meet new people wherever and whenever I can. I recognize, though, that not everyone is like me and certainly not everyone is like Elle Woods.

If you ask a stranger on the street to tell you about networking, the answer will almost always include some mention of networking events. We think of mixers, luncheons, and happy hours organized by various networking groups or organizations as the most traditional form of networking. There's a reason, however, that until now in this book, I have not emphasized events. While they are important and can be incredible opportunities to network, I want to be sure that the readers of *You Know Everybody!* understand first and foremost that events are a part of networking, but they are not your only avenue to develop a network. Networking events can get you on the right path and begin to introduce you to great contacts, but only the tactics I've outlined so far in this book can take the contacts you meet and the muddled faces you picture when you look at the business cards they hand you at an event and turn them into real relationships.

If that's the case, you might be asked, "Why go to networking events at all?" If it's all about one-on-one connections, should you really spend $40 or $400 to attend an event that boasts "great networking"? The confusing answer is: Sometimes. Events can be powerful introductory networking and can grow a massive network with the right amount of time, careful planning, and follow-up. Why are they great? Because they are regularly scheduled, easy to find, generally affordable, and provide attendees with an audience that often varies from event to event. This kind of variability and unpredictability means that with every event, you're taking a chance. You may walk away with business cards from twenty different marketing experts, knowing full well you have no use for a marketing expert in the near future. You could also walk away with the perfect connections, full of synergies that will get you to the next level in your career. It's the risk taking and the "you never know what you're going to get" aspect of networking events that can make them so incredibly valuable. No networking strategy (or networking book, for that matter) would be complete without the inclusion of strategic use of networking events.

The success of an event networking strategy starts in choosing the right event and, sometimes more importantly, avoiding events that might be a waste of time for your networking. The last thing you want to do is spend your hard-earned money and valuable time on attending an event where you walk away and say, "That was pointless."

Types of Events That Are Inherently Valuable

- **Industry Specific.** If you are interested in building your network within your industry, you'll want to be sure you're attending events specific to your industry that include all levels of professionals within your industry. Often, industry specific networking ignores the idea of networking with individuals who are lower on the totem pole. When a leader attends a networking event, she is often there to make specific connections with other leaders in the industry, or to land a client. For this reason, it's difficult for a younger woman to make connections at industry events, but not impossible. When searching for industry events, look for:

▢ **National and state chapters of your industry's main professional organization.** For CPAs, these organizations are a part of the American Institute of CPAs (AICPA). For events professionals, the International Special Events Society (ISES) is powerful industry tool. For marketers, it's the AMA (American Marketing Association), and for fundraisers it's AFP (American Fundraising Professionals). The list goes on. Every industry has one. Find yours both nationally and at a state or local level. Subscribe to their newsletters, follow them on social media, and keep abreast of the networking events they are promoting.

▢ **Follow LinkedIn groups that are specific to your industry.** Often, key players in your field will post to these groups upcoming events that could be of interest to you. When you see that a number of professionals like you are attending the same event, it's a good idea to consider attending yourself.

▢ **Many industries have local women's groups dedicated to the success of women in that industry.** In Illinois, female attorneys have the support of the Coalition of Women's Initiatives in Law, which hosts regular events for female attorneys to both learn and network. Another example is Women in Consulting (WIC), a San Francisco-based organization with multiple chapters for female consultants. These kinds of organizations exist in many industries across the nation and often have their own websites and social media pages, and host events. Follow them and attend when you can.

- **Interest Specific.** Of course you want to grow your network in your industry, but you may also want to expand on interests outside your industry. Consider searching professional organizations of industries parallel to your own or in your new areas of interest. Often, these organizations will have events specific to newcomers to the industry or beginners in the field. Take advantage of mentorship program events and other opportunities to build interest in these new areas.
  - **Use the power of Google Alerts.** If you're a CPA but you're hoping to transition at some point to entrepreneurship, set a Google Alert for your city's name and the words "women entrepreneur events." Your email might just find the perfect networking event for you.
  - **Find your own "Elle Woods" guru in your area of interest.** Peruse the websites of professional organizations and past events in your area of interest, and you'll likely find a few individuals who are present in all of the event photos. Reach out to them and ask which events they recommend attending. They will be your own personal Elle Woods.

- **Women Centered Events.** When expanding your network, women helping women is one key to success. In the same vein, finding events specific to women and networking can act as a jumpstart you won't get elsewhere.
  - **Look for women's conferences.** These kinds of 1-2 day opportunities can be powerful both for your professional development and networking expansion. Often, they are a mix of workshops and mixers/dinners/luncheons

that allow you to network with a wide array of women from countless fields.

- ☐ **Seek out bloggers and online media sites dedicated to women's networking.** Of course, I recommend CareerGirlNetwork.com, as it's my own site, but alongside CGN are countless others – The Daily Muse, Spark and Hustle, Women for Hire, and many more. Search these kinds of resources in your area and find the events they're hosting or the organizations they're partnering with.

- ☐ **Subscribe to local women's magazines.** Even small towns have print publications dedicated to women. My own hometown in North Dakota has "Lake Region Woman," Chicago has "Today's Chicago Woman," Minneapolis has "HERLIFE," and every city around the world has similar publications. These magazines often host their own events and partner with fantastic events in the area, making them great networking opportunities for you.

- • **Nonprofit Events.** When it comes to networking, nothing can be a more powerful connector than a mutual connection to an important mission. When expanding your network, looking for both volunteer opportunities and event-based ways to connect with nonprofits you care about can introduce you to high-level players who are also a part of the work these types of organizations do.
  - ☐ **Both size and format matter.** Many nonprofits host high dollar sit-down dinners and other formal galas yearly. These might not be the best networking opportunities because

you are often seated with individuals who already know each other, and you have little opportunity to move around and meet new people. Instead, look for smaller events hosted by your chosen nonprofit organizations that have a more communal format, like cocktail parties or weekend volunteer days.

▫ **Reach out early to key staff and Board members.** Nonprofit organizations are always on the lookout for new volunteers and potential Board members. By reaching out early to staff and Board, you'll ensure they are looking for you at the event and prepped to potentially introduce you to key players in the organization while you're there.

Types of Events to Avoid

Disclaimer: The following is a short list of events that may not be valuable to you as you build a strategic network. These kinds of events can be valuable for other reasons – social, fun, friendship, etc. When describing them as potential events to avoid, I'm referring specifically to networking.

• **Big, Big, Big.** Bigger isn't always better, friends. Some of the most often marketed and attended networking events are massive in nature. You'll see Facebook updates gloating when over 600 people will be in attendance. And while these events can have value at times, more often than not, they feel more like a club than they do a networking event. Leave these behind in favor of smaller, more strategic events.

• **Descriptions That Are Far Too Specific.** Now, I'm not knocking young professionals groups. They can present phenomenal professional development opportunities. But when it comes to networking, what is the appeal of networking only with someone who is the same age and level as you? Of course, you'll want to make friends as well as connections at these events, but if you're choosing between an event that is age specific or singles specific and one that is more professional and industry specific, you'll find more luck with a broader approach.

- **Social Only.** There's the old saying about someone who is like Elle Woods: "She'd go to the opening of an envelope." Gallery openings, fashion shows, and store openings are often well-promoted events in any city. While valuable for social reasons to attend with friends and have fun, these types of events may not be the best for onsite networking. Most people attend events like these in groups and therefore stick heavily to their groups while attending. Cliques that occur here can be difficult to infiltrate and leave you feeling frustrated.

The price of networking events ranges widely. An evening happy hour with a small group of women might only run the cost of a drink and no admission. More formal networking luncheons could be priced anywhere from $30-$100, and evening events range in price from $10-$150, depending on the content and market the event appeals to. On the higher end of the scale, conferences (especially high-level industry conferences in your field) can range from hundreds of dollars to thousands. Even after deciding which events to attend, you should ask yourself, "Are they worth it?" To ensure you know your money and your time are being spent wisely, be sure to find as many reviews as possible about a specific event prior to registration.

To get honest reviews, ask the top layers of your professional network first. A simple, "Has anyone ever attended a Career Girl Network event" question on Facebook or LinkedIn could garner responses from those closest to you and recommendations for other events to attend. Furthermore, questions about which events to attend should be a staple question in your one-on-one networking; asking "Which networking events do you recommend attending?" can produce fantastic results from high-powered women in your network. These kinds of recommendations will come not only with the name of an event but often with the names of individuals who will likely attend, and a recommendation prior to the event to meet these individuals. This kind of information is gold when walking into a networking event and can make your time there even better.

Now that you know how to find the best events and those that are right for your networking goals, let's jump into the ways you can adequately prepare to make an event a huge success for you. We all want to have the experience of leaving a networking event with a stack of business cards, potential lunch dates and coffee mates, new LinkedIn connections, and even job prospects, thinking to ourselves, "I am ON IT!" The only way you can personally control that outcome is to prepare, prepare, prepare (I'm assuming you're all beginning to see a theme to *You Know Everybody!* at this point. Preparation is key to networking!)

There are three key questions you'll want to ask about any event before you strap on your shoes and head out the door—the tricky part is getting them answered. Have no fear, though. I'm going to walk you through it step by step.

1. **Who is attending the event?**

    Showing up at a networking event with no idea who might be in the room with you can certainly yield interesting connections but *You Know Everybody!* is all about being strategic, and strategically it's much better to enter an event having at least some expectation of the connections you want to make while you're there. To find out who is going to attend the event, consider researching the following:

- Does the event have a Facebook page? You can see on Facebook who is invited, and generally who has responded yes, no, or maybe.
- Does the event have an EventBrite, Evite, or other kind of public invitation website? Here, you can often find the names of those attending.
- Does the organization coordinating the event have an Advisory Board or Board of Directors? It's safe to say many members of this group will be in attendance.
- Ask! Send an email or put out a LinkedIn or Twitter message asking friends in the same industry or interest group if they are attending the event.

2. **Are any of your connections attending, and is there an opportunity for you to attend the event together to help one another network?**

Once you've researched the individuals who might be attending the event, it may be a good idea to find a friend or colleague attending the event to go with you. Going to an event with someone can both help and hinder you as a networker. In a helpful manner, having a friend with you can make ice breaking easier. Rather than walking into a conversation with a group of people singly, it could be easier and a stronger introduction to walk into a group as a twosome. It may also help at the beginning of an event when you feel awkward entering that first conversation or standing at the bar by yourself. Conversely, though, having someone with you at an event cannot give you the excuse to stand in a corner together and avoid actually networking. Be certain the person you're bringing with you is equally or more outgoing than you are, and is ready and willing to network. Also, if you're networking for a job specifically, be sure the person you're with knows that you're looking and what you're looking for. For this reason, networking at an event alongside a coworker who might leak your job seeking to the big boss might not be smart. Think strategically here as well, not just about which events you go to, but about who you stand next to when you're there.

3. **Do the people who are attending the event know you're attending as well?**
    It helps to know who is attending an event, but the most important step in the process isn't just seeking them out at the event, it's reaching out to these individuals prior to the event. What is more powerful – walking up to someone cold at an event and introducing yourself? Or sending a quick LinkedIn message saying something like, "I noticed you are also attending tomorrow's networking event. I've been meaning to reach out to you and would love to meet you while we're both there." Clearly, the preemptive strategy of outreach is much more effective than the cold "hello." Be certain that your targets at the event are aware you're attending the event and want to connect with them.

A few additional notes on preparing for a networking event:

- **Packing Counts Here, Too.** I outlined for you in Chapter 6 the importance of good packing for a meeting. The same goes for an event. Recently, I attended a networking event I believed would be largely sit-down. Because the event centered around fashion, I wore a fierce pair of shoes. I realized quickly, however, that the event was a standing event. I was lucky to have packed an extra pair of flat shoes to spare my poor toes from a night of standing in five-inch heels. Pack for every circumstance. Do you have the right shoes? Also be certain you have adequate numbers of business cards to distribute, pens, makeup if you like to touch up prior to the event, mints or gum, and anything else you might need to ensure you're prepared for any circumstance at the event.

- **Practice Makes Perfect!** Even if you believe you have your elevator pitch perfectly developed, prior to any event you must practice your pitch again and again. Take the time in the hours and days prior to a networking event to practice multiple versions of your elevator pitch in 15-, 30-, and 60-second times. It may sound crazy, but on the day of any networking event, I practice my elevator pitch in the shower while I'm getting ready in the morning. You sing in the shower, right? Why not pitch in the shower?

- **Get Advanced!** If you're really thinking about standing out in the setting of a networking event, consider using a more advanced marketing technique. If you're a business owner, you could pass out a coupon for your product or service rather than a business card. Will the less traditional size or shape of a card or promotion make you stand out to those around you? One of my favorite marketing experts, Ellen Weiss, recently created "text decoders," a business card-sized booklet that allows parents to decode the acronyms their teenagers use while texting. It was genius because Ellen's business, The Impact Elevator, specializes in crafting memorable messaging. Could you make a similar piece that differentiates your skill set from others? While it might not be appropriate at every meeting, these kinds of "gimmicks" are absolutely appropriate in an event setting.

Now that you're prepared adequately to attend the right kind of networking event, let's jump in and tackle the step-by-step guide to success when you walk in the door. Let's not gloss over the end of that sentence, though. Walking in the door can often be the most difficult part of attending a networking event. I hear from women all the time who tell me they register for networking events, they pay to attend, and when it gets to 5:00 p.m. and it's time to get moving, jump in the car, or hail that taxi to head over to the networking event, it's so much easier to stay at the office or steer the car home instead of going to the event. Your desk is calling, your sweat pants are calling, your comfortable couch and the latest episode of your favorite reality television show is calling. All of these things likely sound better to you than standing in a room full of people you don't know and attempting to find connections and sell yourself. If you're reading this book, though, it means you're ready to make networking a priority, and that means taking the steps to bypass the couch or longer hours at your desk, walking through that doorway, and stepping into the room. That's half the battle, and once you've done it you can tackle the event with ease.

Once you've walked in the door, the best piece of advice I can give to you is the same advice your mother probably shouted when you were dipping your toe in the cold swimming pool as a child: "JUMP IN! It won't be so cold once you're in the water." From the moment you walk in the door, start networking. Don't give yourself 10 minutes to check out the bar and hit the bathroom. Jump right in. Introduce yourself to the person staffing the check-in table, shake her hand, and continue that pattern all the way into the room. Introduce yourself to the first group of people you see, and continue to jump into conversations wherever you can. Keep telling yourself why you came to the event. You came to network. You didn't come to stand by the wall and feel nervous.

The biggest obstacle most women have to overcome at a networking event is actually entering the first conversation and the next. The key is looking for friendly groups to walk up to and join. Look for groups in the shape of a U and not an O. Groups that are closed like an O are generally comprised of individuals who have come to the event together and are less apt to network with outside parties. Groups shaped like a U, though, are inherently more inviting. The opening in their shape is a direct invitation to enter the conversation and become a part of the group. Also, look for groups who are starting to introduce themselves to one another. Getting in on the beginning of a conversation can be more comfortable for you than entering an already deep or ongoing discussion. To spot these groups, look for those who are shaking hands or where individuals are walking up to the group. Piggyback the actions you see and dive right into these kinds of circles.

You'll want to start a conversation strong, whether you're talking one-on-one or to a group of 4-5 people. Of course, the best introduction is the same one you learned in kindergarten—your name! A bright smile, an extended hand and a warm "Hi, I'm Marcy. It's so nice to meet you." can take you far in the world of networking. To keep the conversation going, though, you'll need to practice the art of good conversation starters. These ideas will help you to keep conversations going (without feeling or sounding like an idiot):

- **Basic Questions.** To start conversations, these questions are appropriate in any situation:
    - What line of work are you in?
    - What led you to choose your job or industry?
    - What do you do for fun?
    - What projects are you working on now?

- **Sales Tactics Questions.** Tap into the tactics used by the best in sales: Ask questions probing more information about likes, dislikes, wants, and needs in the individual's work life:

  ▫ Are you planning on staying in your current position long-term or are you searching for a job?

  ▫ Tell me more about your team. What struggles have you faced as a leader?

  ▫ Would you recommend your company to someone looking for a job?

- **Networking Experience Questions.** You're at a networking event so it's only natural you would talk about networking. Do your best to keep these questions deeper than surface-level banter. A simple "have you been to this event before" can result in a yes or no answer, something that won't continue your conversation. Ask questions like these, instead:

  ▫ What events have you found to be most valuable in your networking?

  ▫ Tell me about your experience with this organization (especially great in nonprofit networking situations).

  ▫ I'm putting networking on my priority list right now in my life. I'd love to hear your best networking tip!

Conversation starters are just that, starters. These kinds of questions will give you the opportunity to begin a conversation, but it's up to you to continue it. You'll want to have your elevator pitch at the ready to ensure you're conveying your experience, wants, and needs effectively to those you're talking with, and it's a good idea to also keep your wish list in your proverbial back pocket. While you're not having a completely substantive one-on-one networking experience, you may find that someone asks you directly how she can help you succeed or reach your goals. This is the perfect time to request a one-on-one meeting, but you can supplement that request with a few mentions of what's on your wish list that might appeal directly to the individual's mentorship or hiring sensibilities. Something as simple as, "I'd love to get to know you better one-on-one. Could we meet for coffee? I'm currently looking for a job in your industry and would be honored if you'd take a look at my resume and give me your advice on getting connected to key industry players," could get you in the door.

Hopefully now you've got your groove on in any event. You're breaking the ice, starting conversations gracefully, and making quality connections that will result in one-on-one meetings in the future and long-term connections. Be careful of another common hiccup, which is staying in one conversation too long. If you've made a solid connection, exchanged business cards, and agreed upon a follow-up strategy like a next meeting or connecting online, you want to move on from the conversation. A networking event is certainly about quality, but the truth is, it's also about quantity. You have to keep moving to get the most of any single event.

To exit a conversation gracefully, thank the individual for the conversation you've just had and explicitly state your intentions to connect in the future, followed by the only time I'll tell you to say something generic like, "I'm going to grab a glass of water" or "Excuse me, I need to find the ladies' room." More bluntly, you won't offend anyone with, "Great to meet you! I'm going to find my friend who is supposed to be around here somewhere." Both you and the individual you're talking with will want to move around the room and avoid getting stuck in one place or one conversation. Your exit will be welcome and help both of you to keep moving and get the most out of the event.

There are numerous experts in the world of networking who boast the ability to master the art of "small talk." I'll be honest when I tell you these experts drive me crazy. I will never advise you, no matter how awkward you think you might be at a networking event, to use "small talk" to break the ice or make conversation in a networking setting. If you are going to make truly strategic and long-lasting connections with the individuals you meet at networking events, you have to become comfortable with "BIG TALK!" No one ever developed a great relationship by talking about the weather or the traffic on the way to the event. Great relationships are developed when you speak from your most informed place and put your most intelligent, beautiful, charismatic, and eager foot forward. The words, "It's a beautiful day outside" will never do that for you.

What is "big talk" vs. "small talk?" That's easy. Big talk is talking openly and honestly about your ambitions. Big talk is asking for what you need and unabashedly making powerful requests of the individuals you meet. Small talk is "let's get together sometime." Big talk is, "let's look at our calendars and set coffee for next week." Small talk is, "what a great business idea." Big talk is, "I think there are phenomenal opportunities for us to collaborate and I'm incredibly passionate about what you're doing. How can we help each other reach our goals?"

Networking events may seem like throwaway happy hour gatherings, complete with a takeaway of just a stack of business cards. If this is your attitude about these events, you shouldn't be attending them in the first place. You never know the kind of opportunities or connections you could find when you allow yourself to be open to big talk with those who are currently strangers to you in an event-specific setting. If you're an entrepreneur, you may find your future co-founder or a business partner standing next to you at a high-top table. If you're a job searcher, the next hand you shake could belong to your next boss.

If you dive in with big talk, you'll be much more likely to find out that an individual is currently hiring for your dream job than you would while talking about the weather. You could find an investor for your startup, a new financial advisor, a life coach, a lawyer, a CPA, and so much more. You might even run into a future best friend or a spouse. If you can meet your husband or wife online, who's to say you can't meet that person at a professional networking event?

Ultimately, it's up to you to take the right risks, attend the right events, start good conversations, and practice the art of "big talk" instead of small. A few notes, though, for anyone who might say, "But Marcy, I'm terrible at networking! Going to an event and walking into a group of people scares me to death." If you're notoriously "bad at networking" (which, honestly, I don't believe anyone truly is), consider these tips:

- **If you truly believe you're bad at networking, latch on to someone who is good at networking.** Ask a friend to attend with you who you know is great at introductions and "big talk." At the event, follow her lead. Let her help introduce you to groups she might know or feel comfortable approaching.
- This may be controversial advice, but know that I'm giving it with healthy outcomes in mind. **Have a drink!** I firmly believe in what I call the "Patty Stanger Rule." Patty Stanger is "The Millionaire Matchmaker" on Bravo and requires of everyone in her club who go on dates with her millionaires stick to a strict two drink maximum. You should do the same at networking events. If you're truly nervous, though, a glass of wine might help quell your fears and release your inhibitions.
- **Pay attention to the size of the event.** If networking isn't your strong suit, a 200-person holiday luncheon

may not be the best place to start. Consider looking at smaller happy hours that will allow you to connect more specifically one-on-one rather than in small groups in a large event.

- **Ask about format.** There are hundreds of different ways to format a networking event. The most difficult for those truly nervous about networking are the free-for-all, no formal program events that just require you to find your own way. You may find more success in a breakfast or a luncheon with a facilitator at each table, or a speed-networking event (we'll talk more about these kinds of innovative networking opportunities in Chapter 9).

As I said in the beginning of this chapter, event networking cannot be your only avenue to increase your network, but it can be a powerful option to develop first impressions and make lists of potential connections to meet with one on one and develop a long-term relationship with. To be a true *You Know Everybody!* Networker, you must be strategic about the kinds of events you attend and the tactics you use to work the room when you get there. You cannot fake it, you cannot bypass it, and you cannot ignore its importance. We can't all be Elle Woods and love ourselves a good mixer every week, but we can emulate the best qualities women like Elle present at events. Don't worry about your high heeled shoes, perfect makeup, or hitting an event every week. Instead, work the events that are perfect for your networking goals and look for opportunities regularly. If you follow this advice, Elle Woods would certainly give you "snaps."

She Knows Everybody! Narrative: Chapter 7
Cocktails and Connections:
Networking with Strategic Events

Dr. Archelle Georgiou
Nationally recognized physician, advocate,
advisor and author

Find Archelle Online
Website: www.archellemd.com
Twitter: @archellemd
LinkedIn: linkedin.com/in/archellegeorgiou

I met Archelle Georgiou when she joined the Board of Directors of WomenVenture, where I worked at the time. I'll be honest when I tell you that my first impression of her was immediate fondness, but also sheer intimidation. She was wearing a sweater dress that shimmered in the light, and her smile was the biggest I'd ever seen. I knew instantly I wanted to know this woman and, as a young staff member, I wanted to learn from her. Quickly, she eliminated all of the intimidation I felt in meeting her for the first time. Even to a young nonprofit professional, she was the perfect combination of gracious and interested. She made all of the staff at the organization feel liked, supported, and excited to work together to fulfill the mission. She became my friend and my mentor, and her home became a favorite event spot because she always had incredible Greek food and a welcoming disposition.

To introduce you to Archelle formally (and not in my crazy fan girl kind of way that's clearly illustrated above), I need only two sentences, the ones that introduce her on the "About" page of her Georgiou Consulting website: "Dr. Archelle Georgiou is a storyteller, a physician, a former healthcare industry executive, and a data geek. Most importantly, she is a zealot about designing the healthcare system to improve...health."

I sat down with Archelle in December 2012 to talk about *You Know Everybody!* and her advice for the women reading this book and, although I've known her for years, she has perfected her brand so well that when I walked away from our conversation, I realized those first two sentences on her About page were perfectly true. She told me stories I only hope I can capture for you in this short narrative, and she listened with the true heart of a physician in a way that only a tiny fraction of people can.

Let's dive in, shall we?

Powerful Women Are Intimidating....
and Sometimes Intimidated!

Each year, *Fortune* names the "50 Most Powerful Women in Business." While most of us read the list each year, you might not know that in addition to listing these behemoths of the business world, since 1999 *Fortune* has also convened this incredible group of women and special guests at the Most Powerful Women Summit. There are two things you need to know about the *Fortune* summit. First, it's damn near impossible to get invited (only C-level women are added to the list). Second, it's incredibly expensive to attend even if you get invited. Clearly, to get in the room with these women, you have to actually be one of these women. Archelle was just that, and while serving as Chief Medical Officer for United Healthcare was invited for three years to attend the summit. Of course, she went.

Can you imagine? Walking into a room filled with the likes of Meg Whitman, Carly Fiorina, Cathie Black, Indra Nooyi, Anne Mulcahy, and so many more. What would you say to them? What would you do? Archelle, even as CMO at UHC, candidly told me she had those same questions. She said, "Here I am, one of 300 women in a very select group, with the top 50 being those you admire and see everywhere. Intimidation is definitely a barrier." I'll admit, I balked a bit at this point in her story. Archelle is one of the most dynamic and ballsy women I've ever met. Wouldn't her incredible smile and explosive personality mean she wouldn't be intimidated by Andrea Jung? But she was, and I'm purposefully including that point in this narrative because I want you all to know that even the CMO at one of the largest health care companies in the world takes a big, deep, nervous breath before she walks into that kind of event.

My conversation with Archelle about the *Fortune* summit surprised me. I expected her to regale me with stories of her immediate connection with Ursula Burns and how she still exchanges Christmas cards with Irene Rosenfeld. Instead, she admitted to me (and consequently, to all of you) that the *Fortune* summit was "not a great networking experience." She told me that of course, she met some fabulous women, and some were more humble than others. But even as a C-suiter herself, she admitted to being caught up in the comparisons women tend to make between themselves and others. As surprising as it was to hear Archelle Georgiou say these things, it's comforting as well. It's not just women in their 20s and 30s who have self-doubt and constantly compare themselves to the other women in their yoga class. Powerful women, intimidating women, are intimidated at times, too. Take that piece of knowledge with you to the next event, and it might just inspire you to walk up to that C-suiter, introduce yourself, and start the kind of conversation that will lead to mentorship or friendship.

Archelle's Three Word Event Advice: Go for YOU!

As we chatted freely about the *Fortune* summit, I was honored when Archelle opened up to tell me about the way the conference, even with all its shortcomings, changed her life. She told me that somewhere among intimidating lunches sitting across from Meg Whitman and sometimes self-indulgent speakers, she found a session that was not something she needed to attend. It was presented by consulting firm Philadelphia Gap International and called "Discovering Your Genius." Something drew Archelle to that session. It talked participants through the tough process of peeling back the shell of being an "executive" and getting to your core skill set. They asked, "How are you differentiating yourself?" In that session, Archelle says, she realized that in order to truly fulfill her goals, she could not be just a doctor, or just an executive (not that either of those things deserve a "just" in front of them). She was, first and foremost, a storyteller. That session, she says, began a new era of her career and allowed her to focus in new areas – ones that allow her to be a powerful conglomerate of doctor, executive, and storyteller, all at the same time.

By going to that session, Archelle took a leap that most women are reluctant to take. We go to conferences, especially ones paid for by our companies, and we choose sessions based on what makes the most sense for our jobs. In some industries, including law and accounting, we choose conference sessions based on the number of continuing education credits we'll be provided in the hour or two we're attending. We think of our responsibilities at conferences, we think of our job titles, and we think of what our bosses want us to do, but rarely do we think of ourselves. Last year, at a conference for tech entrepreneurs, I spent the first three days attending all of the women-focused panels and speakers. I run a tech startup focused on women so that seemed like a logical plan for the conference. But, like Archelle, halfway through I found myself both disappointed and annoyed. What I really wanted to hear was Ryan Holmes from Hootsuite and Tom Sosnoff from thinkorswim, even thought I didn't need to hear about social media analytics or the history of a stock investing startup. Somewhere in the middle, though, I decided to abandon ship on the women's panels and go to the things I wanted to see. I got more from Tom Sosnoff's presentation that weekend than I did from everything else combined.

This is the advice Archelle is giving all of you in three simple words: "Go for YOU!" You have a duty to your company if they are paying for a conference or event, certainly, but that duty is to become the best employee and the best version of yourself. The only way you can do that is to go to events and conferences for your own reasons. Archelle said to me, with strong conviction, "You will only succeed at events like that [*Fortune* summit] if you do it for genuine personal growth."

After her "a-ha" moment in that "Discovering Your Genius" session at *Fortune's* summit, Archelle completely changed the way she thinks about attending events. She stopped going to the things she "should" go to and instead told me her new litmus tests for events: "Will it massage your brain?" Now, she spends the big bucks on TEDMED and other events like it, those that truly massage her brain as a doctor, as an executive, and as a storyteller.

But Wait, Don't I Have to Make Connections!?

You're probably asking yourself the same question I had for Archelle after the conversation above, "But Archelle, what about networking? Don't I have to make connections and perfect my pitch and all the things Marcy's telling me to do?" Her answer might surprise you (and it's the reason I'm including so many varied stories and opinions in these narratives): Stop worrying about it! If you "Go for YOU!" and you are truly invested in attending an event, Archelle says, "As a result of being truly inspired, you will naturally make incredible connections." She says, "Go and get inspired. Make the goal of meeting anyone to learn something from them. They don't always have something for you, but they always have something you can learn."

Archelle is a physician through and through, and her networking event advice is to "Think like a doctor!" When you're introducing yourself to someone, when you're starting the initial conversation, consider what a doctor might consider the first time she meets a patient – what are the symptoms, what are the issues? Only after you have the answers to those questions can you begin to think about the ways you can be a problem solver for them. Archelle asks herself, "Where do I have knowledge that could help them address that issue?" She's not thinking about business, revenue, or landing a client. She's thinking about her own knowledge, her strengths, and how she can apply them to that individual's situation.

Archelle tells me her favorite question to ask is, "What's your 'stay awake' issue?" The answer to this question, whether personal or professional, allows her to listen like a doctor, diagnose the symptoms, and find places she can apply her knowledge to the "stay awake" issue at hand. Sometimes her ideas to address the problem turn into consulting gigs, sometimes her conversations turn into friendships, and sometimes they're just a conversation. Staying in the mindset of asking questions, listening well, and focusing on being truly inspired will power you through and, suddenly, you'll forget you were ever networking at all.

The "Best of the Best" in Networking Advice

I ended each of the interviews completed for You Know Everybody! by asking each woman to provide to this book's readers her best networking tips and advice. Here are Archelle's tips and tricks.

- **Have coffee with anyone!** Archelle told me about the owner of a small car service she often calls to take her to the airport in Minneapolis from her home in the western suburbs. She regularly has conversations with this man about his business, his life, her business, and her life. In his job, he transports and meets many important people. One of his frequent clients from Seattle happened to be an executive in a hospital construction company. He asked Archelle if he could pass her contact information along to this man. She said yes and the two had coffee the next day, discovering incredible synergies between their businesses. Too many women would think, "I'm not meeting some stranger introduced to me by my valet service!" Instead, have coffee with anyone! You never know where it might lead.
- **Listen EVERYWHERE!** Archelle's theme in this chapter was listening – both to yourself and to others. Meaningful introductions (to your new hair stylist, your business' co-founder, or your next boss) could be anywhere! If you shut off certain situations as personal and others as professional, you'll never find the introductions that can be so powerful in your career.
- **Blog, Career Girls, Blog.** Archelle cited the creation of and careful care of her blog as a huge part of her success. By giving herself a place to regularly share her views and appropriately promoting that place, she has made herself an industry thought leader, someone who is top

of mind for other professionals in her area of expertise, and has shown other media outlets that her blog is a place for a thoughtful, well-written, and unique point of view in the field of healthcare. Archelle's blog and her ability to self-promote have landed her countless television appearances, including a 2012 spot on the Katie Couric Show.

• **Write it down so you can visualize it.** Speaking of Katie Couric, Archelle had a big piece of advice that came from her own experiences. When you want something, put it in writing. Archelle makes a yearly personal business plan (pretty good advice, considering we're giving you the tools in Chapter 4!), and in 2012 she included a photo of Katie Couric in the plan. She followed Katie on Facebook and Twitter, watched her new talk show regularly, and through her spokesperson relationship with Healthgrades, appeared on Katie's show. Whether you believe in "The Secret" or just like the idea of making a plan, write down what you want to do this year with your network. It's much more likely to manifest when it's on paper in ink.

eight

**"I Was Just Talking About You" –
Putting Your Name in the Wind**

*If there is anything more annoying in the world than having people
talk about you, it is certainly having no one talk about you.*

–OSCAR WILDE

Have you ever had a random moment in life where you are certain you recognize someone? Maybe you're in line at a store, or sitting in an airport. You look over, see someone and think, "Where do I know her from?" You may have been on the other side of this kind of exchange as well. Has anyone ever said to you, "You look so familiar to me"? When this exchange occurs, the same process inevitably occurs. You both run through your lifelong history of potential touch points. Did you go to the same school? Did you live in the same neighborhood? Do you know so-and-so? Or perhaps you'll settle on the fact that the two of you don't know one another and say something like, "You must just have one of those faces."

This kind of "haven't we met" moment, especially when you're on the receiving end and not the recognizing end, always feels good. Having someone say to you, "You and I may have met" in any shape or form feels awesome. What happens in that moment is a feeling of recognition, a feeling or connection, and sometimes even a feeling of celebrity. It always feels good when someone thinks they know you and even better if you find out they actually do. Somewhere deep down inside when someone says, "Haven't we met?" you're thinking, "Of course we have! I'm kind of a big deal."

As you strategically build your *You Know Everybody!* Network, you'll find more and more of these experiences happening to you. You may find that you run into more people who have seen you at an event, met you through a friend, know someone you're connected to on social media, or recognize you from somewhere else in your networking journey. These encounters, though, do not often develop without intentional creation of your personal brand and strategic development of your network. If you want to be "kind of a big deal" and have everyone know it, you have to have the kind of face, the kind of name, and the kind of reputation that makes you recognizable.

Those people, the people you look at and say "haven't we met" are usually the same kinds of people. They are the real world's version of the faces on People! Magazine. They are the people you talk about in conversation, the ones you find yourself bringing up constantly in your networking. In your network, no matter how small, you'll find yourself saying "Have you met so-and-so?" or "You simply have to meet this awesome lady." and "You're going to love my friend." The names you fill into these sentences are individuals who truly have their names in the wind. They are the kind of people who, when you run into them at the mall or on the street, you say, "I was just talking about you!"

The tricky thing here is that to be good at networking, and to have that desirable *You Know Everybody!* Network, you have to become comfortable with something almost no one is comfortable with – being talked about. It's easy to feel shy and want to fade into a corner, hoping that the person coming toward you will talk to someone else. It's even easier to keep to yourself, stay in your shell, and hope no one ever talks about you. Being shy, though, won't get your name in the wind. It might protect you from gossip, but not from authentic, practical, and meaningful talk that will get your name out there and enable everyone to hear how fantastic you are.

I started this chapter with a quote from the incomparable Oscar Wilde, and I thought long and hard about which quote would most appropriately fit this chapter. I could have opened the chapter with the famous line from Steel Magnolias, "You know what they say – if you don't have anything nice to say, come sit by me." This chapter is not about gossip, though. It's not about making yourself interesting enough to be talked about in the way the world talks about celebrities and the way we all (admit it, you've done this) talk about our colleague who got too drunk at the Christmas party. I started this chapter with a quote from Oscar Wilde because, ladies, you simply have to be comfortable with people talking about you. Not just comfortable, though, excited! Get in the game and get jazzed about the fact that if you're truly a *You Know Everybody!* Networker, you want people to talk about you. You want everyone you meet to repeat your pitch and sell your brand to everyone else they know. There's no danger in having people talking about you. The great danger, as Oscar Wilde points out, is in having no one talk about you at all. The kind of talk you want to create in your networking journey is heartfelt, it's meaningful, and, if you're doing your job right as a networker, it's the sound of someone singing your praises.

A quick word about gossip, though. It comes with the territory. You will never be successful in life if you haven't broken a few hearts and perhaps even burned a few bridges, and you will never be successful in networking or in business unless someone is trying to talk you down, bring you down, or sabotage your success. These (for lack of a better word) bitches are out there, Career Girls, and they're just one good salacious story away from telling everyone that big fat lie about you. As much as we can wax eloquently about the incredible emotional connections women can make in networking, we also need to be honest that the female sex can be phenomenal at making enemies (or more commonly, frenemies), as well.

The greatest gossip in your career will come during its biggest turning points. You will be hurt by these comments, of course. When you leave a job for another, no matter how great the opportunity, someone will be angry with you for it. Someone will be jealous. Someone will feel you stole it from her. And these people will gossip. Trust me. But if you're good enough to be a *You Know Everybody!* Networker, you're certainly strong enough to deal with the bitches out there who try to pull you down!

The goal with getting your name in the wind is to be networked enough that when you call the "hard to get" person on your list, she'll open the conversation by saying, "I was just talking about you!" Let's break it down and figure out how to get there.

First, some bad news. Again, as I said in Chapter 1, your elevator pitch is not enough. That's the bad news. The good news is, if you have developed a great pitch, you are more than equipped to teach that pitch to others. That's the first step to taking yourself from just kind of networked to "I was just talking about you!"

In every encounter you have, your goal shouldn't be just to sell yourself to the individual you're pitching, but to ensure that person can take your pitch and use it in the future to continue to sell you. If you are the best damn human resources attorney in your city, you want to be sure every person you pitch would remember that when asked. Days, months, years later, that individual could be sitting with a friend or colleague in a Starbucks and that friend says, "Hey, any chance you know a good lawyer specializing in HR? I'm having a heck of a time with an employee contract and would love to bring in another set of eyes." It's that moment where your pitch has to be strong enough to last the days, months, or years since you've seen this individual so she'll say, "You know, I do know someone! You're absolutely going to love my friend Laura. She's the best damn human resources attorney in this city!" I think it's safe to say that kind of endorsement would be awesome for anyone. But how do you teach your pitch to the people you're pitching?

Teaching the Pitch: It's Just as Important as Making the Pitch!

- **Don't Just Say It Once.** If someone hears you rattle off your elevator pitch at an event, the chances of that individual being able to perfectly regurgitate it are slim to none. Your job, then, is to get that individual to hear your pitch again and again. We'll talk more about follow-up in Chapter 10, but be sure you're using the same language in follow-up as you are in the initial encounter. Give them the same brand in the first meeting, the follow-up meeting, and every email, phone call, or tweet you send from there on out! When you repeat your pitch consistently, even when it's in different formats and in multiple places, your target audience is much more likely to remember it.

- **Ask Them to Repeat It!** This may seem strange, but done correctly it can work perfectly. One of my favorite career mentors is the President of an outplacement services company, and her trademark is saying "What I hear is..." When I started Career Girl Network, I met with her, delivered my pitch, told her my plans for the company, and asked for her feedback. Before she gave it to me, she started her sentence with "What I hear is..." and proceeded to distill my pitch into three or four sentences. She then asked, "Did I get that right?" The great news is, she did! In that moment, I learned two things. First, my pitch was clear and she was able to get the right message from it. Second, when someone can immediately distill your pitch, they are more likely to use it again in the future. So go ahead, practice your pitch on some of your closest friends, colleagues, and mentors and then ask them to repeat it back to you. What did they hear?

- **Repeat Other People's Pitches.** Use my mentor's technique from above. When you meet someone at a networking event or individually and hear their pitch, repeat it back to her by starting the sentence, "What I hear is..." This will help the individual you're speaking with clarify her own pitch, and perhaps it will encourage her to repeat your pitch back to you. You might even get a mutually beneficial workshop meeting going about how you might help one another refine and define your brands and perfect pitches.

- **Use Your PMP!** You didn't think I was going to let you just develop a PMP and never use it, did you? If you want people to be a part of your networking-based sales team, then you have to give them the sales tools to close the deal! Perhaps you've met with a corporate power player, walked her through your PMP, and left a copy with her. Months later, when one of that person's employees asks for a recommendation for a consultant or new hire, it will be easy for her to flip through a file and find your PMP. Easier to remember than a business card and more specific to you than a resume can often be. Use it! Anyone who has your PMP will hopefully put your name in the wind whenever they network.

It might be uncomfortable, but you must start thinking of yourself as a brand. In putting your name in the wind, I want you to even go one step further. Don't just think of yourself as a brand. Think of yourself as a product. Here's why: What do you do when you find a new product you love? Hint: This is why women have purchasing power head and shoulders above men, and why every commercial in the world is directed at women – even when the product is for men! It's because when women find a product they truly love, they tell EVERYBODY about it. Think about your favorite pair of shoes or that awesome deal on earrings you got last week. Chances are, you not only told all of your friends about the product, you probably told them about the price, the website, the Facebook page, and a few other details.

Last year, I discovered an incredible company, ErinCondren.com. Erin Condren sells high end calendars, notebooks, iPhone cases, etc., that can be personalized with your name, photos, and more. ErinCondren.com's yearly planners start at $50 and can go up, depending on the amount of personalization you put into them. On first glance, you think to yourself, "What? $50 for a calendar? Does it walk my dog?" Upon further inspection, though, you'll find this is the most sophisticated, fun, and exciting paper calendar you've ever seen. I ordered one immediately after seeing it on a blog I read regularly, and within 30 days, more than 5 of my coworkers had one, too. Collectively, in the span of a month, my office mates and I gave more than $500 to ErinCondren.com, ordering everything from calendars to notebooks and more. If that's not brand excitement, I don't know what is!

Every woman in the world has a story like my ErinCondren.com story (and no, Erin didn't pay me to write this, but that's a good idea). We've all fallen in love with a product and blasted it from the rooftops with word-of-mouth and, of course, social media. I never want to stereotype women, but in this case, it's a gender-wide phenomenon. Spreading the word about our favorite brands is something we all do naturally and without much effort.

Why, then, do we have such a difficult time doing this for ourselves? We can go on and on for entire conversations about a paper calendar. What if, instead, we could say to our coworkers and connections, "OMG! I found this incredible new thing. It's ME! I rock. I am seriously the coolest person I know and I'm damn proud of it." It sounds absurd, but it's the single thing that separates those whose names are in the wind from those whose names aren't. The kind of person who can get her name in the wind is just as able to talk about her own successes as she is able to talk about her favorite products and brands. This kind of "tooting your own horn" is an art, and not a science. It's the person who tells you about a recent award and your first thought is, "That's awesome" instead of "Could you brag any more?" Your passions, your excellence, and your triumphs are just as important to talk about as your shoes, your bags, and your clothing. Start doing it. It may take some time, but you'll find your way if you start slowly. Perhaps open up to a friend about praise you received at work, talk to your family about an award you received, and continue to build your ability to shout from the rooftops, "I'm awesome!" If you can begin to harness this ability in your own speech about yourself, you'll see quickly that others see you as a great new "product" as well. You will become someone's ErinCondren. com, the person talked about, getting someone excited, and keeping interest high!

Like products and great companies who produce them, once is not enough. You must be able to continue to convey your successes, new developments, and brand message over time and throughout changes in your career and your brand. A fantastic example of this kind of branding comes from another favorite brand of mine – lululemon. Over the course of a decade, lululemon moved from a small Canadian clothier to an international monster brand donned by everyone from hardcore yogis to Olympic athletes to the everyday soccer mom. Like other big brands, lululemon has attracted its fair share of controversy and weathered the storm successfully over time. lululemon's ability to product high levels of interest from its customers consistently over time makes it the kind of brand you want to emulate. You may have taken a costly trip to lululemon just a few days ago, but walking into the store 72 hours later often means an entirely new set of merchandise. Christine Day, lululemon's CEO, attributes much of the company's success to the fact that women keep coming back. lululemon slowly works its way out of your workout gear into your life gear, and as the clothing becomes a larger part of your wardrobe, the company becomes a larger part of your life. Women want the newest, the brightest, the best lululemon apparel, which gives lululemon the opportunity to constantly manufacture new styles and colors that fly off the shelf in hours or days, creating incredibly high demand.

While you may not have the ability to make six different colors of what the untrained eye would call "bright pink" and have people lined up outside the door to get it, you can take a lesson from lululemon in continually remanufacturing parts of your brand to ensure you have variety in your networking, consistency in your message, and interest that continues to build among the members of your network about what you're doing and how you're doing it. You want people to think to themselves, "What's that wonderful Career Girl doing these days?" It's in those moments you'll find yourself fondly and appropriately talked about and your praises sung most!

To keep this interest up, talk about yourself. When you're applying for a new job or exploring a career transition, let your network know as much as you can. If you're joining a Board of Directors or volunteering for a new nonprofit you love, tell people. Everyone wants to hear about your philanthropic goals, as it continues to build your own career and reputation as well. If you're nominated for an award or recognized at work, go ahead and make a big deal about it. You deserve it!

Recently, a dear friend of mine joined a very prestigious Board of Directors for a national nonprofit organization. This organization is incredibly selective in the individuals it chooses for its Board. To be selected, each candidate must submit a full application that includes such hoops to jump through as recommendations from current Board members, recommendations from friends and colleagues who are not involved with the organization, and a demonstrated ability to fundraise for the organization. My friend set her mind to join this Board and did everything she could to put her name in the wind. Her friends and colleagues were aware of her goal, and were as supportive as possible. She went above and beyond the requirement of two recommendations from the organization's current Board and spoke to countless Board members, staff members, and interested parties. Her perseverance and excitement about the organization was clear and impressive to the organization's board. Not only did the organization invite her to join the Board, she was offered a leadership position as well. It is that kind of perseverance that will position your name as one people want to be associated with, and your reputation as the positive one that precedes you with grace and ease.

Putting your name in the wind isn't simple and it isn't quick, unfortunately. It takes time and strategy and dedication. To keep you on your toes, here are a few other ways you might consider distributing your branding message to ensure you're being talked about and lauded by your network:

- **Use Social Media to "Toot Your Own Horn."**
Indulgent social media posts are everywhere these days.
We hear about every little thing our friends' children do,
and we see pictures of our coworkers dogs and cats and
gerbils. If they can post indulgent photos of children
covered in snow or spaghetti or some other substance,
what's stopping you from posting about your career?
Nothing! Take to the Internet, Career Girls. Tell the world
what's going on in your life and in your job. Big project?
Tweet it out. Loving your boss because he gave you huge
kudos? Don't shy away from that Facebook status. Let it
be known you rock and you're doing well. Even if no one
notices, at least your mom will be talking about it!

- **Talk to EVERYBODY!** If you want to know everybody,
ladies, you have to talk to everybody. And yes, I mean
everybody! Don't be the person who curtly answers "uh-
huh" and "thanks" in the line at Starbucks or the grocery
store. Be the person who says, "How's your day going" and
"How long have you been working here" to everyone from
cashiers to florists to servers at your favorite restaurant.
You never know what kind of intel these individuals might
have and what kind of *You Know Everybody!* Network
they've built for themselves. One of my favorite groups
in this respect comes from the restaurant business, chefs
specifically. They know EVERYBODY! Think of the kind
of people who want to "compliment the chef." They're high
rollers, CEOs, and foodies with discriminating palates.
Get to know those chefs, and you may just find yourself
with an invitation to join one of the most exclusive clubs
in your city – the foodie club! I love meetinåg chefs and
servers at restaurants, and I'm always excited to learn that
they're great networkers and love connecting people to
other people who love their food.

- **Say YES to EVERYTHING!** Obviously you get my drift, not necessarily everything. Back alley deals and partying with Bret Michaels aside (OK, never mind, go ahead and party with Bret Michaels). What I mean by this is to keep yourself open. When you're invited to a huge networking event that sounds idiotic and annoying to you, GO! It might be idiotic and annoying, but there's a slight chance it could mean huge connections for you. If a person you met at an event asks you to coffee and you simply cannot see any reason to connect with them, say yes! It's coffee, not napalm. You'll be fine. You never know who they might connect you with in the future. As a good friend of mine says, don't just say "yes," say, "Why not?" If there's not a good, solid reason *not* to do something, then do it. Consider it a learning experience.

- **Don't Hoard Your Business Cards.** This is a strange phenomenon I see in women, specifically when it comes to networking with men. We don't give out our business cards. Maybe we think a man is hitting on us, or that it's inappropriate to give a man your phone number when you're married or after the age of 30. It's not. Your business card is just that – a *business* card. It isn't a "call me for sex" card, and it isn't a "feel free to stalk me" card. It's a card with your business information, and invites a business connection. Anyone who doesn't abide by those rules is simply to be ignored. Give them out! That's why you paid to have them printed, right?

- **Get Photographed.** Don't lie, I know you've turned to the social section of your favorite magazine or newspaper and found the photos of those dressed up people at galas and grand openings and thought, "Wish I was there." Getting photographed is one of the best things you can do to get your name out there. Even my doorman commented on a photo he saw of me in the Chicago Sun Times after a charity event recently. No one wants to admit they giddily turn to see that section of a magazine or paper, but they do! Every time you go to an event, get photographed. Don't skip the step and repeat (that's the logo covered sign behind the red carpet) and head straight for the bar. You look great! Make sure someone photographs you and hopefully you'll find yourself a quick member of the society pages. If you can't get photographed, make it happen yourself. Take photos at an event, then tweet them and upload them to Facebook. Tag the people in them and the organization in question, and use the event hashtag if there is one. Get yourself out there in pictures.

- **Look for Opportunities to Be Front and Center.** To truly get your name in the wind, people have to see and hear you. So whether it's introducing your boss at a company event, or speaking on behalf of a local nonprofit organization, or appearing at an open mic night, seize every opportunity you can to stand front and center in a crowd and be the voice everyone hears. The experience you'll get by practicing this kind of public speaking will make you a better networker and a better business professional. If you're truly afraid of this kind of exposure, consider joining Toastmaster's or another group that will help you enhance your public speaking persona.

Above all else, to get your name in the wind, you have to build a reputation that precedes you in its recognition of your excellence and the other positive virtues you possess. Sounds easy, doesn't it? It's not. Ask yourself, though, what someone would say about you if asked. Imagine your best friend is standing at an event and someone says to her, "Hey, you know Annie, don't you? What's she like?" Now imagine someone you met a week ago is in the same scenario. Would the characterization of you be the same coming from your best friend as it would from a new contact? If the answer here is no, you're doing something wrong. Sure, your best friend can speak to your loyalty and love of orange sherbet, but that's not necessarily a part of your brand. Both someone you met last week and someone you've known for years should say the same things about you professionally if you're truly putting your brand at the forefront, delivering a strategic pitch, and putting your name in the wind appropriately.

When it comes to spreading the word about the most important person in your life—YOU—it comes down to one thing: Authenticity. Someone once told me that authenticity is not something you can have or not have, it is an essence you can become more of or less of. No one is authentic or inauthentic, but instead individuals can have more authenticity in one moment than they do in another. Delivering truth in your message and honesty in your excitement about what you're doing, your passions, your mission, your hopes, and your dreams is authentic. Pretending you don't want to sit in your boss' chair when you really do is inauthentic. At the same time, it's OK not to say that to your boss. This is why I love the idea of the sliding scale of authenticity. Authenticity isn't about brutal truth. It's about meaningful honesty given with passion and consideration.

It is only when women are low on the scale of authenticity that talking about someone becomes gossip. If you ride high on the scale of honesty and authenticity, even if someone is criticizing your work, their words are a part of putting your name in the wind in an anti-gossip fashion.

I gave you the bad news at the beginning of this chapter that your pitch just isn't enough. Well, get ready for it, there's more bad news. This plan to put your name in the wind, it isn't foolproof.

I'll give you an example from my own life. A number of years ago, I interviewed for a position that was my dream job at the time. The job was at a corporation I worked closely with in my work in the nonprofit arena. I knew a number of staff members within the corporation, and had glowing reviews from both internal and external partners in the company. On two separate occasions, a friend of mine who was a nonprofit Executive Director and another colleague who worked in the company's New York office reached out directly to the hiring manager to promote my skill set to her. Even more "in the wind" was a random encounter a colleague of mine had with the hiring manager where she talked about me, not knowing I had already applied and interviewed for the job. So here I am, the job of a lifetime, high level networking contacts recommending me without prompting. My name was in the wind, ladies. Guess what? I didn't get the job. I didn't blow the interview, and I didn't have any bad reputation issues. There was another person who was just more qualified and a better fit. That's all. Sometimes no matter what you do, it's not enough. And that's OK.

Years later, the hiring manager at that dream job, the one who didn't give me the job, is a close networking contact and has recommended me for other jobs and consulting gigs since. She's an avid reader of Career Girl and supports me wonderfully in everything I do. The connection I made with her and her team was unique and special, even if it didn't get me the job. Common wisdom tells women to see every networking opportunity as a job interview. I'd encourage you to turn that statement around as well – maybe every job interview is a networking opportunity.

Getting your name in the wind isn't about foolproof planning, and it isn't about landing every job you want or chasing every opportunity 100% successfully. Getting your name in the wind is about networking and building your reputation. Without your name out there, without people knowing who you are and talking about you, you cannot be a *You Know Everybody!*

Networker. You might not get that job you think is perfect, and you might hear "no" here and there from potential contacts. What you will get, though, is a network that is beyond your wildest dreams. We can all envision a network that includes a few hundred people we've met over the course of a few years. Envision your wildest dreams network, though. Does it include CEOs, TV personalities, heads of state? Dream big! Think big! Most of all, talk big!

When I started Career Girl Network, someone asked me how I would know when I'm successful. I said two things: #1, I'm already successful because for me, risk equals success. #2, Melinda Gates will call me for lunch. Don't laugh! I'm serious about that one. Melinda Gates sits at the head of the table in my personal wildest dreams network. So when I toot my own horn, when I post something great on Facebook, and when I talk about my passions and mission and drive to succeed, I sometimes imagine those notions traveling through my network, onward and upward and somehow reaching Melinda Gates. When I'm really down, and can't seem to find my path back to my passions, I think about Melinda sitting at the head of that table, picking up the phone, calling me and saying, "I was just talking about you." Create it! Create your brand, create your pitch, and start putting your name out in the wind, Career Girls. Then, create your own wildest dreams network, your own Melinda Gates, and ask yourself this: What would I need to do, who would I need to reach, and who would need to hear my message to send it onwards and upwards so my wildest dream networking connection would say to me, "I was just talking about you"?

She Knows Everybody! Narrative: Chapter 8
"I Was Just Talking About You" –
Putting Your Name in the Wind

Dawn Jackson Blatner
Registered Dietician, Nutritionist,
Media and Brand Partner

Find Dawn Online
Website: www.dawnjacksonblatner.com
Social: @djblatner

There's an unwritten rule of human behavior, rarely broken, that you're allowed to make fun of a person or a group of people only if you belong to said group. The best examples are jokes about whatever state you're from. No one is allowed to talk about New Jersey unless you're from New Jersey. If you're from New Jersey, go ahead and feel free to call it a hellhole—even Jon Bon Jovi will laugh. For this reason, I feel I'm allowed to start this chapter by telling you that the subject of this narrative, my friend Dawn Jackson Blatner, is exhausting!

That word is not meant as an insult, but rather as a badge of honor. And I consider myself properly allowed to say so because I, myself, am exhausting to many as well. Dawn and I share a fast-moving brain and an even faster-moving mouth that can sometimes make people want to scream, "STOP! Just breathe for a minute!" Suffice it to say that Dawn's energy is one of my favorite things about her, and it's the reason I asked her to be a part of this book. She never stops, she never rests on her past successes, and the fact that she "knows everybody" and everybody knows her is evidence of her relentless energy and drive.

The morning we met to talk about this book, the energy that sometimes gets out of hand crackled around us. Sitting at a restaurant in Chicago's Bucktown neighborhood, we spent nearly 90 minutes talking about everything except the book when I realized I had to get down to business and actually ask her some questions. I know you'll all be glad I eventually gained focus in this meeting, because there is no better illustration of the power of getting your name in the wind than Dawn Jackson Blatner.

Making a Name in a Massive Industry

Dawn's accolades and appearances in the media place her at the top of her field. She's the author of the acclaimed *The Flexitarian Diet* and has been featured in national media outlets including *The Dr. Oz Show, USA Today, Dateline, Newsweek, Cooking Light, WebMD, Fitness Magazine, Health Magazine, Yoga Journal,* and *Vegetarian Times,* and is a regular contributor to *The Huffington Post.* Phew! That's quite a list. It's even more impressive when you consider the size of Dawn's field. Dawn is a registered dietician and certified specialist in sports dietetics. In the United States today, there are approximately 72,000 registered dieticians, and it's safe to say they all haven't been on *The Dr. Oz Show.*

I asked Dawn how, among the thousands of registered dieticians and other nutrition experts in the industry, she has been able to amass the kind of international acclaim and press that makes her business and her brand so successful. Her answers were surprisingly simple. Three sentences touched me in her answer to this question:

- "You're good at this."
- "Mentors are key to my success."
- "I always take my job with me."

The first sentence here comes from Dawn's story about her first television experience. She was, at the time, working for Northwestern Memorial Hospital in Chicago and as she described it to me, "dying to be on TV." She set her sights and began to ask for what she wanted. She pitched stories and ideas to Northwestern's media team and was constantly and consistently turned away. After all, a hospital like Northwestern had public relations and media specialists who were always the people who appeared on TV for the hospital. Dawn said, "Why would they let some dietician step in when the experts were already well known?" A twist of fate came when every single person who normally goes on television for Northwestern got sick on the same day. Finally, her opportunity had come and she appeared on NBC for the first time. As it turns out, the station loved her segment and began requesting her for more interviews.

As Dawn built her reputation in Chicago TV and at Northwestern, a mentor said to her, "You're good at this." That vote of confidence from a trusted advisor gave Dawn even more confidence and drive to continue to speak—at events, and to the media—whenever she could. For this reason, she credits that mentor who pushed her to continue to build her business through speaking, saying "Mentors are key to my success."

I asked Dawn what she thought made her so "good at" media and attractive as a speaker. Her answer, "I always take my job with me." She eats, sleeps, lives, and breathes the mission she stands for. Her mission comes first in everything she does. "I want to inspire and motivate you to transform your health by using the Power of Food. You deserve to know how to feed your body right to wake up each morning with a healthy spring in your step," she said. It speaks volumes in writing, but it's even more appealing when Dawn is telling you about it, talking with her hands, her face lighting up, and the whole world can see her passion. This is why she's talked about, written about, invited on television. It's not because she has the best public relations team out there (in fact, she does her media and press relations herself); it's because she is passionate and believes in what she does.

The Power of Showing Up

Dawn spent the years following her first media spot building her reputation with individuals and the press in Chicago. A huge win came for Dawn when a morning show asked her to appear. The call time? Four o'clock in the morning. She told me, "I think they'd probably called a number of other people, but I was the only one willing to get up and be on TV that early. Sometimes getting ahead is just about being willing to show up." In our society, when it comes to putting your name in the wind, far too many of us want someone else to do it for us. We want our friends to promote us on Facebook and recommend us on LinkedIn, and introduce us to the right people. Unless you're willing to roll your ass out of bed at 4:00 a.m., though, you're not showing up for your own brand and your own career. Dawn Jackson Blatner? She shows up, and she does it with authenticity and gusto.

Dawn said to me, "I'm not putting on a show. I'm showing up and doing what I believe." Can you say that about your own career? If you were like Dawn and your goal was to become a TV expert and a well-respected freelance writer in your field, why do you want it? Could it be that you want to be in the spotlight? That you want to put on a show? Wake-up call here, Career Girls, it won't work if that's the "why" behind it. To be truly successful, you have to show up and do what you believe in. Only that will get your name in the wind in a way that builds a positive reputation and allows you to harness that reputation to build success in your industry.

"I Was Born to Do This"

Dawn tells me, like many of the women in this book have echoed, that authenticity is a massive factor in getting people talking about you. You have to truly and authentically love what you do, and it has to show. People who don't authentically love their jobs spend their time searching for one big success story, and then "ride it 'til they die." Here's an example from Dawn. In 2011, she was recognized as a part of "Lifetime's Remarkable Women" project. This was an incredible honor, and exciting to receive, but Dawn told me, "You can only lean on an award like that for a short period of time. I can't keep touting the Lifetime award for years and expect it to be a big deal!" Someone who truly wants to get her name in the wind has to keep building on successes like the Lifetime award, using its publicity to create more publicity, more wins, and more calls for expert advice.

Dawn says, "If you don't take your job everywhere with you and show up authentically and passionately, why would anyone call you for anything?" I asked her how she does that and she said six words we should all put in our regular vocabulary: "I was born to do this."

Take a moment, pause, and turn that sentence into a question. What are you born to do? Are you doing that? If you're not, it's signal #1 as the reason your name is not "in the wind." Only people who are truly passionate about the work they're born to do will be talked about and lauded for their work. Get on board, if not with promoting yourself, then at least with finding the ways to truly love what you do. Begin, even in small ways, to harness the job you were born to accomplish.

Stop Plotting!

I mentioned earlier that Dawn Jackson Blatner doesn't have a media team. Let that sink in a minute. No PR person, no stylist, no speech coach. Sometimes we think that every successful woman, especially one who is regularly on television, has to have those things. Dawn does it all herself, and incredibly successfully. She credits her success in doing her own press to being open to possibilities. She said, "I don't 'plot.' Everyone in this world wants to plot. I just don't. Instead, I'm comfortable with throwing spaghetti on the wall and seeing where it lands."

Now, don't get me wrong, I'm not telling you to just go into the world spewing whatever you feel like with no direction. No way. Dawn doesn't advocate that strategy, either. Instead, she simply asks you to consider what's driving your plotting. Again, is it fame and fortune? Or is it true passion. Dawn challenges you all to be "driven by the fuel of passion and enjoyment." If you put those priorities first—passion and enjoyment—can you imagine what amazing things might come to you? Can you imagine the incredible people and groups who might be talking about you and the way your name might flow into the wind in the most positive and exciting light? Lace your work daily with the fuel of passion and enjoyment, and stop plotting. Only then will your true desires and needs come to the surface.

The "Best of the Best" in Networking Advice

I ended each of the interviews completed for You Know Everybody!
by asking each woman to provide to this book's readers her best
networking tips and advice. Here are Dawn's tips and tricks.

- **Longevity matters.** She might be beautiful and young in the eyes of her clients, friends, and the world, but Dawn is careful to point out the fact that her career was not an overnight success. "I've been doing this for 15 years! It takes time." You can't allow yourself to get frustrated in your process and give up just because success doesn't happen immediately. When you're frustrated, think about Dawn working at Northwestern and asking time and time again for an opportunity. It took time (and sure, maybe a little nagging) to get even that first opportunity. It takes even more time for the next and the next. You have to be patient and willing to work hard, but also to wait it out.

- **Make time.** There are thousands of things you could do to enhance your career in addition to networking. You have bills to pay and jobs to apply for and family circumstances to consider. We get it! But you have to make time to network, no matter how hard it is. You find the time in your day to watch TV and get together with friends, so be sure you're making time in your day to incorporate networking as well.

- **Think about networking as "friend making" first.** Dawn and I have known each other for a couple of years, peripherally, but not incredibly well. When she and I met on a more one-on-one basis, her exact words to me were "I just want to know you!" That kind of enthusiasm about getting to know someone is difficult to duplicate. Dawn says she thinks of all networking simply as "friend making." Are you going out there and making friends and finding people you want to add to your network? If it scares you, then don't do it with networking in mind. Just go into it looking to make a friend, and you'll go far!

- **Simplify.** Dawn and I laughed together talking about
  people who simply can't find a way to describe what they
  do without using big words and long descriptions. It's
  not uncommon to hear a business owner say something
  like, "We're kind of like the eBay of Groupon. It's hard
  to describe." One of Dawn's best pieces of networking
  advice is to simplify, simplify, simplify. Sometimes, she
  says, when people ask her what she does, she just says, "I
  do nutrition." It might sound too simple, but sometimes
  it's easier than the long description. Don't be afraid to be
  as simple as possible to find success.

nine

New Networking Strategies for Innovative Thinkers

If you never did, you should.
These things are fun and fun is good.

–Dr. Seuss,
One Fish, Two Fish, Red Fish, Blue Fish

There could be no more generic advice about anything than to say, "Think outside the box." The first question I have whenever someone gives that advice is, "What box?" When it comes to the *You Know Everybody!* Networker, though, thinking outside the box of traditional networking will only help you. To build a network that works, you'll need to employ new strategies, and not just new strategies for you but new strategies in general. It's like the buzzword "new media." We're trying to enact some "new networking."

If we're trying to create "new networking," you might be asking yourself what is "old networking"? Old networking is most definitely what you might call "in the box" networking. It's the buttoned up, white business card, black suit wearing, holding a cocktail with a "Hello, My Name Is" name tag kind of networking.

It's the kind of networking that screams, "Don't call me, I'll call you." Conversely, the idea of "new networking" breaks the mold for women in the ways we network, creates meaningful relationships formed both inside and outside cocktail events, and gives all of us the ability to form constituencies around our careers.

Women tend to focus our networking in our own age range, our own location, and our own industry. We network with individuals and groups who feel safe to us, and while it's important to include these groups and individuals in your network, it's also important to consider what others areas we could expand into to truly move the needle, not only for us as individuals in networking but also for women in business across the board. Imagine, for example, that you're an attorney living in Tampa, Florida. Your natural networking instinct is to join organizations focused on female attorneys, or perhaps attorneys practicing in your area of focus. Your instinct is also to network only in Tampa and surrounding areas. Think for a moment about the real logic here. Are attorneys your client base? What happens if you at some point decide to leave Tampa? What if you're offered a position in a firm comprised mostly of men? Do you have the right network surrounding you to make your decisions successful if they lead you outside your city, your age group, or your industry?

The fact of the matter is, lawyers don't always need to meet other lawyers. Sure, you want to network with leaders in your field, but you'll likely do that naturally and with the tips you've received in the rest of this book. What this chapter is about is breaking outside that box and learning ways to get into that "new networking" mode. You'll never regret it! If you're hesitant to try any of the techniques I'm using here, I want you to ask yourself this question: **Do you want to be an industry leader? Or do you want to be a leader?** Think about that long and hard. Being a leader in your industry is incredible. You'll be well respected by your peers, admired by young professionals in the work you do, and you'll rise faster than those who are not considered field leaders. Consider women like Sheryl Sandberg, Hillary Clinton, Meg Whitman, and others like them. Are they leaders in their fields? Or are they leaders period? Creating your network with these outgoing—and perhaps outside your comfort zone—tactics is driving you towards leadership, not just for your industry but for women in business collectively.

Networking that is not classified as "new networking" by this chapter isn't bad. In fact, it's the kind of networking we've been talking about up until this point in the book. It is meaningful and builds relationships that stand the test of time, it is accountable in that it makes you the best version of yourself, and it is authentic to who you are and what you desire in your deepest self. The idea of "new networking" just expands on those notions to include people, places, and ideas that don't fit in the traditional business box.

Take a moment, and think back to the top layers of your personal network. Think about those "move a body" friends, those shoulders to cry on, those individuals who will always be there for a dinner or a cup of coffee when you're having a bad day. Where did you meet them? How did you develop your relationships? Chances are, it wasn't through a traditional networking event where you first swapped your business cards. Most of the top layers in our network are individuals who we've met at key turning points in our lives – high school, college, our first jobs, or influential jobs in our careers. Think, too, about the most influential people in your network who are largely professional friends rather than person. Where did you meet them? How did your relationships develop? Perhaps one of these individuals was your boss, another a mentor, another a friend you attended a conference with years ago.

As you think through your network, you may find that many of your closest connections came not from traditional networking, but instead through the catalyst of a shared experience. Often, we make friends at the office because only those in the cubicle next to us can truly understand our experiences. The same goes for friends from our younger selves. In high school and college, we bond to get through massive changes in our lives. As we age, one of the most difficult challenges comes in making real friends. Do we need to have the shared experience of pimple cream or our first "drank too much" night to truly bond? Thankfully for all of us, the answer is no. The key to making new connections and new friends later in life, though, is "new networking"!

To develop a strong and strategic network using the new networking tactics you'll find in this chapter, you'll need to follow just one rule—the one listed at the beginning of this chapter from the incomparable Dr. Seuss: "If you never did, you should." You'll need only to go beyond your comfort zone and try something new. Or, if you're already a daring risk taker, you'll need to add networking to the scope of the exciting activities you're already a part of. Doing things you've never done may just bring out a side of yourself you've never seen. So let's dive in and look at three new networking techniques you can use to build your *You Know Everybody!* Network.

1. **Using your existing hobbies and connections, and leveraging them in new ways.**
   - **Gyms, Fitness Classes, and Other Physical Activities**
     I started this book by telling you about my own *You Know Everybody!* experiences, but even with those high praises and exclamations from friends and colleagues, being a *You Know Everybody!* Networker is a journey that is never over. I recently attended a workout class in a suburb of Minneapolis, surrounded by powerful Minneapolis women, most of whom work downtown. Under the auspicious notion that I "know everybody," it

would make sense that I knew the women in this class, but I didn't. A traditional networker would have seen this workout class as just that, a workout class. But a new networker saw it as an opportunity. Instead of being afraid because I was surrounded by people I didn't know, I got to know them before and after class, invited them to another event, and excitedly made connections. These are exactly the kind of events you should use, sometimes even more so than traditional networking events, to ensure you're building a strong network in all layers.

If you're a fitness nut, you likely already have natural networks at your gyms and fitness studios that you rarely think of as networking connections. When I moved to Chicago in 2010, I realized quickly it was much easier to make friends at my yoga and spin studios than it was to do the same at networking events. Sure, some of the connections I made at networking events turned into friendships, but relationships that begin while sweating became friendly much more quickly.

How do you harness these connections?
- Consider a gym or a fitness studio that is smaller than the traditional massive sports club. You'll be much more likely to get to know the people working out around you.
- Try to get into a groove with a regular schedule. You'll quickly begin to see the same people every day, and your morning "hello" can more easily morph into "Tell me about yourself." and much more meaningful connections over time.
- Almost all fitness studios and gyms produce events in addition to regular classes and offerings.

Go to that Wednesday night spin class to benefit breast cancer awareness and check out the spa nights at your gym. Take those opportunities to get to know all of the people there.

□ Trainers and fitness professionals have incredible networks, so make use of them. One hour, a trainer might be working with an artist, and the next hour with a CEO. Often, trainers are willing to introduce clients to one another and make great connections. After all, it's a value add for them to ensure clients are getting everything they can out of paying for sessions. Why shouldn't networking be one of those perks?

□ If you participate in races, whether you're a runner, a cyclist, or a triathlete, you can meet phenomenal people through training and completing one of these activities together. Look for training programs in your local running clubs or fitness stores in the area. Find friends through online message boards and training groups who regularly run together or frequent the same trainers or classes. There's nothing racers love to talk about more than racing, and at least this way you're doing it with people who are just as interested in split times as you are.

• **Restaurants and Retail Shops You Love Already**
When I moved from Minneapolis to Chicago, I immediately discovered I had a whole network of people I had completely taken for granted in my former city – chefs, restaurant managers, designers, retail employees, and so many more. Whether you realize it or not, you likely have an incredible number of these

kinds of connections already. These individuals are the kinds of people who, like personal trainers, have massive networks and are always willing to make connections.

In the last few months alone, I've heard two stories about how personal shoppers at J. Crew helped clients land jobs or Board seats with companies of other clients. It's not just J. Crew, either. As a fundraiser, I relied heavily on the networks of my chef friends to reach a number of high level C-suiters with access to discretionary funds. Chefs know everybody; so do retail owners and personal stylists. Take the time to get to know these individuals, introduce yourself, and become more than just "that lady who spends a lot of money here." You never know what kinds of connections these individuals might provide.

- **Volunteer Opportunities**
  Women love to connect with people who are, like credit cards, pre-qualified. It's hard to walk into an event, look around the room, and try to size up the kinds of people who are standing near you. Is someone worth your time? Does she share your passions? Put away those questions the moment you begin networking before, during, or after a volunteer opportunity. By networking directly with individuals who already share your passion for a cause, you're pre-qualifying that individual for your network. You can immediately jump into discussions about your passions, your vision, and the way you hope to achieve it, and avoid all of the small talk about your desk job!

Look for volunteer opportunities that emphasize group activities. Many organizations ask for groups of volunteers to build parks, paint after-school childcare rooms, and other kinds of group beautification. You can have great conversations with the volunteer next to you while planting a garden or building a bench. If you're interested in mentoring young people, you can also find a number of nonprofit organizations that emphasize group mentoring over one-on-one opportunities, giving you the perfect chance to connect not only with adolescents, but with powerful women who share your passion for giving back to the next generation.

- **Parents and Other Family Members**
  Many women, especially the fiercely independent ones who are no doubt reading this book, ignore the option of networking with family members or the connections of family members. We don't want to ask our parents for anything more than what they've already given us, and we ignore their pleas to help us get a job or make connections. The fact is, many of our parents, aunts, and uncles are traditionally successful and themselves have networks built over the course of long careers. Ignoring these connections is not only pigheaded, it's naive. You've relied on your parents and close family members for food, shelter, Christmas gifts, and, for some kids, even cars and college tuition. Doesn't it seem strange to suddenly decide you're better than what they can give you?

There is a fine line between accepting help from your parents and overusing them. In 2012, on yet another Bravo television show featuring the lives of otherwise unknown pseudo-celebrities, we met the ladies of "Gallery Girls." Hardworking women around the country marveled at this strange group, many of whom were pushing 30 and still interning and taking full salaries from what would otherwise be their parents' retirement accounts. It's one thing to ask your well-networked attorney father to introduce you to an industry player after you graduate law school. It's a completely different story to expect your dad's firm to bankroll your party-girl lifestyle. Still, don't be afraid to ask for help when you need it. Connections are easy currency for relatives to provide, and showing the initiative to put your best foot forward in those meetings will not only impress your parents, but may impress the individuals they're introducing you to, as well

2.   Using social media and innovative online connection makers.

There's no doubt social media has completely taken over our world. Many of us spend more time on Facebook than we do on email, and are more likely to send a LinkedIn or Twitter message than pick up the phone to say hello to an old friend.

It would be easy to suggest you use Facebook, Twitter, and LinkedIn to connect with others, and I have throughout this book. When you're focusing on networking innovation, even the staid social media connectors are too traditional for you. Try a few of these more outside the box ideas in your online networking.

- **Meetup.com**
  Meetup.com is the perfect blend of social network and offline community. The website allows local groups to organize face-to-face meetings of like-minded local individuals. It harnesses the power of self-organization and has an impressive 11.1 million members, 2 million event RSVPs and hosts 105,000 groups in 45,000 cities.

You'll find Meetup groups for singles in the suburbs, bootstrapping business owners, authors, adventure seekers, hikers, shoppers, and much more.

Those who have used Meetup regularly will tell you the groups can be hit or miss. You might find yourself sitting in a coffee shop with one other person wondering if anyone else will ever arrive. On the contrary, though, you could be a part of a large group who truly wants to help one another succeed and becomes lifelong connections and friends. The only way you'll ever find the latter instead of the former is to take a chance and go. To increase your chances of getting a great group, look for groups with a longer history of Meetups, a large membership, and specific goals.

- **Tweetups**
  Less organized than Meetup.com, Tweetups can be a fantastic way to meet people on your Twitter followers list and beyond. Twitter is inherently a conversation. You tweet something, someone tweets you back, and BAM! you're getting to know each other. Shortly after Twitter became popular, Tweetup groups popped up all over the world. How do you find them?
  - Watch your circles for Tweetup announcements.
  - Look for Twitter lists in your industry or area of interest. These lists often band together to form Tweetup groups.
  - Google "Tweetup" followed by the name of your city. Larger metropolitan areas often have full websites and organizations dedicated to cataloging Tweetups and handling RSVPs and connections. Check them often!

- **LinkedIn Groups**

  You're probably already using LinkedIn beautifully, but the most common comment I hear about LinkedIn is that many people don't know how to use it beyond updating their profile and connecting with others. The best way to dive deeper on LinkedIn is to first join, and then become active in a number of groups. It's not enough to join one or two. To be truly effective in developing a network using LinkedIn groups, you'll need to join quite a few. Women have an easier go of these choices than men do, as there are some incredible LinkedIn groups specifically catering to women in business. The beauty of these groups is that many women are members of a number of them, giving you the opportunity to see the faces of and converse with the same women in multiple groups. Consider joining the following groups to start your women-focused LinkedIn networking:
  - Connect: Professional Women's Network, Powered by Citi
  - ForbesWoman
  - Marie Claire Career Network
  - Women in the Boardroom
  - The Women's Conference
  - Step Up Women's Network
  - Groups related to women's nonprofit organizations or foundations in your area

- **Online dating**

  It may sound silly, but if you're a single Career Girl, you have a leg up in networking your attached friends will never have – dating! Take it from someone who once called herself a "professional dater." In the two years between my divorce and meeting my now husband,

Charlie, I not only used dating as a fun way to meet men, I considered it a fun way just to meet people and add them to my network. In that time, I met a consultant who later referred me for a job; my best male friend; the catering manager at a hotel that later cut me a huge deal on an event; a baseball broadcaster who always had free tickets to the game; and the owner of a chain of airport restaurants who taught me the best places to avoid security lines at every airport in the country. While none of these men became my husband, each of them became a part of my extended network, some higher ranking than others, of course.

One of the most frequently heard complaints from men about the single women they date is that they're just too damn eager to find out if you're "husband material." I talk to friends and colleagues all the time who rattle off their "must haves" in a man even before a first date. For this reason, you may find you're turning a man off before the end of a first date. Imagine, though, how much stronger your dating life might get if you walked into every date thinking about the person sitting across from you as a potential connection, a potential friend, a potential professional contact, and only after those considerations, a potential romantic relationship. Your dating might get better, and your network certainly will grow!

- **Apps are all the rage**
  Nielsen claims that over 50% of Americans own a smartphone in 2012, so if we eliminate both small children and the elderly, it's safe to assume most of the women reading this book own a phone capable of running either Apple or Android apps. I personally love

that you're likely already an app user, because let me tell you, Career Girls, there are incredible apps to get you ahead when it comes to your career, and networking specifically. To get you in the networking apps mood, try downloading some of the following apps. They'll rock your networking world.

- **Planely**

  You're walking into a massive group of people, many of whom are powerful business professionals and most with a huge amount of down time. You're at the airport! One innovative company is giving us all an opportunity to turn that waiting at the gate and flying experience into a powerful network builder. Planely allows you to check in, tell the app where you're traveling and on what plane, and connect to other Planely fliers on the same flight or in the same departure or arrival time. You can request a seat together on the plane, share a cab home, or grab a cup of coffee. These individuals are a wealth of knowledge and connections. Planely makes the connection. Genius!

- **TripIt**

  TripIt is an awesome travel tool with or without a social connection element. It keeps your itineraries, including flights, cars, hotels, and more, in one access spot. The networking genius accompanying this app, though, is the ability to share your itineraries with your network via Facebook, LinkedIn, and more. This way, you're not connecting with strangers, but with people you already know. In Washington, DC for a few days for work? It may be that one of your college friends just moved there and you didn't even realize it. Now, they'll see you're there and you may have another powerful connection or blast from the past.

- **WhosHere**

  WhosHere is all about proximity. Hanging out at a restaurant by yourself? Use WhosHere to find other individuals who want to interact with you based on your geographic location. Not only can you find individuals, you can use the WhosHere system to send free text messages and even make calls via VoIP without disclosing any personal information. WhosHere is careful to ensure your privacy is protected, while at the same time allowing you to make new connections in your area.

- **CardMunch**

  CardMunch is one of my favorite apps to utilize during and after networking. Somewhere in your desk drawer or home junk drawer, you have a stack full of business cards you just never got around to putting in your contact list. Did you ever connect with those individuals on LinkedIn? Email them to follow up? Probably not. That's OK. Just use the camera on your phone to load each of the cards into CardMunch and the information on it will automatically be converted to a contact you can add to your phone's contact list or connect with on LinkedIn.

◻ **Yelp**

You might think of Yelp as just a site for restaurant reviews, but it's so much more. Behind the scenes are millions of "Yelpers" who not only review businesses and services, but also connect with one another. Yelp has become its own version of Meetup.com. Locals meet with tourists to show them the sites. Women meet with men to grab a bite and perhaps form a romantic relationship. Groups of Yelpers have even band together to get group discounts on plays, sporting events, and more. Take the time to click on the "talk" button on Yelp and hear what people are saying about everything from current events to cell phone service to your favorite new restaurant.

• **Online message boards**

Online forums are great places to network, specifically to learn more about your industry and to perhaps access bloggers, leaders, and others who are the generators of information in your area. The most difficult part of becoming part of an online message board is finding one! There are hundreds of options. I highly recommend the simplicity of ProBoards and its easy to use app. ProBoards has hundreds of online forums on every topic under the sun from travel to entertainment to computers and technology. Find a few forums that appeal to you, save them on your app, and get to know a whole host of new people nationwide.

3. **Engaging your current network in nontraditional ways.**

Finally, aside from using new technologies and out of the box tactics to engage in networking with individuals you don't know yet, I wouldn't be responsible in giving you innovative networking strategies unless I gave you innovative tools for the network you already have. Innovation doesn't always mean new—sometimes it means taking different approaches to the old or stale part of your networking approach.

Consider using some of the following tactics to refresh the relationships you have and are continuing to build with your entire network, from your "move a body" connections to those individuals whose names you might not quite remember.

- **Consider launching a personal website or professional portfolio.**
  Generation Y has been creating websites for as long as we can remember. In the 90s, GeoCities, Expages, Angelfire, and many more. Gen Y created websites for everything from crushes on Jonathan Taylor Thomas to feuds with our best friends. We also pioneered blogging with LiveJournal, Xanga, and the like. This kind of web innovation can be a powerful addition to building your network. Sure, you're employed by Corporation X, but wouldn't it be amazing to send a new networking connection directly to your own website or portfolio? It's not as difficult as it sounds, which any Millennial can tell you. But what should your website contain?
  - If you're a professional searching for a place to display your professional credentials, link some of your work, or give an overview greater than what LinkedIn can provide, consider these resources:
    - ◊ **Wix.com's** tagline is "Easy. Fast. Beautiful." You can quickly create a website in minutes that uses hundreds of cool templates, has

HTML5 capability, and amazing apps to add to your website as well.

◊ An even simpler web creator is **Weebly.com**. If you're looking for something clean, easy, and simple, Weebly is the site for you. You can load a great looking website in minutes.

◊ If you're simply looking for a splash page or one stop, one page website to show people who you are, what you love, and get them to your social media profiles, the best option for you is **About.me**. It's a social media splash page that allows you to upload a photo, description, and then send viewers right off to your LinkedIn, Twitter, Facebook, and more. It's professional, it's simple, and you can have it up and running in minutes.

▫ If you really want a sophisticated and professionally designed website, consider using a **WordPress** template. You can buy WordPress templates on WordPress, of course, but my favorite outside source is Mojo Themes. By following the directions given to you by each designer, and with some diligent work, you can have a professional website created in hours or days, depending on the detail involved.

• If you're an artist, public relations executive, photographer, or in any other business that needs a portfolio, consider the following resources:

▫ Pressfolios gives you the opportunity to put all of your clips in one place and present them in a beautiful tile-based look. You can easily add your portfolio link to your business cards and cover letters when applying for a job.

▫ Carbonmade is another online portfolio site allowing you to add photos to your website in a number of forms, giving you the option to add as many photos, designs, etc., as you need to display your talent to a potential connection.

▫ Behance is the ultimate online portfolio site, meant to connect talent to opportunity. You can seamlessly link your Behance portfolio to your LinkedIn profile.

• **Get your own newsletter. It's free!**
You might think newsletters are only for lonely soccer moms at Christmas or entrepreneurs and businesses. Not true! Some of my favorite newsletters, both simple and elaborate, come from individuals. You don't have to send a newsletter every week or even monthly, but sending even a quarterly update can build your brand, increase your professionalism, and remind people that you're not just another connection, you're a star. Include in your newsletter relevant information about your industry, blog posts you've written recently, articles you're loving lately, or nonprofit events you'll be attending in the future. Anything you're doing professionally should be newsletter worthy, ladies, so go ahead and send one out. Do it strategically and make sure it's well thought out. What do you really want to let your network know about? Those are the key things to include.

The greatest tool for newsletters since email itself is MailChimp.com. Creating amazing newsletters on MailChimp is free for up to 2,000 subscribers and 12,000 emails per month. So go ahead, empty your iContacts or Outlook contacts into MailChimp and send away. Sure, a few people will unsubscribe and think you're a bit crazy or egotistical, but those people frankly suck anyway. The right people in your network will love it and be excited to hear about what's happening in your career.

- **Become an expert in your field.**
  Finally, to truly innovate your networking, you must focus on becoming a leader in your field. True innovators and new networkers are always finding ways to say something new, position themselves as experts, and move the conversation forward in their area of expertise. Consider the following tactics:
  - **Blogging** can be a powerful platform to share your point of view and begin important conversations in your field. You do not need a professionally created website or blog to start the conversation. Log onto WordPress or Blogger and start talking! Over time, you'll find your blogging voice. To be successful as a blogger, though, you'll need to commit to the kind of time necessary to make it good. This requires at least weekly posts that are thoughtfully written, and the time to effectively promote your posts and your blog on industry groups and websites.
  - If writing your own blog sounds far too intense for your schedule, consider the possibility of **guest posting** on another industry blog or one specific to your interests. On my site, Career Girl Network, we host various guest bloggers every week and have regular contributing writers, many of whom are powerful forces

in their fields but simply don't have the time or energy to tend to a full blog themselves. Reach out to blogs you read regularly, submit a few ideas or guest posts, and strive to become a regular contributor. If you later decide to branch into your own blog, you'll have ample material to draw from later.

◻ Earlier, I recommended joining LinkedIn groups, but more important than joining is being active and **starting online conversations.** Be willing to open conversations on groups, message boards, Twitter, Facebook, and more. By asking good questions and responding to feedback readily, you'll quickly be recognized as a leader online and eventually in person. Invite your in-person networking connections to join your groups and engage in conversation. Pairing online with offline will empower your network to get to know you better and to get to know one another.

◻ As you become a recognized expert, it may be time to look for **speaking engagements.** If you're not a great public speaker, join a local Toastmasters group or search for another public speaking opportunity group in your area. From there, reach out to Chambers of Commerce, nonprofit training organizations, or career development resource groups and offer your industry expertise. You'll find quickly that speaking engagements beget speaking engagements beget speaking engagements. One organization will ask you to appear, and the next, and the next. Over time, you'll be asked more and more to speak in your industry and in the topic of your specific expertise. At the beginning, though, speak everywhere and anywhere you can as much as you can. Word of mouth is key for public speakers more than anything else.

Though the tactics above may all be about new networking, the goals you should be setting in employing these strategies remain the same. Your goals here are to develop real relationships both online and off that will sustain over time and produce results in your career and in your life. You should always be strategically thinking about the seven layers of your network and asking yourself, "Which layer does person X fit into?" Developing friendships is difficult normally, and some of these new networking techniques can actually make that process easier and more organic than a business card exchange or LinkedIn connection request.

Continually search for individuals whose authenticity impresses you, who are experts in their own right, and who also stand out as experts in new networking themselves. The person at your fitness studio who talks to everyone? She's the one you want to know. The person on your LinkedIn group whose posts always get the most comments? Get to know her. Schedule a Skype call if you can with her. Let her know you want to be in her network today! That guy you went to dinner with and don't want to date, but really want to hire? Tell him! The relationship will either flourish or it will get swept under the rug. Either way, you've taken the risk to ask for what you want and do everything you can to build your network in both traditional and non-traditional ways. Then, and only then, will someone really believe you're a *You Know Everybody!* Networker. Because you can't just "know everybody" in a black suit armed with business cards. To truly know everybody, you have to know them in all facets of your life and be willing to connect those parts of your life to one another.

She Knows Everybody! Narrative: Chapter 9
New Networking Strategies for Innovative Thinkers

Elizabeth Ruske
CEO, Tiara International

Find Beth Online
Website: www.tiaraleadership.com
Twitter: @eruske_tiara
LinkedIn: linkedin.com/in/elizabethruske

It was clear I picked the right person to talk to about new networking strategies and innovative networking thinking from the first question I asked Beth Ruske. Where, I asked, did she meet some of the best people in her network? Her response: "Weddings. And funerals." I sat forward in my seat. Meeting a connection at a funeral? Clearly Beth knows her stuff when it comes to thinking outside the box in her own networking journey, and she has an incredible amount to teach you about yours!

I met Beth Ruske in 2011 through a mentorship program in Chicago. Beth and her business partner Peg were the presenters at the program's kickoff and goal setting workshop. Her energy, her excitement about the women in the room, and her passion for women in leadership was infectious from the moment I saw her. On top of that, the lady was just funny! I'll never forget Beth telling a whole room of women that day that her goal for 2011 was to be the "hottest 50-year old my husband will ever want to sleep with." This kind of confidence and willingness to share her life and her ideas with others is what immediately drew me to Beth, and draws hundreds of people in her network to her and her business, Tiara Coaching, constantly.

When I went through the massive career change of moving from consulting to entrepreneurship, Beth and her business partner Peg were my first lifeline. Beth became my personal and business coach and helped me to discover what I wanted, and develop a plan to make it happen. Somehow, she always had the confidence in me that I didn't have in myself, and confidence is exactly the reason I chose Beth to illustrate the "how to" of this chapter. To truly be able to network in an innovative way, you have to harness the deepest sense of your own confidence and take it with you. Let's ask Beth how she does it...

Leadership Counts!

You have to ask yourself (and I do, in this chapter), "Do I want to be an industry leader? Or do I want to be a leader?" How would you rather be portrayed? Beth and I discussed this topic specifically and she says, "What you're talking about is innate leadership. Tiara believes everyone has that innate leadership – you are the leader of your own life. It's all about how you manifest it." I wondered, had Beth always been a leader? Or had she learned over time to harness her innate leadership? She told me about being in her first Brownie troop at six years old and being given an award for storytelling, said in the way of, "Oh, that Beth, she's always telling stories." Thinking back, Beth says, that award was a leadership award. Because even as a six-year old, when a true leader, an innate leader, is present, it's obvious. It's not just the Beth Ruske leader. It's every leader.

Being a leader, and not just one in your industry, requires the ability to act like Velcro for great people surrounding you. It requires the confidence and the desire to draw people towards you. In a sense, you have to be attractive – not physically, but personally attractive. You have to attract people to you and bring them into your leadership fold. Be careful, though, Beth says, "You can't be like Velcro inauthentically." True leadership and, subsequently, great, confident, new networking strategies, can only work if you show up in total authenticity to every situation. How does Beth do it? Read on...

How to Really "Know" Everybody

I've had the privilege of seeing Beth network both inside and outside the proverbial box. I've seen her engage in incredible conversations at traditional networking events, and I've also seen her start a meaningful relationship with a server at a coffee shop just by being herself. Of course, I asked her for her "special sauce" in creating these kinds of moments in her life. The story she told me was this one: A while back, Beth found herself standing in her health club's locker room next to a woman probably in her late 60s or early 70s. Beth told me, "She wasn't traditionally beautiful, but something about her was just striking and gorgeous. So I looked at her and said, 'I just wanted to let you know, you are strikingly beautiful.'" Of course the woman replied warmly and told Beth she had just "made her day."

Let's unpack Beth's story. What happened here?

- Beth noticed something special about this woman.
- Beth told the woman the special thing she noticed.
- The woman responded positively.

When you put it in those three little bullets, it seems easy, right? So many women would have noticed that strikingly beautiful woman, thought internally how beautiful she was, and never said a word. Thinking in terms of new networking means recognizing you are having an authentic, honest thought about someone and you want to share it with that person. The biggest leap here comes in actually opening your mouth and saying something.

Beth challenges all of you to "Think about what you're thinking and start acting on it. We're all leaders, and we all have the basic DNA of being great networkers." Is it moxie? Is it confidence? Maybe. But it might also be a little bit of "so what?" Beth authentically recognized something beautiful in this woman and told me she "didn't care if she thinks I'm a wacko." Beth wasn't schmoozing this woman and she wasn't trying to get something from her. She was authentically and with true honesty saying something she noticed.

How can you start to employ this strategy in your own networking journey? It doesn't mean having to tell everyone they're beautiful or extraordinary. Try these tactics to start the process:

- **Go beyond "Thank You."** We're taught to be polite and say "thank you" when someone does something for us, whether it's your assistant, your boss, or a server at a restaurant. What if you started going beyond "thank you" and saying what you really, authentically feel? Try saying, "You have been such a huge help to me, and I want to tell you how much your dedication meant to me just now." That kind of authenticity goes far beyond "thank you."

- **Remember names. No, really!** One of the hardest things for many people in networking is hearing a name and immediately remembering it. To be an outside the box networker and truly excel in your connections, you have to master this task. Beth Ruske told me how she does it. "Whenever I'm public speaking, for instance, I ask every single person's name and I mindmap the room of names. If you're in a room, make a seating chart in your head. I think 'Oh, she looks like my friend Mary and her name is Marian.' I'll also scribble names on a piece of paper. It helps to keep things straight." To be truly authentic, you have to connect with someone personally with her name. Do everything you can to remember it, even if it means asking the individual to repeat it once or twice.

See the Best, Be the Best

One of the best pieces of advice Beth gives women, both reading this book and throughout her coaching and consulting career, is to see the best in everyone you meet. If you can switch one thing in your mindset to become a new networking strategist, this is it. If you walk into a room and you think of the people there as people who could potentially hurt you, annoy you, or let you down, you're immediately damaging the authentic connections you could make. If, conversely, you walk into a room seeing a room full of strangers who are probably kind, caring, and extraordinary people, your view of the room (and possibly the world) will change drastically.

If you know Beth, you've probably heard the story of the gas station robbery. It was summer in Chicago, and Beth pulled her car into a gas station to fill. She grabbed a credit card out of her wallet and exited the car. Windows were down, the sun was beating on the asphalt, and when she turned around at the pump, she saw a young man holding some of her credit cards and cash. Beth's reaction? She said something like, "Oh, my goodness! My cards must have fallen out of my wallet. Thank you for picking them up." Moments later, Beth realized her initial instinct was wrong, and that in fact this man was not a Good Samaritan picking up her credit cards. He was a thief and had just been caught in the process of stealing them. In a hilarious turn, Beth says to the man, "Wait a minute, were you stealing my cards?" The young man, embarrassed, hung his head and said, "Yes, ma'am. I'm sorry," handing her cards back to her. Many of us, in that moment, would have been afraid (and rightfully so) and perhaps even called the police. What did Beth do? She gave the young man $20 and said, "There must be something big going on in your life if you would resort to stealing. Take this $20." What can we learn from Beth's story? Well, first that she was in a public, well-lit, and safe place (I hope she wouldn't have done the same on a dark street corner). Most importantly, though, her initial instinct looking at this young man was to see the good in him, and even when she realized what was really happening, she still chose to see the good in this person, and to treat him with what to him might have seemed like a crazy amount of kindness.

While I hope you're never robbed at a gas station, I want you to take away from this story one thing: See the best in people. If you do, you will inevitably bring out the best in yourself in the process.

Putting It All Together

If you take what you've learned here from Beth, it all fits into a four-step process.

1. Start thinking about what you're thinking. Notice your thoughts and recognize them.
2. Get in touch with your innate leader. Take a deep breath, and recognize you have leadership and confidence within you always.
3. Act on your thoughts! Don't worry about being seen as a "wacko," and instead start telling people the wonderful

things in your head – both personally and professionally.

4.   See the best in people, and expect the best in them. Sure, sometimes you'll be disappointed, but if you go into situations with positive expectations, you're much more likely to get them.

The "Best of the Best" in Networking Advice

I ended each of the interviews completed for You Know Everybody! by asking each woman to provide to this book's readers her best networking tips and advice. Here are Beth's tips and tricks.

- **Do it young!** Don't wait until you're 40, Beth says, and you're figuring out some big career change and thinking, "Oh, damn, I should be networking." By reading this book, you're already ahead of the game. Just starting is a huge piece of the puzzle.
- **Do it in a way that works for you.** Beth and I talked about how so many people are afraid to go to networking events. Her advice? "If you don't want to go by yourself and you know you're never going to go on your own, then do it with a friend. Find someone you admire, who you think is a great networker, and ask her where she's going next. Can you come with?" You don't need to be a great networker on your own, you just have to figure out what will work for you and strategize around it. If that means going in a group, then find that group!
- **Women are already great networkers.** So many times, Beth says, she sees women being networking experts in their own lives, but for other people. "We do it for our children! We do it when it comes to shopping, and so many other areas. But the moment you ask a woman

to network for her own gain, she gets stopped. That's a huge mistake." If you're comfortable asking someone to recommend a daycare for your child or her favorite shoe store or hair stylist, why is it so different to ask for a recommendation for a job or a business opportunity? It's not! All of these propositions are in the same venue. You already have the skill. Beth says, "Go ahead and chat about it!"

ten

The Fine Art of Following Up

*Look, all I'm saying...if a guy doesn't call me, I would like to reserve
the right to call him at 15-minute intervals until he picks up.*

–AMBER, THE DESPERATE SINGLE GIRL FROM
"HE'S JUST NOT THAT INTO YOU"

There will always be commonalities between the process of
networking to advance your career and the process of dating
(presumably to find Ms. or Mr. Right, but no judgment for anyone
searching equally as diligently for Ms. or Mr. Right Now!). If
you've ever gone on a bad date, you know that the bad date doesn't
necessarily end when the date itself is over. It ends when the
person you went out with stops calling you and you stop calling
him. If your date is diligent with follow-up, your bad date can
extend days, weeks, or months (if you're truly unlucky). The same
principles apply to networking. If you meet someone at an event
or connect with someone one-on-one for a meeting and no one
ever calls or follows up with the other party, the relationship is all
but over. Sure, you might be LinkedIn connections or Facebook

friends, and the individual might quickly be relegated to your "What's Your Name Again" networking layer, but effectively the relationship ends when follow-up stalls. This is exactly why I've saved this chapter for last – because it's truly the most important. If you follow every single step in this book, but stop reading at Chapter 9, your attempt to build a *You Know Everybody!* Network will absolutely, without a doubt, fail miserably. So wake up, ladies, it's time for us to talk follow-up!

Sure, it's easy for me to make the dating comparison. Single gals reading this book are cursing me with the "it's not that easy" and "dating sucks" mantras we've all recited at some point in our lives. While I might be a happily married lady, it wasn't so long ago that I, too, was what I referred to as a "professional dater." Trust me. I get it. So I would be remiss if I didn't recognize that following up with a networking connection can be just as tricky as following up with a date who may or may not want to (Fill in the blank here: Date you, sleep with you, love you, marry you, plot your murder). Calling someone you had a casual coffee with and thought was cute last week is just as difficult as calling someone you had a casual coffee with and thought would be a great mentor.

We live in a world of constant stimulus, most of which comes from our mobile devices and various electronics. Telemarketers have been replaced by spam email and texts. Even my in-laws have replaced their home phone with a shiny new iPhone 5 because, really, who needs a landline anymore? Recently, I worked with an advertising agency whose staff doesn't have phones. Why? They don't need them. One of the young women without a phone line said to me, "Who would I call? Everything is done via email, and if someone really needs to talk to me, they'll text."

No wonder we're afraid to pick up a phone. What used to be one-on-one contact has become iPhone-on-iPhone contact. Now, I'm not demonizing devices, emails, texts, or iMessaging, even in the realm of networking. These kinds of connections can be incredibly powerful and effective. But let's compare this phenomenon to dating once again. Let's say you go out with a new guy or gal. You have a great time, you laugh, you might even get a good night kiss. Afterwards, you stare at the phone, minute by minute, and will it to make some kind of noise giving you any indication you weren't alone on some fantasy island and, in fact, the person you find perfect beyond belief feels the same way about you. Which form of outreach would mean more to you? A call saying "I had a great time, and I can't wait to see you again. Can we get together on Friday to live happily ever after?" Or a text that says something like "R u home. U r hott. Would luv to c u again Friday." The answer is quite clear, and it should be for networking as well.

It's no secret that I'm a lover of the phone. After all, I was the daughter of a career telephone man. Perhaps love of the phone has been instilled in me from the day I was born. Of course, I'll give you many options in conducting appropriate follow-up, but in case you haven't gotten it yet, really, seriously, consider picking up the phone. Your voice can say so much more than your typing skills can. Lecture...over.

The good news for anyone who hates talking on the phone is that the most important thing here is not how you do it, but the fact that you do it. Just like I told you that the most important step in attending an event is actually to attend, the most important step in conducting follow-up is to DO IT! That's it. If you take no other advice in this chapter, take that. If you follow up you will be head and shoulders above most of your peers. Now, let's dive deeper and see if we can get you into rock star supernova territory.

When it comes to follow-up, most people fall in what I would describe as a "nice to meet you" category. You attend an event, you shake some hands, you have coffee or drinks, and afterwards you say something like "nice to meet you." Not to harp on the dating point, but if you're as big of a fan of the movie "He's Just Not That Into You" as I am, you'll remember the conversation Ginnifer Goodwin's character has with her coworker. Did he say "Nice to meet you" at the beginning of the date or the end? At the beginning, it's nice to meet you, at the end it's a blow-off. Most women are "nice to meet you" networkers. But hey there, Career Girl, you don't want to be a "nice to meet you" networker. No. You want to be a *You Know Everybody!* Networker, and in that sense, "nice to meet you" doesn't cut it!

Consider this: You just met someone for coffee. It may be that she wanted to pick your brain about your profession or your company. You have a good conversation, you leave cordially, she says "Nice to meet you" and you never hear from her again. Which layer of your professional network does she fit into? Our instinct is to place her in the "What's Your Name Again" category, but that's not usually so. Instead, we put her in the 6th level of our networks, the "Stand Still, Look Pretty" category. The difference here is obvious. Someone who languishes on your LinkedIn connections list doing nothing has never shown you who she is. Someone in the "Stand Still, Look Pretty" layer of your network has often given you a small (or large) dose of who she is and unfortunately have garnished a bit of negativity on your part. You've had coffee, you've given advice, and that bitch (pardon my French, but you know it's what you think) never even said thank you! For better or for worse, she is sentenced to the worst part of your network.

The fact here, Career Girls, is that you're not just "networking" (I put that in quotes to illustrate the idiotic notions most people have about networking, and to set them apart from the networking you're doing when you follow the steps I'm giving you). You're building real, meaningful relationships. They take time. They take effort. They take follow-up. It's not as simple as a "thanks for meeting me" email, either. Like anything else in life, you're going to have to put some sweat equity into your network to get to the stage where *You Know Everybody!*

Let's dive in first to the many channels you might use to ensure you're following up properly.

1. Write it, girl. Like, with a pen!

The handwritten thank you note, some might argue, is all but extinct. Even with the uncertain future of the United States Postal Service and the fact that school children don't learn cursive writing anymore, I may be one of the last modern Career Girls who will tell you the handwritten note is very much alive and well, and should be used often. No matter the occasion – a job interview, a mentoring session, an informational interview, a networking coffee meeting, a holiday gift, a thoughtful hello – handwritten notes are one of the only forms of communication left in the world that *never* feel inappropriate. Whether an action is small or large, everyone loves receiving a thoughtful handwritten thank you note, almost without exception (somewhere, there's curmudgeonly old guy who hates thank you notes...but he's probably not reading this book).

In June of 2012, a bright young woman named Hannah Brencher took the stage at TED@New York and told her story of starting a movement to get the world writing again—not just writing, but writing love letters. Her organization, The World Needs More Love Letters, is a letter writing exchange program developed to connect complete strangers worldwide though simple, easy, heartfelt letter writing. This program, Brencher tells us in her TED Talk, is not about being a pen pal, and it's not about intending to meet the person you're mailing a letter to. Her movement, her experiment, is to get us reaching out to one another again in the form of letter writing. She says, "To sit down, pull out a piece of paper and think about someone the whole way through...is an art form that does not fall down to the Goliath of 'get faster.'"

We live in a world where faster is better. Why write a letter when an email takes one tenth of the time? Especially for younger generations, more and more of us go to meetings without pens and add each other's email addresses to our phones rather than writing them on a piece of paper anymore. We do this to be efficient, but Hannah asks this question: "The ones from my generation, the ones of us who have grown up into a world where everything is paperless, where some of our best conversations have happened on a screen. We have learned to diary our pain onto Facebook, and we speak swiftly in 140 characters or less. But what if it's not about efficiency this time?" What if writing a letter – or in the business world, a handwritten note – can be about connection and building a meaningful relationship? Efficiency has so many places to fit, but this is one place you might consider the longer route, the more difficult tactic.

A few tips when you're writing that handwritten note:

- **Keep it short.** Getting a handwritten letter is great for personal connections, but a shorter note is more appropriate in a business setting. On a 3x5 thank you card, only use one half of the inside to write your note.
- **Sign your full name.** We'd all like to believe all of our contacts remember us. They don't. Take the time to sign your full name legibly. You might consider inserting a business card as well if you know you didn't give one out at your meeting.
- **Thank you is the best message.** If you're sending a handwritten thank you note after a job interview, it's easy to let the whole space be taken up by your qualifications and "why me" statements. Instead, keep the message simple. Thank you. Thank you for the opportunity, thank you for meeting me, thank you for your advice, and the list goes on. Everyone loves to be thanked. Give them what they want!

- **Actually mail it.** A new trend has emerged in job interviewing—writing the thank you beforehand—and it's just plain wrong. I've had countless people over the last few years tell me that job applicants leave thank you notes with the receptionist immediately after an interview. This is just plain wrong! Thank you notes aren't placeholders, they aren't things you must do, and they shouldn't be generic. Sure, you should be timely in sending one (within a day or two) after a meeting. But really take the time to put a stamp on it and drop it in a mailbox. Its impact will be so much greater!

- **Change it up!** This rule applies when it comes to multi-interviewer job interviews, specifically. Do not write the same thank you note to all four people who interviewed you. They may compare them and your thoughtfulness will quickly turn to idiocy. Say something different to a potential coworker (I'm excited to learn more about Project X you mentioned in our conversation.) than you would to a potential boss (I'm confident we will work well together and you'll find I'm a good fit for your team.) or the company's CEO (I'm inspired by the organization's mission and look forward to helping to move the needle forward for the work you do.). The key is thoughtfulness, and carbon copies of anything are never thoughtful.

2. Email it.

As much as I love handwritten notes, I certainly don't love them enough to demonize email. A well-written email can be as powerful as a handwritten note on many occasions, and should definitely be a consideration in most situations. Email correspondence is great follow-up when you want to say a quick hello or thank you following a meeting with an already strong connection. Imaging you're having drinks on Tuesday with a former coworker you haven't seen in years. You catch up, you have a great time, and you want to continue to get together more often. Writing a handwritten thank you is probably too formal for this situation. An email, though, the morning after your meeting with a quick "It was so nice to see you. I'd love to continue to get together more often" can mean a lot to that individual.

Email is also fantastic to outline discussion points or decisions made in your meetings. If your mentor mentions she knows someone in your target company and wants to connect you with her, following up via email is the quickest way to make sure that connection gets onto her to-do list.

A few tips to do email follow-up right:

- **If you're making a request, put it up front.** When you're sending an email for follow-up purposes, it may be that you're asking for something in it immediately. Don't beat around the bush for three paragraphs and then ask. No one reads that far into a thank you email. Put the request in the first few lines. "Thanks for our fantastic mentoring session yesterday! I always take away so much from our conversations. I'm excited to connect with your colleague at Company X. Would you e-introduce us? Let me know if there's anything else you need from me. (Insert a cordial ending blah blah blah and you're done)."

- **Who are you and where did we meet?** If you're sending an email to follow up after a first meeting or event, be sure you're noting immediately who you are and where you met. Maybe you only went to one networking event this week, but your contact could have attended multiple lunches or happy hours. Open with something simple like, "Hi Mary, We met on Tuesday at the Women's Club luncheon. I was the public relations executive in the red jacket!" Then, go on to make your request and suggest next steps just like you did in the cold calling plan in Chapter 5.

- **Strategically use your personal or business email address.** If you meet someone at a networking event, think that you might be able to work with her in your current job, and give her your business card, using your professional email address for correspondence is completely appropriate. If you met someone for coffee and talked about jobs, though, you'll want to stick with your personal address to reach her.

- **Have an email signature.** Often, we have professional email signatures on our "work emails" but not on our personal addresses. If you're emailing a potential employer or networking connection from your personal account, be sure to include a signature that has your name, some kind of title or qualifying statement (if you don't want to use your title, use something like Advertising Professional), your phone number, and any other ways to reach you that might be relevant (your LinkedIn url and Twitter handle are definitely appropriate here).

- **Use your subject wisely.** Too often we agonize over the content of an email, yet completely ignore the subject line. Again, my recommendation here is to put your call to action up front. If you want to meet the person one-on-one, try something like "Coffee next week?" or "Meet for lunch?" Email marketing experts often recommend the use of a question in the subject line to increase interest. Email subject lines are also an appropriate place to name drop or organization name drop. If you meet someone at an event, try "Connection from Women's Club Event" or "We met with Jane Smith!"

3. The trusty telephone.

Warning: Yet another rant about my own generation. How is it, exactly, that the invention of the iPhone meant we would rely totally on the "i" portion of the device and stop using the "Phone" all together? I covered a lot about phones and why you should pick them up in the first section of this chapter, so I won't bore you with all of it again here. Instead, I'll just give you a few tips for effective phone calling here:

- **Practice makes perfect.** If you truly hate phone calls, you're going to need to anxiety-proof your calls. Go ahead and type out a script. Don't think word-for-word, but consider highlights instead. If you're making a follow-up call to someone you met with last week who didn't actually introduce you to the person she said she would, your script might be: "It's Janet. Following up. Great coffee last week. You mentioned Company X. I'd love to chat more about that. Let me know the best way to connect with so-and-so." Of course, you're going to fill in the blanks, but having an outline written down and practiced thoroughly will help with your nerves.

- **Time of day matters.** If you're trying to reach a high level individual via phone, the best times of day are just before 8:00 a.m. and after 5:00 p.m. Usually, these are the times assistants either haven't arrived or have gone home, and a big wig is much more likely to answer her own extension. Don't call during lunch or between 9:00 a.m. and 11:00 a.m. These tend to be times where someone would either be incredibly busy or out of the office at meetings or dealing with the beginning of the day issues. If you do call during proper business hours, try to call around 2:00 or 3:00 p.m. when someone is more likely to be in her office and willing to take a call. Most business meetings are end of day or beginning of day, and that mid-afternoon time slot is usually the best for downtime.

- **Leave a voicemail.** Depending on a person's phone system or voicemail system, someone will generally be able to see missed calls and who called. So don't just hang up. If you're trying to call someone, leave a voicemail if she isn't there. It's just good etiquette. You're then allowing your contact to return your call at her convenience. Calling two or three times without leaving a voicemail could mean you're becoming annoying and pesky. Don't be that girl!

- **Be clear.** Have you ever received a voicemail only to realize the person on the line rattled off a phone number so fast you have no idea what it actually was? Sure. We all have. So make sure you're not that forgotten voicemail. State your name clearly at the beginning, speak loudly enough to be clear, and slowly speak your phone number and name again at the end of the voicemail. If the individual you're trying to reach picks up, don't just say, "Hi, it's Stephanie!" Of course, you know you're special, but that individual may know five different Stephanies. Assume the least amount of knowledge and state your full name and perhaps a few identifiers like company, job title, or where you met, to help the person quickly indentify who you are.

4. New media? New follow-up.

The good news about new media is that it's one of the last places even CEOs manage themselves. Somehow it just hasn't become commonplace for a C-level person's assistant to tweet on her behalf. Sure, the company has its own Twitter account, but its employees are almost always writing and answering their own tweets. The same rules apply for LinkedIn, sometimes even more so, as most individuals have LinkedIn connected to personal and not professional email addresses.

The question remains, though, should you do follow-up on social media? The answer is a bit complicated. Yes and no. Whenever you meet someone you want to add to your network, you should immediately do the following:

- Connect on LinkedIn.
- Follow on Twitter.
- Find her personal website or blog if there is one listed on her other social media channels. Add that to your RSS feed reader.

The grey areas here come with social media platforms that are more personally focused. My contention is that a Facebook friend request is not appropriate with a professional connection in the first or even fifth meeting. Once you've known someone for a number of months, and have corresponded both personally and professionally, you might consider adding that individual as a Facebook friend. But in the first follow-up phase, stay away from this kind of medium. It is always appropriate, however, to like a Facebook Business Page associated with any individuals you meet. Entrepreneurs may not be comfortable becoming your Facebook friend just yet, but they will always love your engagement on the business' Facebook page.

Also, connecting on social media should in no way be a substitute for other methods of following up. Connecting via LinkedIn or Twitter is just that – connecting. It is not chatting or following up. In the rare case, though, where you do not have an email address or phone number, but you have found the individual on LinkedIn or Twitter, you are better off using one of these mediums than sending no follow-up at all. Consider sending a personalized LinkedIn connection message or a personal message on Twitter, but only as a last resort to having no email address or phone number (and you all know I've given you the tools to find these almost always in Chapter 5, so no excuses!).

In Chapter 5, I told you about using the G.I.R.L.S process (**Greet. Introduce. Request. Link. Suggest.**) while making cold calls or composing emails. Here, I'm going to give you a similar acronym to guide you in follow-up communications: S.T.E.P.

- **S – Situation (In what situation did you meet or speak?)**
- **T – Thank (Always say thank you for something. Trust me, you'll find something.)**
- **E – Extraordinary (What makes you extraordinary? Why should they remember you, help you, know you, want to get to know you?)**
- **P – Plan (Make a plan! What are the next steps?)**

Let's dive in with a real world example. Erin just moved to San Francisco. She attended an event for the nonprofit organization Dress for Success where she sat next to Fran, a woman she had never met. Erin and Fran chatted about Erin's experience working with tech startups and her desire to find a job in Silicon Valley. Fran told Erin she had great contacts in that area, and would be glad to help her. The two exchanged business cards, and Erin is following up to move the conversation and potential networking connections forward. How can she use the S.T.E.P. process to leave either a well-positioned voicemail or send a great email to ensure Fran's help is on the way with her job search? Here are two great examples:

Example A – Voicemail:

Hi Fran! This is Erin LastName calling. We met yesterday at the Dress for Success luncheon and after our terrific discussion about the San Francisco tech scene, I wanted to call to thank you for your insight and advice. As I mentioned yesterday, I've spent more than a decade working with Boston tech startups and want to really dig my feet in here in San Francisco. I'd love to meet with you to learn more about how we might be able to help one another. If you could, give me a call back at 555-555-5555. Again, this is Erin LastName, and I look forward to speaking with you!

Example B – Email:

Subject: Great to meet you at Dress for Success!

Fran,

Good morning! I hope this email finds you well. It was such a wonderful experience to be seated next to you at yesterday's Dress for Success luncheon. Being new to San Francisco, I'm so thankful for your willingness to give me such great advice and tips for succeeding here and in the tech industry!

As I mentioned yesterday, moving to San Francisco was the natural next step for me. After years in the tech startup world on the East Coast, I am ready to get in the big tech game here in Silicon Valley. I'm excited to lend my experience and skill set to a new company in California.

I would love to get together to learn more about your suggestions for me in this area, and to pick your brain about your own career. Could I buy you lunch near your office in the next week or two?

Thanks so much. Great to meet you yesterday, and I look forward to speaking soon!

Erin

In these examples, Fran definitely can't mistake who Erin is, what her goals are, and what she's directly requesting. She's respectful, thankful for the advice, and has made an appropriate request to complete the interaction. When you're following up, keep S.T.E.P. in mind and you can't go wrong!

The S.T.E.P. process works best when the person you're following up with is a new connection in your network. The rules change slightly when you're following up with a more long-term contact, perhaps a mentor you've been meeting with regularly, a coach, or a friend. Consider these tips to include in follow-up processes with these kinds of individuals:

- **Include Next Steps.** Often when you meet with a current contact, you'll brainstorm in your meetings together. You might decide you should go to an event together next month, or one of you offers to connect the other to a friend or colleague. Maybe you just want to see her again for coffee in a few weeks, or have some additional ideas to float by her about your own career. Make your follow-up specific to the steps you both decided you would take in your meeting.
- **Think Long Term.** In any networking exchange you want to be sure you're adding as much value as you're asking for. Your follow-up outreach could include a few suggestions of ways you might be able to add to that individual's career or business goals. To brainstorm these kinds of ideas, after every meeting with any individual, think about a few things:
  - Is there a way you might collaborate with that individual on a project?
  - Is that person looking for a job? Do you know of any openings?
  - Is there a new restaurant/spa/movie/play you think she would enjoy?

       ◻   Are there any events you'd like to invite her to?

- **Connect!** If you're truly a *You Know Everybody!* Networker, you'll be the kind of person who not only wants to know everybody, but wants your network to know everybody you know as well. After every networking meeting, you should be full to the brim with ideas of potential connections you could make from Person A to Person B. If you're following up with a current networking connection, but have very little to say in the way of next steps, the best way to continue the relationship and add to the conversation is to introduce that contact to another contact. Soon, you'll find you're doing this naturally and without having to think about it!

We've covered, so far, the ways you might follow up after a meeting or an event, but so much networking and follow-up comes after those initial emails and phone calls are over, the next meeting occurs, and the next emails and phone calls are over as well. To be great at follow-up, you have to recognize that the need for it is ongoing, not static. As relationships in your network progress, you must progress from reactionary following up to more strategic continuing outreach. This kind of continued follow-up is what truly builds relationships, both personal and professional. To compare once again to dating, if an individual you were dating called you only following a date to ask you on another, and never called or texted just to say hello or "I'm thinking of you," would you stick around very long? No. Because sooner or later that relationship would begin to feel transactional rather than organic. You're only calling because you want a companion to accompany you to a play or the grocery store, not because you care about my well-being. Right?

A huge buzzword/phrase in corporate advertising is "touch point." A company might consider where it has multiple touch points with its customers. Some companies have short, succinct touch points. You drive to BP, you buy gasoline, and you drive away. The touch points BP has with you are limited to the time you're at the gas pump. Of course, they advertise to convince you to have more interactions with them, but overall their touch points are limited. On the contrary, consider a theater or music venue you frequent. There's a touch point with you in the ticket searching process, the ticket buying process, later in the ticket taking process, and throughout your evening. Then, the venue might remember the kinds of show you're interested in and email you suggestions, yet another touch point. Like businesses, you'll want to begin to create touch points in your own career with members of your network. This is what "staying in touch" really means – touch points where someone is seeing you, hearing you, identifying with your brand, and keeping you in mind for future partnerships, collaborations, and recommendations.

To close this chapter, and our *You Know Everybody!* Networking process, let's look at a few advanced ways you might consider increasing the number of touch points you have regularly with your network:

- **Congratulations!** If someone in your network does something great, there's no better way to create a touch point than to reach out and say "Congratulations!" How do you know, though, when our friends are often reticent to brag about themselves?
    - Pay attention to the emails LinkedIn sends. In them, you'll find out when someone changes jobs, adds something to his or her profile, or gets a promotion. These are perfect times to reach out to offer kudos.
    - Get on Newsle.com. Newsle connects your social media contacts to a news search that

emails you information when someone in your network is featured in the news. Newsle has sent me reviews of friends' books, information about friends speaking at big conferences, and much more. It's the perfect nudge to reach out to those individuals to offer congratulations. Often Newsle hits publications that aren't super mainstream, as well, so you could be the only person offering congratulations on something that will thrill the individual you're connecting with.

▫ Read the "Who's Who" in your city, state, and industry. Almost every local business journal or women's magazine and truly every industry publication includes a section on promotions, job changes, awards, and other big news for area players. Your friend who just changed jobs at a big women's foundation might not tell you, but your local women's magazine may. Your former boss who is now the CEO of a new company might not have time to call you, but the business journal that featured the transition can let you know. Take the time to read these kinds of publications, search quickly for names you recognize, and reach out immediately.

• **Remember the Date!** This tip is one of my greatest networking tips, and I hope you'll employ it in your own career. When you meet with someone, you're likely to follow up immediately, but then forget and six months later you still haven't talked again. Take it to your calendar! If you met with someone today, set a recurring meeting on your calendar that says something like "Follow up with Robin Henderson (Met first on 1.13.13)." What works best for me is to set this calendar reminder to occur quarterly, or at minimum once every six months. When it buzzes me, I remember that I haven't spoken to that person in a few months, and I evaluate what I might want to follow up with her about. Maybe I have an event coming up I should invite her to or I'd like to meet her for drinks. I don't always act upon these calendar entries, but they're helpful to have set to keep you constantly connecting even when your calendar is full!

- **Be an Information Librarian.** Some of my favorite people in the world are friends who regularly send articles, links, videos, etc., they think might be of interest to me. Now, I'm not talking about "forward this to ten people" emails. For instance, a few weeks back, a friend of mine sent me an article about the business attire of newswomen. She knew I write often about dressing for success and that I love information about powerful women. This exchange had no gain for her and took her just a moment to press forward and write a quick one-line message, but it resonated with me in two ways. #1 – I loved the article and later featured part of it on Career Girl Network, and #2 – It made me feel special that my friend was thinking of me. Easy as that. When you read a great article, find a great resource, or download an awesome new app, tell people about it strategically. Don't just send a mass email, but personally email or call someone to say, "I thought of you when..." It will give you a great touch point and start an even greater relationship.

- **Share Your Passions.** If you are truly passionate about something, spread it around! This can be both big and small. In 2009, I was newly divorced and entering the dating scene when Whitney Houston's new album hit the shelves. I had an "a-ha moment" sitting on my couch watching Whitney sing "I Didn't Know My Own Strength." In that moment, I considered my own life, my own experiences, my own career, and I wanted everyone else I knew to experience it, too. I got in the car, I went to Target, and I bought every copy of Whitney's album they had – something like 23 in total. For the next week, I passed out CDs to everyone I loved. My mother got one in the mail, my best friend, my boss, my personal trainer, a woman I had coffee with to talk about the nonprofit I was working for at the time. I gave it away because it meant something to me. It was a small passion, but sharing it meant a great networking touch point. The same goes for books. If you love one, buy five! Give them out to the women you love. Get those touch points going. On a larger scale, consider sharing your passions for nonprofit organizations, causes, hobbies, and more with your network. You might find that someone who was only a coffee buddy is also an avid marathoner and would love to train with you for next year's race. Score! When you share your passions freely as touch points to your network, you'll increase your relationship's personality with each individual you interact with tenfold.

Here's another important point when it comes to following up. Don't forget your brand! You are who you are and your brand is what it is in every interaction you have. Often, we put our brands front and center with the handshake and the elevator pitch, but lose them somewhere between goodbye and follow-up. Make sure your messages are reflecting who you are and the brand you want to portray when your network has touch points with you. As you put your brand front and center through your first impressions, meetings, and ultimately in your follow-up, you'll find quickly that the layers of your network are filling fast, and you're becoming the *You Know Everybody!* Networker I always knew you could be.

Ask yourself, in every step, but especially in follow-up: Where does this individual fit in the layers of my network? Could she potentially be a "move a body" friend? Maybe. But chances are, you'll start with people lower in the seven layers and eventually move them up. Each follow-up message is an opportunity to bring someone to the next level of your network. Knowing what layer she starts in will help you to ask the question of how to engage her in that layer. And next, how do you move her up, if you want to? What starts as a follow-up email after coffee could become an invitation to attend an event together. That event could turn into a dinner invitation or drinks. Those dinners and regular meetings for drinks could eventually become an idea to go to the spa together or take a theater trip to NYC. And as those things happen and you develop your relationship, you might just find that someone you met passively at an event has moved into the upper echelon of your network. It's that moment, sitting across from someone who cares for you and your career deeply, looking around the room at the layers of your network, realizing you've strategically created it, you've moved people around, you've done the right things, and you've followed up effectively, when you'll suddenly see the effects of *You Know Everybody!*

Don't be afraid to follow up. Pick up the phone, send that email, or write that letter. Everything you do, every message you send, is getting you one step closer to that moment and a network that fuels your career to unimaginable heights.

She Knows Everybody! Narrative: Chapter 10
The Fine Art of Following Up

Angela Elbert
Partner, Neal Gerber Eisenberg

Find Angela Online
Website: www.ngelaw.com/aelbert
Twitter: @RedheadInsGal
LinkedIn: linkedin.com/in/angelaelbert

Of the women I interviewed for these narratives throughout my time writing *You Know Everybody!*, there are many I call colleagues, some I call mentors, and a few that I am blessed and lucky to call my friends. Angela Elbert is all three. She is the Chair of the Board of Directors for Step Up Women's Network Chicago, a Board on which I serve. She is a leader in the Chicago community of women, a mentor to me and countless others, and on top of that, I've had the distinct privilege of participating in a birthday scavenger hunt and subsequent dance party at her home. She is, in the truest sense of the words, a friend and an inspiration to women everywhere.

On top of being an incredible person and a fiery redhead, her list of accolades is long and impressive. In 2013, named to the Top 10 Illinois Super Lawyers list by Super Lawyer Magazine (the only woman on it, by the way), named one of "The Best Lawyers in America" in 2011, a member of "40 Under 40" and "100 Women Making a Difference" as well as the winner of awards from the Coalition of Women's Initiatives in Law and the Chicago Bar Association. I could go on and on about her. I won't, though, because the most inspiring things about Angela don't come from her many lauded achievements. The most inspiring thing about Angela is Angela. You can't be in a room with her without leaving a better person, a more driven individual, and I hope you'll read this narrative and take with you her fire for excellence and drive toward helping women succeed in tandem.

Becoming a "Rainmaker"

Angela graduated from Indiana University's Maurer School of Law and worked her way up quickly in the vast field of Chicago lawyers. Finding her home at Neal, Gerber & Eisenberg LLP, she settled into work she loved and a firm that was supportive of both her personal and professional goals. Angela says, "I had always served as the loyal lieutenant to some terrific mentors and lawyers." She was the "go-to-gal" for numerous partners and had developed great relationships. Something changed, though, when Angela returned from maternity leave after the birth of her first son, Robert. One of the partners she supported heavily had decided to leave the firm, and Chicago. While he invited her to go with him, her priorities as a wife and new mother based in Chicago kept her tied to the city. She said, "I had no idea what was going to happen to my career at that point, and I was afraid. However, I had always wanted to be my own boss with my own clients, and I thought then that I had it in me to do just that – be a rainmaker."

Becoming a rainmaker for the firm didn't happen overnight. In fact, Angela gave birth to her second son just 16 months later, and following a second maternity leave in as many years, decided it was time to "jump off the cliff." How did she do it? Here's how. Angela says, "I had a plan. I looked at what other successful insurance coverage attorneys in my field did to develop and build their practices, and I made my own business plan. I have to admit it was pretty scary, and I felt the fear and thought about what my other options might be. However, I thought I could be pretty good at it and would enjoy it if I really gave it a fair go. My plan was to learn a newer niche area of insurance coverage counseling. I read up on everything I could to become a real expert. I wrote articles. I looked for speaking opportunities everywhere that would have me. I worked really hard internally to sell my services to my partners and their clients. I took that experience and knowledge and used it to sell myself and my services externally. I targeted clients I wanted to do work for and I went after them. I made it a goal to get involved in several external boards of directors, and I researched and talked to my friends and colleagues and looked until I found the right fits for me. I went after leadership positions on each of my boards and with the ABA. I slowly built a strong network. The whole time, I had a good deal of fear in my belly, but I worked hard to overcome that fear and grew more confident with each step I took."

I tell you this story of Angela becoming a rainmaker for a very specific reason in this very specific chapter. Rainmakers are, by their nature, if they want to be successful, great at following up. No one ever won a piece of business (law firm or otherwise) with one email or phone call. It takes diligent follow-up to make it happen, and Angela is an expert in it. She told me, "Follow-up was a very important part of my transition. When I decided I wanted to be a rainmaker, I had to move from being a worker-bee to going out and getting work. To get work, you have to go after it, and you don't always get the first thing you go after. I reached out to as many people as I could to develop relationships."

The other key to being a rainmaker is to recognize that inherent in the process of landing business is the process of losing business. Angela says, "They didn't always respond! It's hard to find the fine line between pushing too hard and not. Finding just the right amount of follow-up is looking at something you want to get, going after it, and getting it. But you also have to recognize when it's over."

I asked Angela how that feels – the moment you feel you've lost someone, a piece of business, and she responded hilariously with, "It's a big 'oh no, I think I stalked her' moment. But I don't just let it go! I let it go for a while, and then call back on a whim. You never know what kind of reaction you'll get. Sure, sometimes you do have to give up – recognize that you don't get everything, and you sometimes have to ask yourself, 'What did I do wrong? What would I have done differently?' That's ok! There are a ton of people out there, and a huge amount of business to be had. The more irons you have in the fire, the more likely you are to 'make it rain.'"

It's Not All About the Money

Becoming a rainmaker, you probably have visions in your head of rappers at a Las Vegas club and the image of cash falling on the crowd, "making it rain." I hate to break it to you, but the best rainmakers in the world, lawyers and otherwise, realize that being a moneymaker means it's not all about money. Angela being named a Super Lawyer likely has little to do with her ability to make money, and much more in her ability to create long lasting and meaningful relationships both with her clients for her firm and with connections nationwide who support her causes and consider her a friend.

How, though, does someone whose day is stacked with client engagements, nonprofit board service, and a family manage to find time to follow up in order to create these kinds of relationships? I asked Angela this question, and she smiles as she said, "I love it! So I make the time. I love personal interactions. It's the most fun part of my day." For Angela, meetings don't mean money—they mean personal connections. She says, "Some people think of it as business development, and it is! If you're going to be a rainmaker you have to make time for business development and follow-up every day. You're only as good as the next piece of business you bring in the door. You have to go out to lunch even when you're busy, you have to keep meeting people all the time."

Are you doing enough follow-up to get your lunch dates full this month? Are you finding enough ways to reach out to create meaningful relationships in order to fuel your pipeline? Whether you're developing business for a firm or just want to strategically build your own network, you have to actually *do it!* Angela lamented to me, "A lot of women think that sitting at their desks and working hard is enough, but it's not. Even if you're great at what you do, it's not enough. You have to sell, and follow-up gets you the sale." You're not always selling a product, but you are always selling yourself. Being good at your job or good in your field doesn't sell you, does it? So get out there, Career Girls, follow Angela's advice, and damnit, make some rain!

Follow-Up: The Tricks of a True Rainmaker

I figured (and was right!) that someone like Angela had some great "tricks" to give women about making follow-up work. Here are just a few tactics she's used that get her in the door and on someone's calendar, rather than having her initial message or follow-up relegated to the spam folder:

- **Switch it up.** Angela admits, "I'm most comfortable emailing, but sometimes that's a mistake." Call people if they don't respond to emails. Sometimes you might even know they're going to be at an event. Go to it. You have to try multiple means of communication if one doesn't work. Try multiple times, but not too close together in time. Don't keep emailing if emailing doesn't seem to be working.

- **Suck up to the assistants.** They are the true gatekeepers. The truth is, though, assistants are sometimes treated as if they're not people. Far too often, we don't look them in the eyes or use their first names or ask them how their days are going. Take the time to stop, say hello, treat them like people, and invest in your relationship with them as much as the people you're contacting. When an assistant likes you and appreciates your approach, she'll help you get time on the calendar.

- **Have a plan.** Angela says, "Know who you want to meet and what you want to go after. If you know what you're trying to do, then you can back into the steps you need to take to get there. If my goal is to get McDonald's as a client, I'm going to contact the people at my firm who already work with them, ask to help me set up a speaking engagement at their offices. Then, I follow up with the people I met and invite them to lunch, and eventually ask them for work. In this instance, I asked for work, and I got it. But if you didn't have the goal in mind, it's hard to even know where to start your connections and lead your follow-up."

- **Follow up when you don't need something.** "Put people on your list," Angela says. "Invite them to things, send them tips, give them information or articles you think they might be interested in. Ask them to lunch. Send them a Christmas card." Doing these kinds of things throughout the year when you don't specifically need something will mean more effective follow-up when you do!

The "Best of the Best" in Networking Advice

I ended each of the interviews completed for You Know Everybody!
by asking each woman to provide to this book's readers her best
networking tips and advice. The section below is an excerpt
from a speech given by Angela Elbert to the Coalition of
Women's Initiatives in Law in 2012.

"Here is how I do it and my own personal manifesto that I do
my best to live by:

- Work hard, but know that you can't do it all yourself, so
  surround yourself with really smart and talented people
  and freely rely on them for help, and ask for what you
  want and need.
- Stop expecting things to go perfectly or for yourself to
  be perfect. Be willing to allow "good enough" where
  appropriate, while always striving to improve.
- Say "no" or impose limits when you need to – while we
  sometimes play one on TV, we are not superheroes.
- Be in control and act intentionally. Live in the present
  and focus your attention on what needs to be done at
  the moment or what you are doing at the moment.
- Shamelessly cheer for and promote yourself while you
  make many new relationships with people and, if and
  when appropriate, ask them for work.
- Hug and snuggle with my boys – all three of them –
  almost every day. They ground me.

Putting my manifesto into action, slowly, my plan seems
to be working. It hasn't happened overnight, but it is growing,
as are my wonderful sons and as is my network of support from
family, friends and colleagues. I'm not as afraid now as I once

was. I feel more confident that this path is the one I was meant to be on and that I can do it. Because I am doing it."

Epilogue

You (Yes, I'm Talking to You!) Know Everybody!

Writing this book has truly been one of the most joyful experiences of my career, so much so that I can't believe I waited so long to do it! Many, many people told me that writing a book will be like birthing a child; that it will be the hardest, most intense experience of your life. This was not my experience. Writing this book was fun and so much easier than I anticipated. Sure, I saw many a late night clock chime 3:00 a.m., but on the whole I found great joy in giving to women a book I believe is missing in the marketplace.

I started *You Know Everybody!* by telling you about the genesis of writing this book, my "a-ha" moment. When my friend turned to me in November 2011 and said, *"You Know Everybody!,"* I knew with every fiber of my being that I needed to write this book. What I didn't expect, however, was that writing this book would produce two additional "a-ha" moments that would fundamentally change the way I look at networking, and at business in general. To serve as a conclusion to this book, I want to share these new and meaningful "a-has" with you:

- **We *are* the stereotype! And that's OK.**
  The ten women I interviewed as a part of the *She Knows Everybody!* narratives you see in each chapter gave me the greatest joy in writing this book. To be able to learn

from and give to my readers the advice of women who are authors, CEOs, Fortune 50 key players, law firm partners, and more was a blessing for me, and I hope the narratives you read here were for you as well.

During every interview I completed for these narratives, one notion became constant. Women just do some things differently than men. I heard women like Mary Blegen and Linda Descano, who have fought their way up the corporate ladder, speak openly about the fact that what got them there was not acting like, dressing like, or emulating men, it was being uniquely and sometimes even stereotypically female. The thing is, the stereotype is generally correct: women are more caring, we are more sensitive, we are more emotionally intelligent. It's true. And the beauty of that truth is this: Women are naturally great networkers. Beth Ruske said it best when she said, "We do it for our children! We do it when it comes to shopping, and so many other areas. But the moment you ask a woman to network for her own gain, she gets stopped. That's a huge mistake."

You are already an incredible networker. Why? Because you're a woman. Use it! Don't be afraid to be feminine, to be emotionally intelligent, to be open and honest and authentic. It's what we, as females, do best. Sure, we can put on a suit and saddle up to a conference table with the old boys' club, too, but the beauty in our leadership and networking power is entirely and perhaps even stereotypically feminine!

- **Your way is the right way.**

  I told my husband and friends so many times, "Thank goodness I wrote the whole book *before* I interviewed any of the ten women in the narratives." Why? Every single time I interviewed one of them, I had this intense desire to rewrite the entire book. I distinctly remember coming back to my in-laws' home in Minnesota after talking to Archelle Georgiou and saying, "I need to rewrite the whole thing. It all has to be just like Archelle does it!"

That same doubt and fear in me ensued after nearly every interview. Somewhere in the middle, though, I had another "a-ha" moment. The fact of the matter is, there's no one right way. The ten women featured in *You Know Everybody!* have massive and powerful networks. They are connected nationally and internationally and have risen to the tops of their fields. Yet no two in the group followed the same path to building that network. Each of them employed different skill sets, different tactics, and experienced different types of success in building what resulted in a *You Know Everybody!* Network.

You have to do the same. This book is subtitled *A Career Girl's Guide to Building a Network That Works.* Two things should stand out to you in that sentence. First, it is a *guide.* This book is not a textbook, and it is not a Bible. It is a *guide,* meant to make you better at the skills you are born with naturally, and to give you a framework with which you can strategically center your goals and make them happen. Second, this book is not about building a network that looks just like everyone else's. It is about building a network *that works.* The end of the sentence missing in our subtitle is "for you." You have to build a network that works...for you! There are thousands of ways to accomplish that goal. The "a-ha" moment for all of us here should be to take the tactics in this book, blend them with the advice of the ten women in this book, and find the path that works for you to create the network and ultimately the career and life you love.

The key takeaway from *You Know Everybody!* is kind of a no brainer. Go with me here. You. Know. Everybody. You might not feel that way now, but it's the truth. At this moment, you know everybody you need to know in order to build your network. When you begin to build, at that moment, you continue to know everybody you need to know. Soon, your network will amass hundreds of colleagues, friends, and acquaintances, and what you'll realize is that because you built it, you knew the right people to get there. With the risk of sounding like Glinda the Good Witch, the truth of the matter is, you have the tools you need to build the network you want. You've had them all along. The beauty of *You Know Everybody!* is simply giving you a roadmap to get there.

My hope for all of you, as I said at the beginning of this book, is for you to know the joy and sense of accomplishment you'll feel when someone turns to you and says, *"You Know Everybody!"* The journey to building that network is ongoing and lifelong, but damn it feels good to hear those three words every now and again. Go out and get them for yourself!

Acknowledgements

This book, from idea to completion, would not have been possible without the driving support of my husband, Charlie. In moments of darkness when I sat staring at a blinking cursor with doubt and fear, he provided the light that guided me to harness my mission and passion and write the best book I know how. This book is a massive passion project, conceived by me, but driven largely by the support and love of this incredibly patient and loving man.

This book is also blessed by a caring and supportive family. It was written from my office and home in Chicago, but just as much from my mother's kitchen table in North Dakota, my in-laws' couch in Minneapolis, and various vacation coffee shops with great encouragement from my family. To my parents Kathy and Tim, my brother Jeremy, my sister-in-law Brandi, and my amazing nieces and nephew Jenica, Bryson, and Josie, your love and unconditional support made my life, my career, and this book possible. To my dear in-laws (but so much more than in-laws) Bob, Mary, Carolyn, and Jeff, thank you for your encouragement and curiosity when my computer sat on my lap through many bottles of wine and nearly an entire Christmas vacation.

I must thank, with incredible gratitude, the women who gave so freely of their ideas and expertise to help me develop ten *She Knows Everybody!* narratives. This book would not be the same without each of you! Thank you Robin Fisher Roffer, Cindy

McLaughlin, Mary Blegen, Julie Cottineau, Aleen Bayard, Linda Descano, Archelle Georgiou, Dawn Jackson Blatner, Beth Ruske, and Angela Elbert for your honesty and willingness to teach me and all of the women reading this book your tricks of the trade.

I thank, with incredible gratitude, the publishing team who made *You Know Everybody!* a reality. Kim Bookless, book consultant and editor extraordinaire, whose excitement about this project kept me moving. Mill City Press, for turning my words on a page into something tangible and real. Megh Knappenberger, for rescuing me when the words "book cover" made me physically ill and for capturing beauty in this book.

Finally, to a litany of friends and colleagues whose "How's the book coming?" and "I can't wait to read it" statements motivated me more than you will ever know – Shayna Cook, Linda Konop, Betsy Kroon, Sadie Simcox, Lauren McCabe, Melissa Foster, Kelley Long, Rebecca Niziol, Emily Rolkowski, Nicole Wetzell, all of the ladies at Levo League, Kickstart Kitchen, the incredible women of the Career Girl Network advisory group, and many, many more.

Book acknowledgements are like a tiny version of an Oscar speech – I'm sure there are many forgotten. Please know I am grateful beyond measure and thank you all deeply for your support and love.

About the Author

Marcy Twete authored this book during her tenure as Founder and CEO of Career Girl Network, an initiative that began in Minneapolis in 2007 with the blog "Minneapolis Career Girl" and later moved to Chicago, Illinois with "Chicago Career Girl." After building blog readership in Minneapolis and Chicago, Career Girl Network became a national platform to connect women nationally and internationally, providing resources to women who want to excel in their careers.

Marcy spent her childhood and adolescence in rural North Dakota, the granddaughter of farmers, and daughter to parents who instilled a strong work ethic and dedication to excellence at a young age. She worked her way through high school and college, waiting tables, taking tickets, making coffee, and completing multiple internships during her time at the College of St. Benedict in St. Joseph, Minnesota. Always the "Career Girl," Ms. Twete graduated college in 3.5 years, eager to jump into the working world, quickly landing in the political realm in Washington, DC and later Minneapolis, Minnesota. Later, armed with a dedication to public service and the female electorate, she took the skills harnessed in politics and moved to the nonprofit sector, where she spent nearly a decade leading and advising annual and capital campaigns ranging from $3 million to $4 billion.

Following the publication of this book, Marcy used her own "You Know Everybody" network to transfer her experience as an entrepreneur and nonprofit leader to the for profit sector. In 2014, she joined ArcelorMittal, the world's largest steel and mining company, where she led a team responsible for the company's sustainability and corporate responsibility function in the Americas region from 2014-2018.

Marcy remains a recognized leader in corporate responsibility and sustainability for multinational Fortune 500 companies. Graduating Kellogg's Executive MBA program in 2018, Marcy calls herself a CSR leader turned "finance geek" and a passionate advocate for the intersection of societal value and responsible practices across sectors.

Since her time as Founder of Career Girl Network came to a close, Marcy has remained dedicated to womens issues and causes that support the next generation of women and girls. She has served on Boards of Directors for Step Up Women's Network, the Girl Scouts of Greater Chicago and Northwest Indiana, Girls on the Run Twin Cities, and Chicago Architecture Center.